Contemporary Irish Writers

Contemporary Irish Writers and Filmmakers

General Series Editor:
Eugene O'Brien, Head of English Department,
Mary Immaculate College, University of Limerick.

Titles in the series:

Contemporary Irish Writers

Brian Friel

*Decoding the Language
of the Tribe*

Revised and Updated Edition

Tony Corbett

The Liffey Press

Published by The Liffey Press
Ashbrook House, 10 Main Street,
Raheny, Dublin 5, Ireland
www.theliffeypress.com

© 2002, 2008 Tony Corbett

A catalogue record of this book is
available from the British Library.

ISBN 978-1-905785-22-3

Revised and Updated edition; first edition published 2002

Front cover photograph © *The Irish Times*
Reproduced with kind permission

Printed in Ireland by Colour books

Contents

About the Author

Tony Corbett is an independent scholar who has had an involvement with all aspects of the theatre since his early teens. He has published articles on many facets of literature and drama, from the Middle Ages to the present day, and in journals as diverse as *Medieval English Theatre*, *Research Opportunities in Renaissance Drama*, and *The Brazilian Journal of Irish Studies*. He is an associate editor of *The Irish Book Review*, and is presently working on a study of late medieval English mystery plays.

Series Introduction

Given the amount of study that the topic of Irish writing, and increasingly Irish film, has generated, perhaps the first task of a series entitled *Contemporary Irish Writers and Filmmakers* is to justify its existence in a time of diminishing rainforests. As Declan Kiberd's *Irish Classics* has shown, Ireland has produced a great variety of writers who have influenced indigenous, and indeed, world culture, and there are innumerable books devoted to the study of the works of Yeats, Joyce and Beckett. These writers spoke out of a particular Irish culture, and also transcended that culture to speak to the Anglophone world, and beyond.

However, Ireland is now a very different place from that which figures in the works of Yeats, Joyce and Beckett, and it seems timely that the representations of this more secular, more European, and more cosmopolitan Ireland should be investigated and it is with this in mind that *Contemporary Irish Writers and Filmmakers* has been launched.

This series will examine the work of writers and filmmakers who have engaged with the contemporary cultural issues that are important in Ireland today. Irish literature and film has often been viewed as obsessed with the past, but contemporary writers and filmmakers seem to be involved in a process of negotiation between the Ireland of the past and the Ireland of the coming times. It is on this process of negotiation that much of our current imaginative literature and film is focused, and this series hopes to investigate this process through the chosen *auteurs*.

Indeed, it is a sign of the maturity of these *auteurs* that many of them base their narratives not only in the setting of this "new Ireland", but often beyond these shores. Writers and filmmakers such as Seamus Heaney, John Banville, William Trevor and Neil Jordan have the confidence to write and work as *artists* without the necessary addendum of the qualify-ing "Irish". Their concerns, themes and settings take them outside Ireland to a global stage. Yet, as this series attests,, their "Irishness", however that is defined, remains intact and is often imprinted even in their most "international" works.

The role of the aesthetic in the shaping of attitudes and opinions cannot be understated and these books will attempt to understand the transformative potential of the work of the artist in the context of the ongoing redefinition of society and culture. The current proliferation of writers and film-makers of the highest quality can be taken as an index of the growing confidence of this society, and of the desire to enun-ciate that confidence. However, as Luke Gibbons has put it: "a people has not found its voice until it has expressed itself, not only in a body of creative works, but also in a body of critical works", and *Contemporary Irish Writers and Filmmakers* is part of such an attempt to find that voice.

Aimed at the student and general reader alike, it is hoped that the series will play its part in enabling our con-tinuing participation in the great humanistic project of un-derstanding ourselves and others.

Eugene O'Brien
Department of English
Mary Immaculate College
University of Limerick

Acknowledgements

I need to thank several people and organisations for their help and support. My wife, Sinéad, as always, has my thanks for her patience, proofreading, and suggestions. Eugene O'Brien, general editor of the series, I thank for his diligence and encouragement, which often went far beyond what was required of him. Brian Langan and David Givens at The Liffey Press were enormously supportive of the book in all its stages. I would finally like to thank my father-in-law, Ray McElhinney, himself an Inishowen man, for help with Donegal sayings and dialect words.

For the second edition I need to thank again those who helped with the first, especially Eugene, whose idea it was to include the chapter on Friel's Russian plays. Some of my own errors have been expunged; doubtless others remain.

To Sinéad
And, this time, to Sarah too

Chronology

1929	Brian Friel born on 9 or 10 January near Omagh, County Tyrone.
1939	Family moves to Derry.
1941–46	Secondary Education at St. Columb's College, Derry.
1946–48	Seminarian in Maynooth. Leaves before ordination.
1949–50	Teacher training at St Joseph's College, Belfast.
1950–60	Teacher in a number of schools Derry.
1952	Publishes first short story, *The Child*. Writes first play, *The Francophile*, later renamed *A Doubtful Paradise*.
1954	Marries Anne Morrison. They will have four daughters and one son.
1958	*A Sort of Freedom* broadcast by BBC Northern Ireland.
1960	*A Doubtful Paradise* is produced at the Group Theatre, Belfast. Friel retires from teaching to write full-time.
1962	*The Enemy Within* performed in the Abbey Theatre, Dublin. *A Saucer of Larks* (short stories) is published.
1962–3	Writes weekly column for *The Irish Press*.

1963	*The Blind Mice* opens at the Eblana, Dublin. Friel spends time at the Guthrie Theatre, Minneapolis.
1964	*Philadelphia, Here I Come!* opens at the Gaiety Theatre, Dublin.
1966	*The Loves of Cass McGuire* opens at the Helen Hayes Theatre, New York. *Philadelphia, Here I Come!* opens on Broadway. *The Gold in the Sea* (short stories) is published.
1967	*Lovers* opens at the Gate Theatre, Dublin. *The Loves of Cass McGuire* opens at the Abbey. Friel moves from Derry to Muff, Co. Donegal, in the Republic.
1968	*Crystal and Fox* opens at the Gaiety. New York production of *Lovers* at the Lincoln Centre.
1969	*The Mundy Scheme*, rejected by the Abbey, opens at the Olympia.
1971	*The Gentle Island* opens at the Olympia.
1972	British soldiers kill 13 civilians in the Bogside area of Derry during an anti-internment protest. Friel elected a member of the Irish Academy of Letters.
1973	*The Freedom of the City* opens at the Abbey, and at the Royal Court Theatre, London. New York production of *Crystal and Fox*.
1974	New York production of *The Freedom of the City*.
1975	*Volunteers* opens at the Abbey. American Film Theatre TV movie of *Philadelphia, Here I Come!*
1977	*Living Quarters* opens at the Abbey.
1979	*Aristocrats* opens at the Abbey. *Faith Healer* opens at the Longacre Theatre, New York, and closes after one week. *Selected Stories* published.
1980	Founds Field Day Theatre Company with Stephen Rea. *Translations* opens at the Guildhall, Derry.

1981	*Faith Healer* opens at the Royal Court. New York production of *Translations* at the Manhattan Theatre Club. London production of *Translations* at the Hampstead Theatre. Friel's version of Chekhov's *Three Sisters* opens at the Guildhall.
1982	*The Communication Cord* opens at the Guildhall. Friel moves from Muff to Greencastle, Co. Donegal. Elected a member of Aosdana, The National Treasury of Irish Artists.
1983	Awarded honorary D.Litt. by the National University of Ireland.
1985	First Belfast production of the 1977 *Living Quarters*.
1986	Edits and writes an introduction to *The Last of the Name* by Charles McGlinchey.
1987	Friel's version of Turgenev's *Fathers and Sons* opens at the Lyttleton, London. Friel appointed to Senate.
1988	*Making History* opens at the Guildhall. Transfers to National Theatre after Irish tour. Revival of *The Gentle Island* directed by playwright Frank McGuinness. First London production of the 1979 *Aristocrats* at the Hampstead Theatre. Receives *Evening Standard* Best Play award.
1990	*Dancing at Lughnasa* opens at the Abbey. Transfers to the National Theatre, London.
1991	*Dancing at Lughnasa* receives Play of the Year at the Olivier Awards. Opens on Broadway in October.
1992	*The London Vertigo* (a version of Charles Macklin's *The True Born Irishman*) opens at the Andrews Lane Theatre, Dublin. *A Month in the Country*, after Turgenev, opens at the Gate. *Dancing at Lughnasa* wins three Tony awards.
1993	*Wonderful Tennessee* opens at the Abbey. Broadway production closes after nine performances.

1994	Friel resigns as a director of Field Day. *Molly Sweeney* opens at the Gate, directed by Friel himself. Transfers to the Almeida, London.
1996	*Molly Sweeney* named best foreign play by New York Drama Critics Circle.
1997	*Give Me Your Answer, Do!* opens at the Abbey, directed by Friel.
1998	London production of *Give Me Your Answer, Do!* at the Hampstead Theatre. Friel's version of *Uncle Vanya* opens at the Gate. Movie version of *Dancing at Lughnasa* released.
1999	Friel celebrates his seventieth birthday. A Friel festival in Dublin marks the occasion. *Give Me Your Answer, Do!* opens in New York.
2001	Friel presents the archive of his work to the National Library of Ireland. A short play, *The Yalta Game*, based on a Chekhov story, *The Lady with the Lapdog*, opens at the Gate as part of the Dublin Theatre Festival.
2002	*The Yalta Game* appears with *The Bear* and *Afterplay* as *Three Plays After* at the Gate.
2003	*Performances* opens at the Gate.
2005	*The Home Place* opens at the Gate.

Introduction

The original aim of this book was to interrogate Brian Friel's fictive Ireland, to discover the extent to which his plays reflected or critiqued the Ireland in which they were written. As the writing progressed, it became apparent that Friel's view of Ireland was linked at a very fundamental level to his art as a whole, and that no picture of his social and political themes would be complete, or could even make sense, without setting it in the context of Irish social and political development. The depressed, repressed, inward-looking country in which Friel wrote *A Doubtful Paradise* or *The Enemy Within* was a very different place from the prosperous European country in which he wrote *Wonderful Tennessee* or *Give Me Your Answer, Do!*

A number of themes reappear throughout Friel's plays, from the earliest to the most recent. Memory is important, especially false and inaccurate memories, which, without any connection with reality, become part of the essence of an individual. Many critics refer to Friel's plays as "memory-plays", in that the action is over before the play begins, and is recalled by one or more of the characters.

Communication is at the root of almost everything Friel has written. Communication between individuals, between cultures, between languages, between past and present, between the self and external reality; all of these are interrogated and problematised in the plays. Although I deal with communication specifically in Chapter Two, the theme permeates his whole canon, and consequently the whole book.

The Irish psyche is another important theme. In *Translations*, Friel pinpoints the moment at which the Irish psyche divided. As the language of the people no longer matched the landscape in which they lived, so the people became displaced in their homes. This shift becomes the basis of Friel's interest in the composition of external reality, and its connections with the perceptions of individual minds, a theme that, although nascent in the early plays, evolves throughout the canon, and emerges in *Faith Healer* and in *Molly Sweeney*.

Friel has much to say about loyalty, whether the familial, tribal loyalty in *The Enemy Within* or *Aristocrats*, or the expedient political loyalty in *Making History*, or loyalty to God, or to the past, or to an idea of Ireland. As with most of Friel's themes, a resolution is not possible, for Friel as an artist recognises the ambiguities of any loyalty.

In a book of this length, the most difficult choices are the omissions. I have chosen to remain silent on the short stories, although themes that appeared in them have reappeared in the plays. I have also omitted biographical material, except in the chronology, as a great deal of this material is available elsewhere. In the material I have dealt with, the choice and arrangement is loosely thematic rather than chronological, for reasons that I hope will be clear. This approach has its own dangers, as themes overlap to a large degree, but I hope it illustrates the different ways in which Friel deals with his material, and the emerging concerns of his work.

Chapter One, "Historical Tribes" deals with Friel's plays based on Irish history: *The Enemy Within*, *Translations*, and *Making History*. In each of these the element of tribalism appears, but with different political ramifications. In *The Enemy*

Within, the conflict is between Columba's familial duties and his commitment to what Fintan O'Toole calls "Christianity as a supra-tribal force" (O'Toole, 1993: 202). In *Translations*, loyalty to the Irish language is scrutinised, while in *Making History*, the historical process itself is problematised. *The Home Place* examines the nature of Irishness from geographical, historical and ethnic perspectives, using Victorian pseudo-science as a catalyst.

Chapter Two, "Talking to Ourselves", takes as its subject the evident discontinuity of communication between characters in almost all of Friel's plays. This discontinuity is one of the main themes of *Philadelphia, Here I Come!*, and is expanded on in the later works. In *The Communication Cord*, confusion over foreign languages becomes a vehicle to explore contemporary attitudes to Irish heritage. A return to *Translations* illustrates how communication in Friel's plays is pushing at the boundaries of language and linguistic possibilities, a theme that is taken up in many later plays. In *Living Quarters*, a family tries to communicate with its own past, but finds that, although the details might be assembled with precision, reliving the mistakes of the past gives little relief in the present.

Chapter Three, somewhat ironically entitled "Wonderful Ballybeg", looks at the idea of place in Friel, beginning with the location of his fictional Donegal town, Ballybeg, *locus* for many of the plays, and central to his fictive Ireland, past and present. Several plays are set in once-grand houses, now decaying; and the theme of decay, and the social and political symbolism of the big house, is discussed at length in relation to *Aristocrats*. This chapter also explores Friel's view of peasant Ireland, in relation to *Philadelphia, Here I Come!*, *The Gentle Island*, and *The Communication Cord*, and contrasts it with the normative Catholic and isolationist views of Eamon de Valera. The chapter concludes by examining the symbolism of the setting in *The Freedom of the City* and *Volunteers*.

"The Grammar of Reality", Chapter Four, traces the development of one of Friel's most fundamental themes. Friel's doubts about the possibility of communication crystallise in an interrogation of the nature of perceived reality. When one looks at plays such as *Faith Healer* and *Molly Sweeney*, and relates the themes found in them to Friel's earlier work, it is possible to see a continuum. In meditating on the possibility of communication, Friel begins to examine the way in which human perception affects the external world. *Molly Sweeney* is a masterpiece of enunciation on the uncertainty of knowledge, and of the persistent need of humanity to construct its little corner of the world in a way which gives them comfort, despite the discontinuity between them and any perceived "external reality". Playing again with notions of reality, *Performances*, Friel's play about composer Leoš Janáček is simultaneously real and unreal. Janáček is dead, Anezka lives in the computer age, but they discuss his work while his String Quartet No. 2. rehearses offstage.

Chapter Five, "The Schizophrenic Community", takes its title from a broadcast that Friel made in 1971. It looks in detail at two plays, *The Freedom of the City* and *Volunteers*, because these two deal overtly with republican and nationalist ideals. Both are based on political events in modern Ireland, and both were criticised for political bias. A side issue in the chapter is Friel's first attempt at political drama, *The Mundy Scheme*.

Chapter Six, "From Moscow to Ballybeg", deals with Friel's adaptations of Turgenev and Chekhov. His work is both a homage to writers that he considers his mentors, and an act of artistic inclusiveness. In considering *Three Sisters*, *Fathers and Sons*, or any other of his translations or versions, Friel has as much to say about the modern Irish dilemma as about the Russian provincial gentry of the nineteenth century. The translations also provide an artistic background against which Friel's "Big House" plays can be read.

Chapter One

Historical Tribes

> In some way the inherited images of 1916, or 1690, control and rule our lives much more profoundly than the historical truth of what happened on those two occasions. (Brian Friel, *Magill*, December 1980)

There are two kinds of history at work in Friel's plays. The history of pre-famine Ireland may help one to understand the background to *Translations*, for example, but a knowledge of modern Irish culture and *mores* is just as important. Friel uses historical times and places to weave ambiguous arguments about Ireland in the present. He not only contrasts past and present, he also makes use of the assumed knowledge of the audience or reader about subsequent events. He is contrasting the virtual history of the dramatic text with the actual history of the island of Ireland in order to comment on, or to interrogate, the present. His virtual history does not always match the actual history — a fact which, more than once, has brought Friel into conflict with historians.

In the earliest of these plays — the earliest, in fact, of his plays that Friel wishes to acknowledge — *The Enemy Within*, Columba's present, as abbot of his monastery, is always assaulted by his past as a prince of Tirconaill (modern west Donegal). The plot turns around two visits which the abbot, in voluntary exile on the island of Iona, receives from Inishowen. The first, from Brian, a messenger, is to request Columba's help in an impending battle between two clans. Columba assents. The second visit, from Columba's brother, Eoghan, and his nephew, Aedh, is to request help in a much more personal dispute. Aedh's wife, a Pictish pagan, has returned to her people. Aedh wishes to take her back. This time Columba, having renewed his vow to remain in his monastery and out of the affairs of his home place, refuses. He is cursed by his family as a result of this resolve.

Likewise, his reputation as a holy man, itself a kind of history, is at odds with his self-image, which is one of doubt about his own worthiness. Columba strives, for much of the play, to satisfy the demands of both families: his kin and his monks. Early in Act I, Columba tells of a waking vision, in which he imagines himself back in his home place, with the monks around him in the fields of Iona becoming characters from his past. Far from taking comfort in a homely *déjà vu*, Columba feels threatened, feels too attached to the place in which he was born. The inner man, he says, is "chained irrevocably to the earth, to the green wooded earth of Ireland" (21). Towards the end of the play, in a melodramatic speech, he articulates the feelings he has towards Ireland and his kinsmen in an apostrophe to Eoghan and Aedh:

> Get out of my monastery! Get out of my island! Get out of my life! Go back to those damned mountains and seductive hills that have robbed me of my Christ! You soaked my sweat! You sucked my blood! You stole my manhood, my best years! What more do you demand of me, damned Ireland? My soul? My immortal soul? Damned, damned, damned Ireland! — (*His voice breaks*) Soft, green Ireland — beautiful, green Ireland — my lovely green Ireland. O my Ireland . . . (75)

Both the rhetoric and the imagery are compelling, if unsubtle. The threefold repetition of "get out" is intensified by the expanding terms of reference: *monastery . . . island . . . life*. The mountains and hills of Ireland are characterised sensually, both damned and seductive; they fulfil the role of tempter in the religious sense and also of seductress. The imagery of coition is continued throughout the speech, but added to it is the idea of the blood-sucking stealer of manhood, a combination of the idea of vampire and *succubus*, the demon in female form who has intercourse with sleeping men.

There is a great deal of tradition and history at work in this short speech, not just mythic and Christian tradition, but Irish literary and political tradition as well. At its simplest, the sentimental notion of "Mother Ireland" is being invoked and rejected in favour of a far more predatory female form, one who consumes rather than nourishes. The image of Ireland as a mother who devours her children had already occurred in Joyce, who referred to Ireland as "an old sow who eats her farrow" (Joyce, 1992: 157).

Another female form which is related to Ireland occurs in a type of Gaelic poetry known as the *Aisling*. In this *genre*, the poet falls asleep and is visited in his dream by a young and beautiful girl. She identifies herself, or is identified, as the embodiment of Ireland, and recounts her woes to the sleeper, before exacting a promise of help. The form itself dates from the eighteenth century, and was used to encode overtly political messages, notably about Stuart help for the beleaguered Irish (Ó Tuama and Kinsella, 1981: xxvii). As the *Aisling* tradition developed a political rhetoric, the sleeper usually awoke with his resolve to help Ireland renewed. Columba finds not clarity of purpose, but moral confusion in the waking visions and visitations from Ireland.

The assertion that the land robbed him of his manhood must recall Patrick Kavanagh, particularly in *The Great Hun-*

ger, and individual poems such as "Stony Grey Soil of Monaghan", in which the poet apostrophises the land: "O stony
grey soil of Monaghan / You burgled my bank of youth"
(1964: 82). Kavanagh's savage indictment of the casual
drudgery of Irish peasant life is echoed here in Columba's
words, together with a deep, perceived rather than articulated attachment to the landscape. An ambivalent attachment to places appears again and again throughout Friel's
plays: for example, place names in *Translations*, or the changing accent of Hugh O'Neill in *Making History*. Gar Public's
uncertainty at the end of *Philadelphia, Here I Come!* is the
same unspoken and, largely, unutterable attitude towards
Irish native places. It is apt that Friel's only attempt to make
his characters speak of this attachment emerges as deliberate, mawkish, and insincere sentimentality in *The Communication Cord*. Columba's fear for his soul in the face of the
political demands of his country recalls Stephen in *A Portrait
of the Artist as a Young Man*: "When the soul of a man is born
in this country there are nets flung at it to hold it back from
flight. You talk to me of nationality, language, religion. I shall
try to fly by those nets" (Joyce, 1992: 157). Even in Iona, the
nets of kinship and religion are spread to trap Columba.

The constant reference to Ireland as green is iconic.
Apart from the Irish tourist board's marketing of Ireland as a
green, rural paradise, the adjective is used throughout modern Irish history as a synonym for republicanism, particularly
militant republicanism, and as a synecdoche for the country
as a whole.

Columba's speech, then, in terms of its artistic purpose,
is built on multiple layers of tradition in Irish social and political writing from the eighteenth to the twentieth centuries.
It looks for its resonances, not in the medieval history of
Ireland, but in its early modern history, in its emergent nationalism and in ambivalent social theories which recall de

Valera at his most bucolic. It is this element, more than any other, which makes *The Enemy Within* a history-play, rather than a historical drama, and, as a history-play, it uses political and literary traditions to add significance to its theme.

The Enemy Within is also a memory-play; indeed, memory is, to an extent, the "enemy" of the title. As Columba is disturbed by memories of his past, the elderly monks contend with their conflicting memories of their pre-exilic life. It is memory that binds Columba to his dual past, as founder of monasteries and leader of soldiers. Columba is a divided soul, as much as Hugh O'Neill in *Making History* is split between Gaelic Ireland and Renaissance England.

The Enemy Within is a good starting-point for Friel's plays, because his concerns with the modern Irish psyche are not masked as well by the art of the dramatist as they are in later plays. In *The Enemy Within,* the concerns that still exercise his mind nearly forty years later are present in embryonic form. He begins here to question accepted views of Ireland as nurturing, as edenic, or even as Christian. His Ireland has its share of Pictish pagans, and its Christians are violent and tribal, and look to the Christian church to bless their bloodshed. Brian, in his attempt to persuade Columba to lead the army claims: "We need a priest to lead us. They have a priest." (30). Eoghan, near the end of the play, is of similar mind: "it is in God's cause that you are going to lead us — to save Ita and the baby from the heathens" (70). This is not far removed from the rhetoric of religion and sacrifice for one's country espoused by Patrick Pearse.

In *Making History*, twenty-six years later, Friel's touch is more sure, and his target different. In *The Enemy Within*, he interrogated Ireland as an ideal, as an uncomfortable fixed point in the mind of a good man. In *Making History*, Ireland, represented by Hugh O'Neill, is not a fixed idea, but a country which is in flux. The O'Neill at the beginning of the play is quite distinct from O'Neill at the end, and neither bears much resemblance to Lombard's idealisation of him in his *History*. It becomes clear in the opening scene that *Making History* is a history-play in the Shakespearean sense. It represents figures from history, but radically alters characters, dates, times, and events to force the past to interrogate the present. In O'Neill, O'Donnell, and Lombard, Friel presents three different versions of the Irish patriot. O'Neill is charismatic, complex, and deeply flawed. His English upbringing and accent contest with his native Irish lordship. He is cautious; his motives are unclear, even to himself. He has fought alongside the English against the Irish, and alongside the Irish against the English. O'Neill himself anachronistically refers to this as "the cold pragmatism of the Renaissance mind" (*Plays 2*: 283). Friel uses the conceit of changing accent to demonstrate that O'Neill is, in one body, two people. He speaks with an educated English accent which becomes, in moments of emotion, "*pure Tyrone*" (338).

O'Donnell, on the other hand, is drawn with broader strokes. He is a simple, emotional patriot. He follows the leader, but cannot fathom the subtleties of the leader's mind. To him it is a matter of good and bad, black and white, them and us. Friel uses him as a comic counterpart to O'Neill, but the serious purpose of the dramatic construction of this kind of patriot must not be overlooked in the bluster. In Act I, Scene I, his mind appears to be skipping from place to place. He interrupts Lombard's exegesis on Ireland, Europe, and the Counter-Reformation to talk about his mother's floor, salvaged from the Spanish Armada, and "the shit O'Doherty up in Inishowen" (258). F.C. McGrath is of the opinion that O'Donnell is drawn too broadly: "Friel's Red Hugh is a one-dimensional buffoon, a stage Irishman" (1999: 233). While there is some substance to the claim that: "[a]s a chieftain, second only to O'Neill in his time, he is not believable", this is, I think, to miss at least some of the point, and to confuse history with art. O'Donnell's antics are all good, comic material, but the contrast is necessary if the complex and calculating O'Neill is to be seen in the context of the simpler attitudes which surround him. Furthermore, O'Donnell's composition as a character supports one of the self-consciously dramatic constructions in the play.

During his first appearance, a dialogue takes place in which O'Donnell and Lombard speak to O'Neill, but seemingly at cross-purposes. Friel constructs this dialogue as a composer of chamber music or opera might. Marked by Harry's exit, O'Donnell's tangential prattle takes the form of a musical counterpoint to Lombard's report on his *Commentarius*. While Lombard pronounces on England's mismanagement of Ireland, O'Donnell grounds the conversation in domestic rows. Two conversations take place, and two views of historical process are presented simultaneously: the partisan historian's view, which imposes pattern and purpose on events, and the equally partisan view of the participant, who on occasion cannot see the big picture at all. This is why Friel introduces O'Neill's questioning of Lombard's *History* at this point, while the other speeches are taking place:

> **O'Neill**   And when your checking is done?
>
> **Lombard**   Then I suppose I'll try to arrange the material into a shape — eventually.
>
> **O'Neill**   And interpret what you've gathered?
>
> **Lombard**   Not interpret, Hugh. Just describe.
>
> **O'Neill**   Without comment? . . .
>
> **Lombard**   I'm no historian, Hugh. I'm not even sure I know what the historian's function is — not to talk of his method. (257)

The duet between Lombard and O'Donnell turns into a trio, with O'Neill at this point making artistic and dramatic sense of the other two by drawing attention to the structure of the conversation. Harry, the fourth participant in what then becomes a quartet, returns to strike a chord from one of the earlier themes: O'Neill's marriage to Mabel Bagenal. The use of the form gradually subsides as Harry takes control of the meeting, but surfaces twice again in the course of the play, in Act 2, Scene 1, and again in Scene 2.

Lombard is the myth-maker, and as such is the one who makes history in the play. Lombard, as a cleric, is writing not a history of O'Neill, but a hagiography. Quite apart from the discussion of the merits of style over truth, Lombard's earlier thesis, *De Regno Hiberniae Sanctorum Insula Commentarius* (A Commentary on the Kingdom of Ireland, Island of Saints), makes clear the nature of the political force he represents. The Island is holy, and must therefore be treated in religious terms. This is a theme which has surfaced and resurfaced in the course of Irish history.

There was, for a long time in Irish politics, a tendency to confuse republicanism and Catholicism. They developed a common rhetoric, one of sacrifice and submission, of saintly mothers and holy peasants obedient to a higher power. In one case, this was God, in the other the ideals of the republican movement, and later, of the Fianna Fáil party as the perceived inheritor of those ideals. Although, historically, O'Neill did have the tacit support of Pope Clement VIII, his was not a Catholic nationalist uprising against English tyranny, but an attempt by a local lord to hold his independence and prestige, by whatever means possible. Lombard's *History* is, one may assume from its opening, cast firmly in traditional, redemptive form. A hero is longed for, is predicted by prophets, and is born to free an oppressed race (339).

Lombard may owe some aspects of his character to the myth-making elements of Pearse, who, when he spoke of Ireland and of rebellion, did so in terms better suited to epic poetry or religion. Pearse was both myth-maker, in that he invoked the spirit of Wolfe Tone during the 1916 rising, and myth, as his own cult, and the need of the new republic for simplified heroic figures, grew following his execution. In an oft-quoted passage, Pearse said: "bloodshed is a cleansing and sanctifying thing, and the nation that regards it as the final horror has lost its manhood . . .". The passage was used by Sean O'Casey in *The Plough and the Stars* to counterpoint the action in the public house (O'Casey, 1980: 162). Specifically, since the Easter Rising, patriotism, in the sense of republican patriotism, has become imbricated with Catholicism. The chosen day for the rebellion and the act of rebellion itself, which was doomed to failure from the outset, was a deliberately manipulated echo of the blood sacrifice of Calvary and the Resurrection of Christ on Easter Sunday. The reality is that the Catholic Church automatically excommunicated members of the Irish Republican Brotherhood, and that the Rising itself was badly organised, poorly equipped, and had, in fact, been called off by the IRB leadership.

In Lombard, Friel has assembled the essence of the historical vindicator. Lombard writes history as an idealised *exemplum* for the present. He acknowledges this in his opinions on the status of truth and falsity: "But are truth and falsity the proper criteria? I don't know. Maybe when the time comes my first responsibility will be to tell the best possible narrative. Isn't that what history is, a kind of story-telling?" (257).

This is more than simply a statement of Lombard's intention to glorify O'Neill, whatever the actual outcome of his life. The question has resonances for scholarship, art, and politics. The question affects the status of scholarship. If

scholars of any kind try to find patterns in a life, or a work
of art, are they then guilty of "a kind of storytelling"? Friel is
alluding here to postmodern theories, which cast doubt on
the existence of an objective "truth", divorced from the subject who utters it, an important theme in many of his plays.
Lombard's question also affects art and politics, because, if
the same is true for them as for scholarship, then there are
equivalences between them. Politics becomes another scholarship, and another art, in which patterns are imposed on
random events, and stories of various kinds are told, for
whose practice truth and falsity may not be the most important criteria. This is very true in the Renaissance, during
which politics came to be seen as an art to be practised.
One thinks not only of Machiavelli's *The Prince*, but also of
Castiglione's *The Book of the Courtier*, both of which seek to
inform the cold, pragmatic Renaissance mind, to paraphrase
O'Neill himself.

Musical forms appear again in Act 2, Scene 1, as a disbe-
lieving Hugh O'Donnell reads from the letter of submission
that O'Neill is composing to Elizabeth. An extended stage-
direction marks the importance of the exchange:

> *At first O'Donnell reads his portions of the submission in*
> *mocking and exaggerated tones. He is unaware that*
> *O'Neill is deadly serious. But as they proceed through the*
> *document — O'Donnell reading his sections, O'Neill*
> *speaking his by heart — O'Donnell's good humour*
> *drains away and he ends up as formal and as grave as*
> *O'Neill.* (310–1)

In this duet, the theme is the same, but delivered with different emphases, the music gradually blending at the end of
the letter. As the phrases become shorter, the tone is one
of gradually merging sadnesses. It is concluded by
O'Donnell: "To whom I now most abjectly and most obedi-
ently offer my service and indeed . . . my life . . . *Silence* . . ."

(312). The movement is counterpointed by the discussion which follows. O'Donnell suggests that it would be "a good one" if Elizabeth were to believe O'Neill's letter. He misses the point, again allowing O'Neill to deliver the play's message of political relativism and expediency: "Belief has nothing to do with it. As Mabel says, she'll use me if it suits her" (313).

The play ends, in Act 2, Scene 2, with the final duet, this time between O'Neill and Lombard. It is a reprise of the theme, announced earlier in the Act, of submission. Lombard's theme is the opening of his *History*. O'Neill's speeches are, *verbatim*, the letter to the Queen he had written in Scene I. Lombard begins his *History* with a highly conventional portrait of the romantic hero:

Lombard	Son of Feardorcha, son of Con Bacagh, son of Conn Mor, noblest son of noblest lineage, who was fostered and brought up by the high-born nobles of his tribe —
O'Neill	I do with all true and humble penitency prostrate myself at your feet and absolutely submit myself to your mercy . . .
Lombard	He continued to grow and increase in comeliness and urbanity, tact and eloquence, wisdom and knowledge . . . (338–9)

While Lombard's histrionics are effective as conventional hagiography or romance, they are also exaggerated enough to indicate that Friel has another idea in mind. The lines, which are based on Luke 2: 40, 52, recall not so much Christ, or any Gaelic hero, but a pastiche, such as the description of Finn MacCool in O'Brien's *At Swim-Two-Birds*:

The arms to him were like the necks of beasts, ball-swollen with their bunched-up brawnstrings and blood-veins, the better for harping and hunting and

> contending with the bards. . . . Three fifties of foster-
> lings could engage with handball against the wideness
> of his backside, which was wide enough to halt the
> march of warriors through a mountain-pass.
> (O'Brien, 1980: 14–5)

By exaggerating the description of the ideal Hugh, while the figure of O'Neill is present on the stage to be compared to it, a poignant and bathetic ending is created. By undercutting Lombard in just the same way, Friel is commenting on those who make history, including, as playwright, himself.

Musical constructions abound in the work of Friel, and it is not unusual to find him structuring sections of his drama after musical forms. As early as his introduction to *The Loves of Cass McGuire* he speaks of the characters' soliloquies as "rhapsodies". He continues: "to pursue the musical imagery a stage further . . . I consider this play to be a concerto in which Cass McGuire is the soloist" (7). Music and dancing punctuate *Dancing at Lughnasa*, and music pervades *Aristocrats*, *Wonderful Tennessee* and *Give Me Your Answer, Do!*, while in *Performances*, an entire string quartet is played during the course of the play.

In *Making History*, the musical forms tie the main themes together, but their function is not merely structural. By giving the story of O'Neill a structure, which is evidently formal and artificial, he eschews realism. This is not untypical: he has done so in many plays, but here it has an additional poignancy, not to mention irony, in that one of the main discussions in the play is on the merits of truth over style. In his introduction to *Plays 2*, Christopher Murray quotes Friel from the programme note, when he says: "history and fiction are related and comparable forms of discourse and . . . an historical text is a kind of literary artifact" (xii). By saying so, and by consciously changing the facts of history, Friel draws attention to his play as an artefact, as a piece of fiction.

Early in Act 1, Scene 1, Harry Hoveden mentions: "Bad news from London. Young Essex's been arrested and thrown in the Tower" (*Plays* 2: 251). There follows an exchange on the charges facing Essex, and on O'Neill's affection for him. This could not have happened. The scene is set specifically in late August 1591. At that time, the first Earl of Essex, Walter Devereaux was dead (1576), and the second earl, Robert, would not be appointed Lord Lieutenant in Ireland until 1599. The charges mentioned by Harry were not brought until the summer of 1600 (Guy, 1990: 448). This is neither accident nor the misinformation of his sources. According to Murray, Friel used Seán O'Faoláin's book *The Great O'Neill* as his primary source. O'Faoláin sets out the participants in the book at the beginning, like a cast of characters. Under "Essex" is the note:

Walter Devereux, 1st Earl of Essex.

Robert Devereux, 2nd Earl of Essex. Lord Lieutenant of Ireland, 1599–1600. (O'Faoláin, 1942: x)

It is inconceivable that Friel would not have read the *dramatis personae*. Likewise, the arrival of Lombard and O'Donnell is historically impossible. O'Donnell was a prisoner in Dublin Castle until his escape at Christmas 1591, and his return to Ulster in January 1592 (Morgan, 1993: 131–2). This, and the fact that he did not become chieftain until May 1592, is also recounted by O'Faoláin (122–3). Friel also adapts the relationship between O'Neill and Mabel Bagenal to suit his theme; she becomes the obsession of his decline in exile. The historical Mabel left O'Neill because he kept mistresses, and died two years later than her fictional counterpart, in 1595.

Friel, it is acknowledged, is not writing a historical account, and is thus free to change details and events as they suit his purposes, but why these seemingly trivial changes to history? I would contend that it is connected precisely to the theme represented by Lombard, and the main theme of the play, namely, the writing of history and the status of truth. Friel changes these details simply because he can, and because it draws attention to the play's status as a self-conscious artifice. In this way the dramatic text itself becomes a piece of made history. Friel has O'Neill make a wry reference to this process in his conversation with Mary Bagenal when he makes the comment that "art has precedence over accuracy".

There is the suggestion that history is "made" in other ways, too. In Act 1, Scene 2, O'Neill purports to explain his purposes to Mabel: he is trying to hold a confused people together by keeping them in touch with their former traditions. The speech is not unlike the manifesto of a modern politician. O'Neill is honouring the traditions of the past, but he does not claim to believe in them; he is trying to keep the old ways as a means of social cohesion, but he is cautiously nudging them "towards changing evaluations and beliefs" (*Plays* 2: 299). The climax of the speech is the statement that "the formation of nations and civilizations is a willed act, not a product of fate or accident" (299–300). O'Neill is trying to shape his people with deliberation, because he believes that the "slow, sure tide of history" is with him (283). This is surely a deliberate anachronism. O'Neill is speaking like a modern statesman, a founding father; a de Valera, a de Gaulle, or a Jefferson. Friel is making the point that the modern state, and in particular, we must assume, modern Ireland, is the product of the deliberations of a few minds, as opposed to the organic and evolutionary will of the people. O'Neill's tribe are there to be led, not to be consulted.

Hiram Morgan points out that O'Neill is a divided self, in the way in which all modern Irish people are divided: being Irish, but speaking in English, having one foot in a Celtic past, and one in the European present (Morgan, 1990: 61–3). This is, one presumes, a common position in which post-colonial countries find themselves. They are divorced from their culture, in that their current language is not the language of their ancestors. They are not, and, according to Friel, cannot be, integrated into the language of the conqueror. It becomes more intense for those post-colonial northern Irish nationalists whose emotional allegiance is to the Irish Republic, yet whose legal duty is to the British crown.

Morgan points out that *Making History* and *Translations* dramatise two of the crucial historical episodes which produced colonial Ireland: the flight of the earls and the renaming of the country, alongside the inception of the National School system. Homi K. Bhaba, in "The Discourse of Colonialism", proposes that: "the construction of the colonial subject in discourse, and the exercise of colonial power through discourse demands an articulation of forms of difference . . ." (Bhaba, 1986: 150).

In terms of *Making History* and *Translations*, the construction of British colonial power is established through the kind of difference Bhaba mentions. In the sixteenth century, it was by re-establishing the Irish chieftains as English barons and earls, with the legal protection of primogeniture. This inserted a lever of difference between the newly created Irish nobles and those members of their septs who might have been eligible for election to the leadership under the Brehon Laws. In *Translations*, the country is renamed in English, inserting a discourse of difference between the people and their localities. By this method, ironically, *Dún na nGall*, "the stronghold of the foreigners", becomes the meaningless *Donegal* in a foreign tongue.

The repercussions for modern Ireland of these historical events cannot be underestimated, and Friel does not disregard their power. His O'Neill was, historically, an attempt at a fusion of the two cultures. Instead of synthesis, Friel portrays Hugh as a conflicted body, representative of the Irish body politic. The ethnic conflict is played out in the body of Hugh, and, one might imply from Morgan's remarks, in the body of every modern Irish person.

The most renowned of all Friel's history-plays is *Translations*. From its first production by the Field Day Company in 1980, it was apparent that something significant had happened in Irish theatre. The drama critic of the London *Times* noted at the time that he was "witnessing the birth of a classic" (*Irish Times*, 10 November 2000). Field Day itself had been founded with an overtly political purpose. In another *Irish Times* article, playwright Thomas Kilroy spoke of the company's work exemplifying "the way in which . . . theatre could cast a light upon contemporary politics in Ireland, north and south" (*Irish Times*, 24 April 1999; also Kilroy, 1999: 87). This is broadly corroborated by Seamus Deane in the introduction to *Selected Plays* (1984: 20–1).

The plot of *Translations* deals, in its broadest terms, with the effect of the Ordnance Survey expedition of 1833 on Baile Beag, County Donegal. It also pits the learned Gaelic tradition of the hedge school against the developing National School system. Fluid, traditional Irish toponyms are contrasted with official, registered English ones; unofficial, localised traditional schools of Latin and Greek are compared with the new institutionalised system of education.

The hedge school, it must be said, was by no means as primitive as its name implies, although the *OED* definition suggests the opposite: "an open-air school, esp. in Ireland; (later) an inferior type of school". The schools were, at their best, neither open-air nor inferior. The facilities were basic, when compared to the building designs that followed the 1831 Education Act, but they compared well to the houses in which their pupils and masters lived. The 1831 Act made elementary education available to all, but forbade the use of the Irish language, and taught English history and customs. It is this system which Pearse called "the murder machine" for its attempt to eradicate Gaelic customs and language.

Translations is an intensely political play, yet Friel says that he did not set out to write one: "the play has to do with language and only language. And if it becomes overwhelmed by that political element . . . it is lost" (McGrath, 1999: 181–2). However, it is disingenuous to believe that any work dealing with the Irish language in the context of colonialism can be apolitical, or that the issues raised by the suppression of Irish culture by British rule will not cause an emotional response in at least part of the audience.

The politicisation of the Irish language begins quite early in Irish history. The Statutes of Kilkenny in 1366 enacted that the English in Ireland should not use Irish, or Irish customs. The Statutes also forbade intermarriage between English and Irish-speakers, though the practice still continued. These laws were the beginning of the separation of the Irish language from political power.

Following O'Neill's defeat, James I followed a policy of plantation in Ireland. The effect on the language of the introduction of English-speakers with titles to large tracts of land was obvious: it equated Irish-speaking with poverty.

The Penal Laws had the same effect, although they were specifically anti-Catholic rather than anti-language. First enacted in 1625, they forbade Catholics from teaching schools, bearing arms, and buying land, among others. As most Catholics were still Irish-speaking at this time, the result was a further alienation of the language from the centres of political control. The Irish language remained outside the structures of power until the Gaelic revival of the late nineteenth and early twentieth centuries.

Pearse and his contemporaries sought to make the Irish language a political instrument, a means of differentiating "Gael" and "Gall" (Irish and foreigner). The phrase "Tír gan teanga, tír gan anam" ("a country without a language is a country without a soul") encapsulates the Pearsean nexus of language and identity. Even still, Irish language organisations remain a powerful political lobbying force, influencing education, sport, and culture, and exercising influence on politicians at local and national levels.

The Free State, and later the Republic, structured itself in such a way as to re-empower the Irish language. The Constitution of the new republic enacted that: "The Irish language as the national language is the first official language" (*Dréacht-Bunreacht*, 1937: 8), a slightly less robust translation of the inversion in Irish of: "Ós í an Ghaedhilg an teanga náisiúnta is í an phrímh-theanga oifigeamhail í" (As Irish is the national language, it is the official principal language (9)). "[P]rímh-teanga", furthermore, carries with it a semantic undertone of superiority which is lost in the translation. The civil and public services, the police, primary and secondary teaching, and even access to third-level education were inaccessible without knowledge of Irish, whether or not this knowledge would ever be relevant to the job or discipline. This requirement persists in some areas to the present day. This, in part, is the linguistic and cultural baggage carried by *Translations*.

Thus we may say that language in *Translations* is an indication of separation, a sign of cultural and political distinction. In this, Friel appears to follow Pearse. In fact, he echoes many writers on post-colonialism who see language as a means both of colonisation and of subjugation. However well the colony speaks the language, it will never belong to them. In *Portrait*, Stephen muses on this fact after a conversation with the Dean of Studies, an Englishman:

> The language in which we are speaking is his before
> it is mine. . . . I cannot speak or write these words
> without unrest of spirit. His language, so familiar and
> so foreign, will always be for me an acquired speech.
> I have not made or accepted its words. My voice
> holds them at bay. My soul frets in the shadow of his
> language. (Joyce, 1992: 146)

The premise of *Translations*, then, is that there are two
pieces of English legislation threatening the *status quo* in Baile
Beag, both of which require a transition from Irish to English. The characters may be presented in terms of their linguistic allegiances: Sarah, who, at the beginning of the play,
cannot speak at all; Jimmy Jack, who is lost in classical antiquity; Máire, who wants to learn English in order to emigrate;
Hugh, who refuses to teach English, and rarely speaks it;
Owen, for whom his knowledge of Irish and English is a tool
to be used; Yolland and Lancey, who are linguistically isolated in the play because they cannot speak Irish; and Manus,
who speaks all the languages used in the play, but is ill-at-
ease in any of them. He is an outsider in his own home, as
all of Baile Beag will be by the end of the play, linguistically
and physically, by reason of the anglicisation of names and
Lancey's evictions.

The touchstone of the play is Manus, who from the beginning is given the role of outsider, although he is part of
Ballybeg. He is isolated by his physical imperfection — he is
lame — and by his ability to see the broader implications of
the cartographical survey. In Act 1, he elevates Doalty's
prank to the status of a gesture of defiance. Doalty has been
surreptitiously moving the surveyor's staff, causing them to
dismantle the theodolite. Máire is merely exasperated by his
antics:

Máire	You must be proud of yourself, Doalty.
Doalty	What d'you mean?
Máire	That was a very clever piece of work.
Manus	It was a gesture.
Máire	What sort of gesture?
Manus	Just to indicate . . . a presence.
Máire	Hah! (*Translations*: 12)

The pause before "presence" draws attention to the word and gives it weight. Manus feels, already, that they have lost their presence in Baile Beag. As the opposite of presence is absence, one may surmise that Manus, even at this stage in the play, is beginning to feel in some way absent from his home place, in some way displaced. Máire's inarticulate "Hah!" indicates that she does not understand the gravity of the point. The writing exercise set for Bridget feeds directly into the irony of the scene: "It's easier to stamp out learning than to recall it" (15).

Another presence in the opening scene is the possibility of potato blight. *Translations* is set in 1833. In 1845–47, the crop failed repeatedly and led to the death or mass emigration of millions. There had, however, been severe potato famines in the years 1720, 1739, 1741, 1800, and 1822 (Kee, 1976: 173), so the sweet smell Bridget mentions would be available in living memory. An audience, in particular an Irish audience, would be aware that the Great Famine will, in just over a decade, complete the work of anglicisation begun by the Ordnance Survey translators. Of course, Manus cannot be aware of this, but he shares with Hugh O'Neill and, indeed, with his own father, the capacity to see that he is poised between two cultures which are about to clash, and that when that clash happens, he will be on the losing side.

It is with the entry of Hugh that the elements of the play are put into a fluid motion. He converts his drinking bout into a lesson in etymology, turning the events of his life into a translation exercise. He it is who introduces Captain Lancey, who wishes to address the class. Lancey, however, cannot speak Irish. According to Hugh, Lancey was surprised:

> that we did not speak his language. I explained that a few of us did, on occasion — outside the parish of course — and then usually for the purposes of commerce, a use to which his tongue seemed particularly suited . . . (23)

Friel is setting up a number of stereotypes here: the Englishman who expects all foreigners to speak English, and the native Irish speaker who scoffs at English as an inferior and bastardised tongue, suited only to buying and selling. Both are stereotypes current in modern Irish society, and Hugh and Lancey exemplify these types particularly well.

Hugh's disdain for English takes a distinctly political turn when he is challenged by Máire. She wishes to learn English, as money has arrived for her passage to America. She refers to Daniel O'Connell, the Liberator, who had little time for the Irish language, believing it to be an obstacle to political advance. The reaction of Doalty and Bridget is almost choric. Doalty comments that O'Connell was not averse to using Irish "when he's travelling around scrounging votes"; while Bridget adds: "And sleeping with married women" (24). Consistency and sexual morality were attributes demanded from Irish politicians. One thinks immediately of Parnell, crushed by the exposure of his affair with Catherine O'Shea. In a way, the reaction of Doalty and Bridget is a very Irish one. The Irish have always classed themselves as "begrudgers", those who cannot simply admire success. Faults must be found and articulated, the exalted must be humbled. Doalty and Bridget are the "chorus" who articulate this feeling.

Máire's announcement that she is leaving after the harvest is met by silence and a change to a not-unrelated subject. Hugh is confident that he will take over the new National School, and that it will be run just as the hedgeschool was, teaching Latin and Greek, but no English.

This attitude is contrasted with the work of the Survey, in the person of Owen. His comment that "My job is to translate the quaint, archaic tongue you people persist in speaking into the King's good English", allies him with Máire in his attitude to Irish, although the fact that he speaks both Irish and English undercuts the implied criticism in the King's "good" English (30). Lancey is presented somewhat comically as the "little Englander", one who is continuously frustrated by the persistence of foreigners in not speaking English. It is a cruel stereotype, and probably, as much as anything else, gave rise to the objections to the play that were voiced after its first production. Friel uses Lancey's stereotypical character to advance the plot later in the play. Here, he introduces the linguistic convention that has become the hallmark of *Translations*. All the actors speak their lines in English, but through the adroitness of the dialogue and action, characters can be speaking either English or Irish, depending on the context. Latin and Greek are the only languages spoken in their own right. The stage direction here is very specific: "*He speaks as if he were addressing children — a shade too loudly and enunciating excessively*" (32). Friel is working a well-used cliché here, and cannot resist making Lancey reply, when spoken to in Latin by Jimmy Jack: "I do not speak Gaelic, sir". In his speech about the Survey, and in Owen's brief translations, the comedy is continued. However, the subsequent conversation between Owen and Manus dilutes the humour of the scene by concentrating on the military and political nature of the operation:

Manus	You weren't saying what Lancey was saying!
Owen	"Uncertainty in meaning is incipient poetry" — who said that?
Manus	There was nothing uncertain about what Lancey said: it's a bloody military operation, Owen! And what's Yolland's function? What's "incorrect" about the place-names we have here?
Owen	Nothing at all. They're just going to be standardised.
Manus	You mean changed into English? (36)

The coming linguistic and cultural changes are indicated by Owen's name. Although he is called Roland by the English, he claims to be the same person. The end of Act I is ambiguous about this. Manus says that he is, indeed, the same Owen, but then watches as he "confidently" introduces Máire to Yolland. In performance, much could be said by Manus's reactions at this point. Is he sceptical about Owen's assertion? On Owen's entry to the schoolroom, the stage-directions are particular about his clothes; he is dressed like a city-dweller. Manus's clothes are, on the other hand, "shabby" (1). That change, we can assume, has come about since Owen left Baile Beag. But are the outward trappings the key to the character? Friel is too canny a playwright to make such definite statements so early in the play.

In the opening of Act 2, Owen and Yolland discuss their translation methodology, and while they do so, Yolland reveals his growing sentimental attachment to the Irish countryside. Friel introduces this aspect of Yolland's character as a counterbalance to the bullishness of Lancey, and yet it is another developed cliché. This is not a criticism: Friel is using a theatrical shorthand to enable the audience to recognise certain "types" before developing them further. Here,

Yolland is the type of sentimental Englishman who looks on Ireland as a rural paradise. This is a modern type, but it existed in the nineteenth century also. Yolland, for all his sentimentality and readiness to fall in love with the country, has an almost post-colonial awareness of himself as an outsider: "I may learn the password but the language of the tribe will always elude me . . . The private core will always be . . . hermetic . . ." (48). Friel here transcends the political elements of the play to approach one of his core concerns: the limits of spoken language as a medium of communication. It is here, and in Scene 2, that Friel exploits to its fullest the linguistic convention he established in the first act. Here, we see just how much Yolland is cut off from the Irish who surround him. Owen translates, explains, and takes him through the steps of the process, a mixture of translation and transliteration, until they find a suitable English version of the place names.

The lore of place names, or *dinnseanchas*, was an important part of Irish culture from the Middle Ages, beginning as early as the ninth century. *Dinnseanchas* professes to explain how and why features in the landscape came to be so named. Many of the explanations were at best spurious and at worst invented, but they achieved a kind of impetus of their own, an authenticity by use and acceptance. Place names acquired a narrative and a tradition of their own, and a set of associations which could be evoked by writers. Many of these *logainmneacha* (place names) survive: Teamhair (Tara), in County Meath evokes the ancient seat of the High Kings of Ireland. Benedict Kiely cites another such location:

> In Columcille's Glen of Gartan, near Letterkenny, you can still see the Flagstone of Loneliness, Leac an Uaignis, on which, tradition held, the saint had slept penitentially on the night before he sailed from Ireland. (Kiely, 1982: 98)

This one site is of particular interest, because Friel uses it himself in *The Enemy Within*:

> It appears that one night, years and years ago . . . I slept on this great slab of rock. Needless to say, I don't remember doing it. But it seems that ever since a pious practice has grown round the spot and all the young Tirconaill emigrants spend their last night there. (21)

Friel's slightly ironic tone mirrors that of Owen in his description of the origins of Tobair Bhriain. Owen's disdain for the etymology of place is abruptly arrested by Yolland:

Owen   [D]o we keep piety with a man long dead, long forgotten, his name "eroded" beyond recognition, whose trivial little story nobody in the parish remembers?

Yolland   Except you. (53)

Yolland's sentimental passion for Irish *logainmneacha* is also undercut by Friel. A moment earlier, while enthusing on the use of Greek and Latin, he glossed the place name "Termon" as coming from *Terminus*, Roman god of boundaries. In fact, "Termon" is a common Irish toponym, and is more likely to derive directly from the Irish, "tearmann", a safe place, refuge, or sanctuary, which was used in a religious sense, and thence from the Latin "terminus", meaning simply a boundary or a limit (Greek $\tau\varepsilon\rho\mu\alpha$, a boundary). While the Latin etymology was personified as the "god of boundaries", it is unlikely that any Irish place name would be so constituted, as Latin was introduced to the Irish language not through the Romans, as in Britain, but through its status as the *lingua franca* of the Christian church. Yolland's apparently straightforward etymology is false, whereas Owen's story, told in order to justify the changes to the name, is a more than adequate piece of *dinnseanchas*, albeit on a very homely level.

The two pieces of etymological *dinnseanchas* are put into context by Hugh, in a short pithy sentence that occurs in the text between Yolland's and Owen's. It is so charged with political significance that it is worth quoting in full:

> But remember that words are signals, counters. They are not immortal. And it can happen . . . that a civilisation can be imprisoned in a linguistic contour which no longer matches the landscape of . . . fact. (52)

These lines are at the core of the play, as far as the decline of the Irish language is concerned. Languages, Hugh is reminding Yolland, do not last after they have outlived their use. Typically, we are not told whether the Irish language has outlived its use naturally, or whether it is a forced death brought about by British imperialism. Hugh's words are borne out by the curious scene at the end of the play in which Jimmy Jack announces that he has arranged to marry Athene, and was seeing Zeus the following week to arrange the ceremony. That comic little scene can be played as the ravings of a drunken autodidact who has lost control of his own life and become unhinged, or as a stern warning against sentimental judgements about dead languages.

The Greek and Latin in the play are not just an indication of the level of learning of the inhabitants of Ballybeg, although it is a historical fact that some hedge-schools did foster an appreciation of those languages. They are also dead languages, studied for their rich literature and their influence on the events and thought-processes of the present. Hugh sees them as the product of an Arcadian age, of the "warm Mediterranean". He denigrates English as the language of commerce, ignoring the fact that his Latin and Greek are almost useless for communication with the living.

His attitude is quite close to that of some Irish language groups in the Republic today. The tendency to look at Gaelic Ireland as a kind of pre-British Eden is very common among *Gaeilgeoirí* (Irish-speakers outside the Gaeltacht) in present-day Ireland, but it is not a view to which Friel subscribes, having said clearly in an interview that he had "no nostalgia for that time", adding the caveat that: "one should look back on the process of history with some kind of coolness" (Agnew, 1980: 148).

The Donnelly twins have a similar function. Never appearing on the stage, they represent the violent underbelly of the society that Yolland thinks of as Eden. Doalty's suggestion that the twins would know how to defend themselves against a trained army gives them a vague paramilitary, terrorist resonance. These elements of the play should serve as a brake on the tendencies of critics and audiences alike to see the play as an elegy for a lost, Gaelic society. Edna Longley has remarked that the play "does not so much examine myths of dispossession and oppression as repeat them" (McGrath, 1999: 195–6). Lynda Henderson, in *Theatre Ireland*, called it a dangerous play because it "oversimplifies the cultural and political oppression of an 'innocent', 'untroubled', 'good-humoured' people by the 'militarily superior, imaginatively undernourished and relatively illiterate English'" (ibid, 196). This is, I think, to miss the point. It is only Yolland who sees the Irish in these terms, and he is killed for it. It is Hugh who accuses the English of a paucity of imagination, but he has not heard of Yolland's one-time neighbour, Wordsworth. Ignorance, it would seem, is culturally relative.

Neither are the Irish "untroubled": Hugh is alcoholic, Manus is lame, Sarah is mute, Jimmy is filthy, Doalty is "thick". Innocence, certainly in the sense of sexual innocence, is not a feature of Friel's landscape. Nellie Ruadh has

had a child out of wedlock, or at least by a man not her husband; the baby subsequently dies. Furthermore, at no point
are any of the English characters in the play portrayed as
illiterate. They are certainly militarily superior, and are, in
the person of Lancey, portrayed as oppressors.

Friel came under some criticism for his portrayal of the
sappers. J.H. Andrews, from whose book *A Paper Landscape*
Friel adapted some of the characters and situations in *Translations*, took him to task for his historical inaccuracies. Andrews pointed out that the sappers did not use bayonets,
and would not have been used to evict tenants. In a reply to
the criticisms, Friel pointed out that: "[y]ou don't go to
Macbeth for history" (Murray, 1999: 119). Friel's admission
of culpability in relation to historical accuracy was unnecessary, given that his plays, before and after *Translations*, have
so much to say on the nature of absolute truth, and the impossibility of finding it in language. Murray points out that
Andrews returned to his theme nearly ten years later, in an
article entitled: "Notes Towards a Future Edition of Brian
Friel's *Translations*" (Andrews, 1992–3), thus attempting to
place historiography above art, and suggesting by implication
that *Translations* be revised.

This small controversy is not in itself significant, being
based on a fundamental misunderstanding between the functions of art and history, but it is emblematic of the way in
which art becomes imbricated with politics in the Irish context. From the ballads of 1798 and the political *aisling*, Irish
art has always had a political dimension, so much so that the
poet Seamus Heaney had been criticised for not being more
overtly political, for not allying himself with his tribe. Friel
never had the intention of writing an overtly political play, as
an extract from his diary for May 1979, when he was writing
Translations, shows:

> The thought occurred to me that what I was circling
> around was a political play and that thought panicked
> me. But it is a political play — how can that be
> avoided? If it is not political, what is it? Inaccurate
> history? Social drama? (Murray, 1999: 74)

We have seen that Friel subsequently denied that the play
was about politics. Both statements are essentially true.
Translations is not *about* politics, but it is a political play, because of the political and cultural accumulations around the
Irish language, and the uneasy relations between Britain and
Ireland which existed in the early years of the Thatcher government (Margaret Thatcher was elected as British Prime
Minister on May 3, two days after Friel's play diary begins).
A play which ends with the large-scale eviction of a community by British soldiers, and whose first performance was in
the Guildhall in Derry, was certain to provoke political reaction. The play's first run, beginning in September 1980, was
against the backdrop of "blanket protests" by republican
prisoners in the Maze prison in Belfast. The protest got its
name from the practice of cutting holes in blankets and
wearing them, poncho-style. It is unsurprising that, under
such conditions, those who were predisposed to see the
play as republican or nationalist propaganda would read political meanings into the text. In an interview with Paddy
Agnew, Friel noted that *An Phoblacht* (The Sinn Féin/IRA
newspaper) published an article suggesting that Doalty was
the central character: "that a man who does not know the
seven times table, can still have a deep instinct which is true
and accurate" (Agnew, 1980: 147).

The play ends, as many of Friel's plays do, on a sombre
note. Ultimately, Friel's vision is a dark one, and many of his
characters are forced into self-denying or self-destructive
paths. In *Translations*, Manus decides to leave, and, although
his motives are never explained, it can be inferred that sus-

picion about Yolland's disappearance is only one factor. Manus has been displaced throughout the play. He is merely now giving a physical form to an established fact. The gathering in the schoolroom balances the scene at the beginning of the play: Máire, Bridget, Doalty, and Sarah are present, but Manus has been supplanted by Owen; the Gaelic scholar by the colonial hireling.

Máire's recital of the English place names given to her by Yolland has a particular poignancy, as it is followed shortly afterwards by Lancey's list of the places around Ballybeg that are to be razed. The final scene between Jimmy Jack and Hugh is reminiscent of the final scene of O'Casey's *Juno and the Paycock*, where Joxer and Captain Boyle return drunk to the empty tenement, and agree that the whole world is in a state of "chassis" (chaos). Christopher Murray has written more extensively on this parallel (Murray, 1999a: 19–21). He notes the "definite echo of the ironic closure of *Juno . . .*" (21). Hugh's *"urbs antiqua"* is also the victim of imperialist expansion, and he fails to notice that Rome, which produced much of the literature he admires, was an imperial, colonial power.

Friel returns to nineteenth-century Ireland in *The Home Place* and, inevitably, comparisons will be made between it and *Translations*. The tragedy in *The Home Place* is more domestic, even if it has social and political resonances for Ireland in both the nineteenth and twenty-first centuries. It is not a memory play, nor one which interrogates perceptions like *Translations* or *Making History*, but is more concerned with tribalism, race, loyalty, belonging, and exile from the centre. The question posed by the play is the question of whether Irishness is defined by birth, political affiliation or tribal loyalty; by anthropometrical measurement or genetic code; by fierce conviction or maudlin sentiment.

The play is set in 1878, the year before the Land War, and the year before Parnell became president of the Land League. The year is significant, because Friel is able to allude to the tenant unrest that gave rise to the campaign against landlordism without becoming directly involved in the politics of the period.

In the late 1870s, poor agricultural conditions in Ireland and cheap grain from America had depressed prices, with the inevitable consequence that many tenant farmers could no longer pay their rents. Evictions "more than doubled" in 1878 (Kee, 1976a: 70). By 1880, due to widespread eviction, more than half the population was dependent on private charity (70). In 1878 and 1879 agrarian unrest increased, with attacks on landlords and their agents becoming more common. Irishmen who occupied lands from which others had been evicted were also targeted. It is against the background of rising agrarian protest, after a long period of comparative calm, that *The Home Place* is set.

As the play opens, Christopher Gore, landlord and master of Ballybeg Lodge, is returning from a memorial service for Lord Lifford, who had been murdered on his way to evict a tenant. The Anglo-Irish gentry of Ballybeg and its surrounding areas are obviously shaken by the murder, and Christopher is concerned that there may be a list of intended victims. Almost immediately Friel introduces one of the main themes of the play: the past, and its influence on the present. This is not only the past in the sense of historical sweep, but also in the sense of a personal past, which can be both nurturing womb and enclosing prison. Personal past and historical dialectic invariably come into conflict in Friel. The catalyst in this case is Christopher's reminiscences about the past. He reminisces about Penny Pasco, who became Lady Lifford; about the past of Lifford himself, merciless to his tenants and, it is implied, abusive to his wife; about the eponymous home place in Kent, to which he was sent every summer as a boy, in order that he might become friends with his cousin Richard, who is his house-guest at the moment.

Richard Gore is the archetypal Victorian imperialist. Doctor by profession, gentleman scientist by inclination, he is currently engaged in an anthropological project. He is *en route* to the Aran Islands, where he proposes to measure the heads and bodies of the inhabitants. Richard is an adherent of craniometry and anthropometry, sciences which sought to classify people according to head and body measurements respectively. The "scientific" assumption behind craniometry is that skull size relates to brain size, and that skull shape determines other factors such as intelligence and predisposition to criminality or morality. In this it is not altogether different from the Victorian parlour pseudo-science, phrenology, which claimed to be able to predict character traits and intelligence from cranial bumps and hollows.

Craniometry is still a tool of anthropologists, who claim to be able to determine the continent of origin of a skull with reasonable accuracy from measurement alone. Anthropometry is now used benignly in the design of furniture, and the measurement of nutritional levels in populations. In the nineteenth century, it was being used to classify racial and sub-racial groupings. Anthropometry and craniometry reached their lowest point in the mid-twentieth century, when they became part of the Nazi arsenal of racist pseudo-sciences. Aryans and non-Aryans were classified according to craniometric measurement, and other physical features.

The Aran islanders were actually measured by anthropologist A.C. Haddon in the nineteenth century, and a paper on the subject was read to the Royal Irish Academy in 1892 (*The Home Place*, 77-9). Richard Gore's aims are more ambitious than mere scientific enquiry, and he is clear about his ultimate aims:

> Crack our code and we will reveal to you how a
> man thinks, what his character traits are, his loyal-
> ties, his vices, his entire intellectual architecture . . .
> If we could break into that vault . . . we wouldn't just
> control an empire. We would rule the entire uni-
> verse. (36)

This is science in the service of Empire, to be used to extend and preserve the British Dominions.

It is the mensuration theme which connects *The Home
Place* with *Translations*. In *Translations*, the British were concerned with mapping the Irish countryside; here, with mapping the populace. Both plays are concerned with the
attempt by the outsiders to "get the measure" of the Irish
race. In *Translations*, the measuring and renaming of the landscape captured and tamed its shifting, mythical essence, iso-
lating the population from their linguistic and topographical
past. In *The Home Place*, the mensuration is doomed to failure, not because its science is a sham, but because it offends
subversive elements in the local population. Its failure is the
catalyst for Christopher's realisation that he does not have
the measure of his tenants any more than does his cousin.
After three generations, the Gores of Ballybeg Lodge are still
called "the lodgers". "There were no locals?" asks Margaret
of attendance at Lord Lifford's memorial service, provoking
the cry from Christopher: "What am I, Margaret?" (17).

Richard Gore's attempt to classify the Irish race, or
races, by measurement, has resonances for the twenty-first
century. There is an element of the nature/nurture debate,
determinism having been reinvigorated by the claims of the
Human Genome Project, which, it has been claimed, has discovered the genes for belief in God and for infidelity, among
other things. Friel deals with it comically quite early in the
play. Describing Richard as a boring and graceless snob,
Christopher wryly remarks: "Must have something to do

with India. . . everyone who does even a short service there comes home gross. Father was convinced the climate did it" (19). The line is a throw-away, but neatly presents the nurture aspect of the argument. Furthermore, Richard's observations are bathetically deflated by local knowledge. He remarks that Clement O'Donnell's close-set eyes and short arms mark him out as not native to the area, to be told: "The O'Donnells have been here for close on two millennia" (43). Richard's language is sprinkled with casual racism, but Friel is careful to note that Richard consciously plays up his stereotype (29). By creating a character with the appearance of self-awareness, Friel has addressed some of the distaste a modern audience might feel. Using terms such as "nigresence" (20, 49) is deliberately provocative. Friel wants us to feel some of the offence caused by the measuring process, the humiliation of being treated like a specimen, and being rewarded with the equivalent of glass beads (32).

Of all the characters, only Richard Gore is most at ease with his place in the world. He is absolutely assured of the moral and economic superiority of the British Empire, and confident in the ability of science to classify, and thereby subjugate, the world. He is outraged rather than frightened when ordered to leave by the murderers of Lord Lifford, as if the sudden inversion of the social order was a personal affront rather than an expression of the misery and discontent of the population.

The play raises timely political questions also. In 2004 the Irish electorate was asked to vote on changes to Article 9 of the Constitution, one of the key citizenship articles. The 1937 Constitution had stated that citizenship belonged to everyone born on the island of Ireland. In the light of increased economic migration from Eastern Europe and Africa, the government proposed to deny automatic citizenship to children born on the island unless they had: "at the time of the birth of that person, at least one parent who is an Irish citizen or entitled to be an Irish citizen . . .". Human rights groups and the Irish Refugee Council were outraged at the proposal, and campaigned against it, calling it retrograde and racist. Nonetheless, it was passed by a majority of four to one. While the play may not have been influenced directly by the referendum campaign, the question of Irishness had been debated for many years before that, focusing on issues such as one's adherence to republican politics, the level of one's anti-Britishness, or one's ability to speak the Irish language.

Friel reduces all of these attempts to measure Irishness to absurdity with his insistence on anthropometry and craniometry, thereby problematising the question once more. Even the home place of the title is difficult to locate. Christopher refers to his home place in Kent, but Ballybeg Lodge is the only home he has had. He is tied financially and emotionally to his Irish estate, but sentimentally to Kent, which he visited as a boy. Other colonists are referred to by their English places of origin: Penny Pasco is from Devonshire; Tristram Brooke, a relation who lives in Kenya, has his home place in Warwickshire (26). The play raises the question of how many years or generations it takes to become Irish, or Kenyan, or anything. In the case of Christopher Gore, the attachment to Kent is a reminder that he does not belong in Ballybeg, even after three generations. His past is a reminder of his colonial and social superiority, and acts as a brake on his "marrying down" or "going native".

The home place exists in the play as an idea, rather than as a geographical location. After three generations, Christopher would be no more at home in Kent than he would be in Kenya. The home place is a symbol of the necessity to be rooted. It is, in anthropological terms, an "architectonic symbol of the centre" (Eliade, 1974: 8), a fragile expression of putative belonging. It is the same feeling, grossly sentimentalised, which drives the Irish when abroad to look for the nearest Irish pub, or the often-satirised need of the English to find fish-and-chips everywhere.

Christopher Gore's son, David, wants to break free of the house and its *genius loci* and concocts implausible dreams of eloping with Margaret and working as a tattie-hoker in Glasgow, teaching cello in Edinburgh, or emigrating to Africa, but is equipped neither physically nor intellectually for any of them. They are merely other locations into which he will not fit, as he does not fit in the Lodge. His past has formed his present, and is inescapable because he carries it with him. Whether this is a genetic/racial past or a socio-cultural past is left unclear. Christopher treats his son with mild contempt and condescension, not least because they are both in love with Margaret.

Margaret's love for David's ostensibly weak character is implausible unless one considers her situation as a servant. Her position in the house is unusual, given that she addresses everyone in the house by their first names, including the visitors, and behaves almost as their social equal. Richard refers to her as a "chatelaine" (21). She is herself dislocated from her origins. Sally asks: "[d]o you never go home now at all, Maggie?" (13); but the question remains unanswered. There is no home to which she can return. Clement O'Donnell claims that she has "cut herself off from her home and her people" (40). The discussion of her marrying Christopher is used to exercise some of the social and ethnic theories of the time. Richard, in his guise as man-of-the-world, is of the opinion that they should marry, and that Christopher should not concern himself about "marrying down". Richard, the guardian of racial purity, a few pages later in the text, is of the opinion that Christopher will: "marry an Irish woman and whatever is still Kentish in you will be extinguished" (33), neatly overturning his own theories on racial features. Introducing English blood into Irish stock he refers to as "evolution working progressively" (33).

Margaret's father, Clement O'Donnell, the drunken schoolmaster, articulates the emotional view of Irishness, all Tom Moore and mawkish sentimentality. It is as if Hugh Mor O'Donnell had wandered in from *Translations* for one scene. Friel is using a kind of self-referential literary shorthand here, as Hugh articulated much of the play's central dissociative power in *Translations*. Clement, his literary descendant, is an accomplished choirmaster. His music, drawn from *Moore's Melodies*, is an ambiguous trope. On the one hand, Moore has, Clement tells Richard with more than a touch of dramatic irony, "our true measure" (42), and his work "reproduces features of our history and our character". Friel's choice of "measure" and "features" in close proximity is richly ironic. Clement claims that the music enables the children to transcend poverty. The music, Friel implies, reflects a national collective psyche, unmeasurable by science. On the other hand, he has Clement use the songs, and his choir, to ingratiate himself with the local gentry, and the only reference to an Irish soul in the play is made by a maudlin drunk. On his exit, Richard dissects his character and his physical features splenetically. He is clearly affronted by Clement's appearance, demeanour, and opinions, and uses his scientific discourse as a weapon to reinforce his sense of his own superiority.

The local peasantry are presented on a continuum from the violently discontented Con Doherty, through the comical posturings of Tommy Boyle to the dismal wretchedness of Mary Sweeney. Con Doherty drives the plot of the play. He is presented as an agrarian agitator, one who is active politically as well as physically. He has recently returned from England where he had been "Meeting people; travelling around; addressing small groups" (14). Friel manages to make the terse lines sound like guarded understatement. It is impor-

tant to the structure of the play that he is not simply presented as a thug, but as one who is intellectually committed
to revolution and who has a love interest in Sally. His threats
to Christopher are all the more sinister for being low-key
and polite. Friel also contrives to make him Margaret's
cousin, once again problematising the idea of tribal loyalty. It
becomes apparent late in the play that Ballybeg Lodge de-
pends on the tacit and fragile goodwill and passivity of the
local populace. Once that disappears, as many landlords discovered, the system becomes unworkable. Both sides suffer,
and the implicit symbiosis is destroyed.

Tommy Boyle, aged fourteen, appears in Act Two, and is
a stage-Irish creation. Apart from the totemistic "Bejaysus"
he is irritatingly familiar and determinedly comical in his dealings with the Gores. In him, Friel creates another shade of
racial stereotype, yet another way in which the Irish national
character coped with colonisation: by becoming a burlesque
of itself for the amusement of the ascendancy. In performance, Tommy Boyle would probably be mildly charming to
one who was not aware of the elements of parody in his
character, and exceedingly irksome to those Irish who are
sensitive to the national image.

The silent Maisie McLaughlin, with her "amazing head of
curls" (46) is another picture-postcard image of Ireland, who
is overshadowed by Mary Sweeney. She, in turn, is emblematic of a significant section of the Irish peasantry of the time.
Despite occasionally kindly landlords like Christopher Gore,
the peasantry lived in filth and squalor, with little hope of
remedy other than by charity. Even those who suffer the pri-
vations of callous landlordism are given little sympathy.
When, in the opening scenes of the play, Margaret asks who
Lifford was evicting at the time of his murder, Christopher
answers: "Some welsher. Does it matter?" (17), dismissing
the grave social crisis as a problem of economic discipline.

The end of the play is problematic. As with many of Friel's plays, the final thrust which brings down the delicate social and psychic edifices in which his characters live is an apparently small one. Christopher Gore does not suffer a grave physical trauma, or a financial loss, or a personal bereavement; he is merely threatened. The threat of violence, given its proof in the case of Lord Lifford, is enough.

The measurement scene in Act Two is the fulcrum of the play. Typically Friel, the dialogue imitates music, in that the spoken parts are discrete but interconnected. Each speaker enunciates their own theme, and is not necessarily speaking to any other. In this fashion a maximum amount of information can be conveyed, and the themes of the play, having been introduced in Act One, are played before the audience with the efficiency of an operatic septet. Perkins, Richard Gore's assistant, delivers his smooth scientific message as a background against which the other themes emerge: Christopher's ineffectual "twittering", Mary Sweeney's beggarly whine, Richard's callous disregard, Tommy's stage-Irish turn, Margaret's commonsense, and Con Doherty's sudden "stop".

Richard's conciliatory attitude appears as variously sensible to Con, cowardly to Margaret, or traitorous to Richard. It is unresolved whether his motivation was any of the three, or just the realisation that his position was a very fragile one. As the play draws to a close, he oscillates between nostalgia, self-pity and impotent belligerence, doubting his position in the world:

> He [Lifford] bellowed at people as if they couldn't hear him. Maybe they didn't. That's how a landlord had to behave, he believed; as do most of the huddled eleven that turned up for the service. Always knew they were wrong. And I believed I could do things differently . . . . Fell flat on my face, didn't I?
> (66)

He doesn't question his right to be a landlord, merely the way in which that authority was exercised. His conclusion is that he and the locals "don't share a language" (67). This realisation, in Frielian terms, is crucial. There is no shared symbolic order between the planters and the natives. It is a trope that was central to *Translations*, but is here somewhat forced. The theme of Christopher's lack of knowledge of the Irish is only developed in Act Two. Friel places some lines in the text that emphasise the trope. He apologises to the assembled peasants because he has "thrown your routine into disarray" (45), asks if Maisie's curls are natural (46), objects to Margaret's subject and predicate inversion (60), and suggests Sally should buy herself a parasol and silk gloves (64).

The trees that are referred to in the opening and closing of the play probably owe something of their literary genesis to the destruction of the trees in Chekhov's *The Cherry Orchard*. Planted by Christopher's grandfather, they are scheduled for felling. The trees are specified by Friel as part of the stage set: "[a] crescent of trees encloses the entire house and lawn; it seems to press in on them" (8). They are a visible symbol of the way in which the past trespasses on the present. Planted by the "marvellous people", they now cut out the light and encroach on the house. The classification theme is played out in a minor key as it is applied to the trees. Their Latin names, the planting record, the countries of origin, colours, shapes, estimated root depth. The theme is connected to the mensuration theme by the discovery of a Black Walnut tree: "A Juglans nigra, yes! A nigrescent juglans!" (71). By using the provocative 'nigrescent', the marking of the trees suggests the marking of people for segregation: seats at the back of the bus, separate drinking fountains, or the marking of Jews with stars of David by the Nazis.

The play begins to gather its themes and tropes for the finale. The trees, the classifications, the mensuration, the songs of Tom Moore, the return of the falcon, the dependence of Christopher on Margaret all recur in a few moments of stage time. The finale is low-key and enigmatic. David, having spilled whitewash on his father, is fetching a new shirt. Christopher is overcome with confusion and Margaret rocks him in her arms like a child. David re-enters to witness this:

Margaret:	Sit quiet and listen.
Christopher:	I know you won't betray me, Maggie. I know that.
Margaret:	Don't talk. Listen. Pay attention to the music.
Christopher:	Maggie –
Margaret:	Shhh. Just listen. Because in a short time Father will come up here for me. Shhh.

In the first production in the Gate Theatre, Dublin, the play ended with David's re-entry, and omitted the lines above. There was no indication that Margaret would leave. Instead, the three of them were poised in a moment of unresolved uncertainty. By including the final lines, Christopher's tragedy is deepened, and the fate of Ballybeg Lodge is clear.

Friel's history-plays have in common with most of his work a concern for language, and a grave doubt about the existence or expressibility of an absolute truth. They are also imbued with the spirit of Irish history and literature. I do not mean that his plays are naively "Irish", or worse still, "Oirish", but that they are anchored in a social and literary history that makes them stronger by their use of, and questioning of, received historical traditions. The impact of history on the psyche of a country has little to do with the facts of history, insofar as they can be established. Friel shares this opinion, as evinced in the quotation used as the epigraph to this chapter. In his interrogation of the space between fact and its transformation by utterance, Friel is at once evoking the postmodern deconstructive project and the origins of what he considers to be the Irish dramatic tradition. In postmodernist terms, the space between fact and the effect of those facts on the psyche of the population is the point at which the deconstructive lever can be inserted. In the words of J.M. Synge: "there's a great gap between a gallous story and a dirty deed" (Synge, 1968: 169).

In speaking about *The Enemy Within*, Friel commented that he did not consider it a "historical play" (Maxwell, 1973: 55). Neither, for that matter, is *Making History*, nor *Translations*, nor *The Home Place*. In calling them "history-plays", rather than "historical plays" a crucial distinction is being made. A historical play is one from which a historical accuracy can be expected, although "historical accuracy" as a term is itself somewhat of an oxymoron. From a history-play, one can expect artistic integrity. Some historians have failed to grasp not only the difference between the two in relation to Friel, but have also neglected to notice that a large part of Friel's project is the questioning of the status of, or, indeed, the possibility of, any kind of accuracy or truth.

Chapter Two

Talking to Ourselves

. . . it may be considered, and carefully examined, whether the greatest part of the disputes of the world are not merely verbal and about the signification of words; and whether, if the terms they are made in were defined and reduced in their signification. . . these disputes would not end of themselves and immediately vanish. (John Locke, *An Essay Concerning Human Understanding*)

Communication in all forms is a fundamental theme in Friel, and is linked to his scepticism about the existence of external, objective truth. Characters attempt to communicate in various ways, and in various ways they fail. Communication appears to be at its most fragile when it is verbal. Words slip, and lose their meanings between languages, between individuals, and between the event and the recounting of it, through misunderstanding, misrepresentation, and lying. Communication — between individuals, between cultures, between past and present, or between the self and external reality — is a concern in all of Friel's plays.

Communication, too, is about a sense of Irishness. Eugene O'Brien has written on the way in which Irishness is defined by its opposite. He uses Lacan to illustrate the proc-

ess by which the Irish have come to define themselves: not
British, not English-speaking, not Protestant (2001: 115).
Friel problematises the way in which several Irelands (the
Ireland of the 1960s, republican Ireland, the Ireland of Big
Houses and faded gentility) communicate with themselves,
with outsiders, and with their sense of their own identity.

In *Philadelphia, Here I Come!*, Friel deals with what might
have been called, at the time of the play's first production,
"the generation gap" — that inability of adjacent generations
to understand their mutually exclusive *argots*. Gar and his
father rarely speak of anything other than the events of the
day and the commonplaces of commerce. As critics have
pointed out, the play has only the most rudimentary of plots,
concentrating instead on the emotional interplay of characters (Maxwell, 1973: 63; Dantanus, 1985: 123). The play
combines the custom of the American wake with the meaningless prattle of Beckett's tramps in *Waiting for Godot*. A
wake was a gathering of friends and neighbours who sat
through the night with a corpse before a funeral. Drinking,
card-playing, and storytelling were integral to the custom.
An American wake was similar, but to honour the living,
who, once they had gone, would most likely never return. In
Philadelphia, the schoolmaster and the priest call, friends of
Gar stay for a while, and the past returns in the form of
memories and stories. Yet, at the end of the play, none of
the characters has revealed anything important to any other,
and the most vital question is unanswered:

Private   . . . why do you have to leave? Why? Why?
Public   I don't know. I-I-I don't know. (*Plays 1*: 99)

Even Gar's communication with himself is difficult. By split-
ting the character into Public and Private, Friel is able to
present a parallel commentary on Gar's actions. The commentary, however, is not merely conscience, nor a stream of

consciousness, any more than the commentary of Sir in *Living Quarters* is straightforward and unquestionable.

In Episode One, Gar's excitement is conveyed by his song, and by his attempt to dance with Madge. The dialogue between Public and Private when Gar returns to his room, where he imagines himself spitting down on the inhabitants of Ballybeg, and watching himself play Gaelic football, is more appropriate to a teenager. It is Gar Private who then reveals that Gar is twenty-five. In reading the play, this is unexpected. This first twist in the commentary exposes the fact that Gar's emotional development is stunted. The rest of the dialogue is exposition mixed with fragments and fantasies, which serve to illustrate Gar's repression and his discontinuous inner life. The fragment of Burke's *Reflections* — "It is now sixteen or seventeen years since I saw the Queen of France, then the Dauphiness, at Versailles . . ." — is repeated eight times, with variations. Gar Public speaks the lines three times, Gar Private, five, completing the quote only once. Seamus Deane claims that the piece is used:

> to display the fact that the Ballybeg which Gar
> O'Donnell is trying to leave is indeed the remnant of
> a past civilization and that the new world, however
> vulgar it may seem, is that of Philadelphia and the
> Irish Americans. (Deane, 1984: 14)

This is, I suspect, an over-complex explanation. At one level, it is an Eliotesque fragment to be shored against the ruins of Gar's thought process. Constant manic internal posturing leaves little time for the question that can only be asked as the play closes. When the memory of his mother's unhappiness becomes too unpleasant, he uses the fragment to block it out (38). The use of the piece by Private during Katie's visit suggests that he is romantically transferring the description of a distant exotic female to Katie, who has married a doctor. It is also, to borrow from Deane's explanation, part of the posturing of Gar the pseudo-sophisticate. It is consistent with his fantasies about fashion shows, Chinese spies and Russian princesses, daydreams which lift him out of the drudgery of life as his father's assistant.

When Katie leaves, at the end of Episode Two, Private uses the quote as an unsuccessful attempt to calm the distressed Public. Private then breaks into a fragmentary recapitulation of the dialogue of the first two episodes. The effect is clearly of thoughts beyond control hammering at Public, and concludes with Private's unheard apostrophe to his father: "Screwballs, say something! Say something, Father!" (80). The absence of communication between exploitative fathers and weak sons is a theme which recurs throughout Friel: Manus in *Translations* cannot apply for the teaching job because his father has; Philly is damaged by his father's strength of character in *The Gentle Island*; the gloomy, dying spirit of Father broods over *Aristocrats*; Ben in *Living Quarters* has an affair with his stepmother, which precipitates the suicide of his father. Here the stubbornness of Gar and the inarticulateness of S.B. make communication impossible, except in a stunted, circuitous way, through Madge.

Both Gar and S.B. use Madge as a sounding-board for their recollections, and it is she who is the recipient of whatever vestigial emotions they share. In Episode One, when Gar discovers the newspaper in the suitcase, and realises that it dates from his parents' wedding day, his recollections of his mother are interspersed with "Madge says": "She was small, Madge says, and wild, and young, Madge says" (37). It emerges that Madge is his only channel of information about his mother, and that the case has been untouched since the honeymoon trip. This is accompanied by the second movement of Mendelssohn's *Violin Concerto in E Minor*. The shift from the fast First Movement (*Allegro molto appassionato*) to the slow Second Movement (*Andante*) is signalled by Friel just before the discovery of the paper (36).

The combination of massed strings and mellow woodwinds, and the high solo violin in the early section of the *Andante* conveys a feeling of irrecoverable loss. The contrast between the slow Second and exuberant Third Movements parallels Gar's progression from sadness to manic high spirits. He breaks out of his thought-sequence by removing the record, and lapsing into "Philadelphia, Here I Come!".

It is typical of Friel that the memory of his father that means most to Gar might be a figment of his imagination, while the memory S.B. has of him is equally faulty. In Episode Three, Gar plays the Mendelssohn again, this time while S.B. and the Canon are playing chess. Private becomes frenzied and, according to the stage direction: "*thrusts his face between the players*" (89):

> D'you know what the music says? . . . It says that once upon a time a boy and his father sat in a blue boat on a lake on an afternoon in May, and on that afternoon a great beauty happened, a beauty that has haunted the boy ever since, because he wonders now did it really take place or did he imagine it. (89)

S.B. cannot recall the incident, or even the boat. He misses the significance of the episode, infuriating Gar by listing the boats he could remember from the lake (95–6). S.B.'s own memory is different. He remembers Gar, dressed in a sailor suit, refusing to go to school, wanting instead to work in the shop. S.B. remembers taking the child to school by the hand, the two of them "as happy as larks". By the time he finishes, Madge has already cast doubt upon the memory, claiming that Gar never owned a sailor suit. The only connection between the two memories is the vague nautical motif, but this makes the missed connection all the more poignant.

The scene is based on an incident from Friel's own childhood. He tells the story of walking home in the rain with his father from a fishing trip. He remembers the lakes, the boat, the road, the weather, the singing. But in musing on the experience something different happens:

> [t]here's something wrong here . . . what is it? Yes, I know what it is. There is no lake along that muddy road. And, since there is no lake, my father and I never walked back from it in the rain with our rods across our shoulders. The fact is a fiction. Have I imagined the scene then? Or is it a composite of two or three different episodes? The point is: I don't think it matters. . . . For some reason the mind has shuffled the pieces of verifiable truth and composed a truth of its own. (Friel, 1971: 101)

It may not matter for Friel, but the memories are significant for Gar and S.B., although neither can articulate why. Each memory gives an imaginary shared sense of ease with the other that they cannot replicate in the reality of their existence.

Communication between the other inhabitants of Ballybeg is equally difficult. Gar's friends, when they call, appear to specialise in lying to one another about their sexual exploits, in order to cover up the fact that they haven't had any. Ned begins, boasting that he "had" Big Annie McFadden. The tone thus set, the scene becomes a series of false reminiscences of girls they have seduced from Greenock to Dublin to the "English bits" staying in the local hotel on whom they set their sights that night. Gar Private exposes the fiction by presenting parallel versions of the stories:

> you know what they'll do tonight, don't you? They'll shuffle around the gable of the hotel and take an odd furtive peep into the lounge at those English women who won't even look up from their frigid knitting! (*Plays 1*: 77)

Avenues of communication are restricted among this generation, too. Ned, whom Friel makes clear is the leader of the group, will brook no contradiction when challenged by Gar Public, and is supported by Joe and Tom:

Ned	Are you calling me a liar? . . .
Tom	(*Quickly*) Oh, by God, Ned was there, Gar, many's and many's the time. Weren't you, Ned? . . .
Joe	(*Nervously*) And maybe she got the squint straightened out since I saw her last. (71)

The directions are important. Tom reacts quickly to avoid upsetting Ned. Joe, uncertain of his place in the hierarchy, retracts his assertion that Big Annie had a squint. Private makes the point, jeeringly, that the memory of whatever fun they might have had will soon be shorn of its coarseness, and "what's left is going to be precious, precious gold" (77). The gold of memory, even false memory, transmuted from the dross of everyday life, is fools' gold, Private implies, trying hard to maintain the façade of cynicism.

Master Boyle is introduced, along with the Canon, S.B., and Madge, to epitomise the older generation, who have refused to relinquish power to the ageing younger one. They are characterised by repetitive speech, strangled by the demands of their lives and the need to keep going. Boyle, the schoolmaster who wants to write for American magazines, is an example of what Gar might become, were he to stay, but he may also be a parody of Friel, who, for ten years, was a teacher who wrote for *The New Yorker*. Boyle, a dissipated alcoholic, at odds with the Canon, always on the point of losing his job, still fantasises about a future in the same way that Gar does. He has, he claims, been offered a post by an American university, head of education in Boston (52). Although he is never contradicted, his story has the same resonance, and the same currency, as Ned's conquests.

The Canon communicates in comfortable clichés. Private plays the same game he played with S.B. at the beginning of the play, predicting what will be said next. On one level, it is a theatrical device for extracting humour from an everyday scene. On another, it reflects the paucity of communication that takes place in Gar's world. For Private, however, the Canon's lack of communication is more serious, given that his vocation is to convey eternal truths: "you could translate all this loneliness, this groping, this dreadful bloody buffoonery into Christian terms that will make life bearable for us all. And yet you don't say a word" (88). This is one of the few direct references to religion in the play, and it is invoked only to be dismissed as "insane". The religion of the old is of little consolation to the young.

The situation in which these young people, Gar, Ned, Tom, and Joe, find themselves was not unusual in rural Ireland. Many parents retained control of the family farm or business, and thereby controlled the lives, economic and social, of their children. As Lee put it succinctly, rural Ireland controlled population:

> through restricted and delayed marriage. . . . A callously efficient socialisation process postponed marriage and effectively denied the right to a family . . . by the simple device of parents disinheriting a high proportion of potential grooms and brides among their children. (Lee, 1989: 71)

This led to a high resentment factor against parents, seen not only in Gar's non-existent relationship with his father, but in Madge's warning that the "boss" would not like to see beer-bottles strewn about, and in the comments of Ned, the self-styled womaniser, who is just as dependent as the others on his father's sporadic generosity:

Ned   I meant to buy you something good, but the aul fella didn't sell the calf to the jobbers last Friday . . . and he could have, the stupid bastard, such a bloody stupid bastard of an aul fella! (75)

The alternative to the non-communicative world of Ballybeg is the constant prattle of the New World, embodied in Lizzy Sweeney. Even before she appears on the stage, she is characterised by Public's reading of her letter, and by her slightly inappropriate use of "desist", which strikes a discordant note in her vocabulary. She is everything that Ballybeg is not: she talks constantly about her feelings, her dwelling on the past is anecdotal rather than imprisoning, and her flitting, shallow mind constantly changes subject, unable to remember if Ben Burton is Lutheran, Baptist, or Episcopalian. She says more than she intends, both in her story of Gar's parents' wedding day, and in her story of why they came to Ballybeg. In the first, she lets slip that Maire may have been crying on her wedding day. In the second story, she parades their childlessness on the same level as her possessions, as a means of securing Gar's promise to emigrate. Private is, according to the notes, *"Terrified"* (65). Lizzy is a grotesque stereotype of what in Ireland is still termed "the returned Yank": vulgar, materialistic, and sentimental about the old country. It is to Friel's credit, and illustrates his integrity as an artist, that he never attempts to make his eponymous Philadelphia attractive. Gar's fantasies about his sexual adventures in America have the same status as Ned's bragging. One can infer that Gar will take his repression with him.

Repression and sexuality are also major themes in *The Gentle Island*, which exposes as spurious myths about the saintly lives of islanders, myths to which almost every schoolchild in Ireland was exposed until quite recently. The play, produced in 1971, was not a box office success, per-

haps because it dealt openly with homosexuality and homosexual acts, the latter still illegal in Ireland at the time.

Quite early in the play, it becomes apparent that Anna
and Joe have feelings for one another, but that these feelings
had never been expressed. As she leaves the island, helping
her drunk and incapable father, Joe seizes the moment:

Joe   Anna, I will write to you, Anna.

Anna   You hadn't that much to say to me when I
               was here. (*The Gentle Island*: 14)

He is unable to pursue the conversation, as she is occupied
with her father, and he, embarrassed by the slight show of
emotion, turns to talk to his. In that scene, many of the concerns of *Philadelphia* are played out. The would-be lovers are
kept apart by emotionally strangled inarticulateness and the
demands and expectations of the older generation. Like Gar,
Joe and Philly's mother is dead, and they depend on the
memories of others for an image of her. The absence of a
mother as a conduit for emotional communication between
fathers and sons occurs in many other Friel plays, including
Translations, *Living Quarters*, and *Aristocrats*. For Joe, looking
after Anna's house is a substitute for caring for Anna.

When the visitors, Shane and Peter, arrive, Joe is anxious that they be told the story of the Monks. Manus, his
father, the self-styled King of Inishkeen, refuses, so Joe begins himself. It becomes apparent very quickly why the story
is so important to him: "There used to be a monastery here
hundreds of years ago . . . and the old monk in charge of it
was very stern and very powerful" (32). All emotions and
urges, all important ideas are sublimated on Inishkeen. Joe's
invocation of the old, stern monk exacting vengeance on the
younger monks is simply another version of what is happening to him and to Philly. Manus, however, is of the opinion

that Joe will destroy the story; even the allegories have to have his *imprimatur*.

Joe's attempt to write to Anna is ultimately futile; he cannot write. Although he would have preferred Sarah to write for him, it is his father who bullies him into beginning dictation, and it is Manus who intervenes between Joe and his attempt at communication, by beginning without him:

> **Manus**   "Dear Anna, my father is writing this letter for me".
>
> **Joe**   That's smart. She'll know it's not me, won't she? (59–60)

Manus's motives soon become clear. He is trying to precipitate a marriage between Joe and Anna in order to repopulate the island. What the letter, or rather Joe's reporting of it to Sarah, does precipitate is the revelation that Shane and Philly were having sex in the boathouse. An attempt to create a normative heterosexual relationship has become skewed into the disclosure of a homosexual one.

In the play as a whole, the repression seeps out in the language, in the form of a Freudian return of the repressed. What might have been a useful strategy is, in fact, one of his less successful theatrical devices. When Shane and Peter arrive, Sarah responds to his momentary reluctance with the line: "No one going to eat you" (30). Shane's pretence that his mother is "principal boy in the Lap national pantomime", (35) hints at the gender-confusion which follows. Joe's invitation, at the dancing, for Philly to give a "buck-lep", with its connotations of rampant male sexuality, becomes a source of friction between the brothers (44). Probably the least successful use of the device is Joe's response to Philly's question about Peter's turf-cutting skills: "You're a bugger, too" (47).

Shane is a nexus for linguistic repression also. His changing accents are, among other things, a token of his ambiguous sexuality and of his dislike of straight questions, something at which Sarah excels. She asks many questions of
Shane, only some of which he answers appropriately. Even
with Peter, his alternative *personæ* contrive to keep others
at a distance, what Peter calls "the great protection" (27).
His response to Peter's initial rapture on the beauty of the
island is "Apache". His re-naming of Inishkeen as "scalping
island" is closer to the truth than he realises (26). As scalping is the violent removal of the hair and scalp, so the protective layers of the characters will be stripped away violently. His renaming is a reinforcement of the casual violence
that lurks beneath the seemingly idyllic surface of the island,
a violence indicated in Manus's missing arm, and the attempts to kill the stray dog. His response to Sarah's greeting
is "Hiawatha", which at once evokes the scalping island, and
the gender/sexuality confusion which is part of the play.

Sarah too, has difficulty with language. In the scenes with
Manus and Philly, she speaks like any other character. In her
expository scene with Philly, attention is drawn to her vocabulary in the line: "I won't be able to *thole* it, Philly, I know
I won't" (24). "Thole" is a Donegal dialect word, meaning to
suffer, but it comes, not from Irish, but from Old English
"*þolian*", to endure (Seamus Heaney makes the word a
lynchpin in the introduction to his translation of *Beowulf*
(Heaney, 1999: xxv)). The importance here is not etymology, but the oddity of the word, which serves as a marker in
her speech. When she speaks to Shane and Peter, her language becomes distinctly odd: "How did youse get in to the
island?" (28). The "youse" is repeated five times. When
Shane does one of his accents, which Sarah cannot understand, and Manus enters, speaking Irish, we realise that
Sarah's English is uncertain, and that in the early scenes she
was speaking Irish. The theatrical conceit, to use Friel's own

term, is never made explicit, or ever exploited, and was abandoned after one scene, but it is there, waiting to be developed in a mature fashion in *Translations*.

Not all communication in Friel is futile, although it is ultimately tragic. In *Translations*, the short love-scene between Yolland and Máire is a triumph of theatricality, and a major element in Friel's developing theory of communication. Yolland has no Irish, and Máire only one stumbling phrase and a few odd words of English, yet they manage to communicate their affection perfectly, their contrasting languages, although expressed entirely through English, merging and diverging like themes in a duet. They begin to communicate through the mechanics of the languages, rather than through their content. Thus:

Maire	The grass must be wet. My feet are soaking.
Yolland	Your feet must be wet. The grass is soaking.
	(*Translations*: 62)

The involved chiasmus is extremely effective when played carefully, but it can be lost in performance if not acted and directed skilfully. The simpler, but no less effective, "what what?" and "sorry-sorry?" and the mutually used phrase "O my God", draw them closer, but for the audience, not for the characters themselves. One might infer that Friel is using the similarities of the human thought process to indicate that understanding and closeness are possible without language, even though the speakers of language are unaware of these possibilities.

They move from the constructions of language to the sounds of language: water, fire, earth, Druim Dubh, Poll na gCaorach, Lios Maol. Maire joins in Yolland's recitation of place names as they map out an imaginary topography which brings them physically closer together. They appear, by the end of the scene, to be aware of what the other is saying:

Maire	Don't stop — I know what you're saying.
Yolland	I would tell you how I want to be here — to live here — always — with you — always, always.
Maire	"Always"? What is that word — "always"?
Yolland	Yes-yes; always.
Maire	You're trembling.
Yolland	Yes, I'm trembling because of you.
Maire	I'm trembling, too. (67)

The writing is adroit, because it is just possible from the context that what they are saying is generated by the passionate repetition of "always" and the action of trembling. If that were the only purpose of the writing, then it would be merely appealing and clever, and could be admired or even dismissed as such. It works because both languages, at this point, are seen to comprehend the world in the same way. The rest of the play is taken up with the recital of the differences in perception between the Irish and English, with the impossibility of decoding the language of the tribe. Here the decoding process becomes, at least, simple; at best, irrelevant. Maire and Yolland move beyond language, speaking only in separate signifiers, without recourse to a shared signified. The language process becomes foregrounded again in the person of Sarah, who discovers them kissing. It is Manus who has taught her to speak, and now the words she speaks will precipitate the tragic ending of the play.

In *Living Quarters*, Friel creates a family living with the consequences of a long-ingrained inability to communicate. The Butlers repeat endlessly the day of their father's suicide, minutely examining their situation and motivations. To this end they have "conceived" Sir, who is part of the action, but outside the play. The story has been over for "some years" when the play begins, and the implication is that the family has been replaying events ever since. Sir is unlike Gar Private in two major respects: he is visible and accessible to every character, and he is aware of the presence of the audience, to whom he speaks. He is also the narrator, or perhaps, given the epigraph "after Hippolytus", the Chorus. Sir is charged with recording and interpreting every detail of the events leading up to Frank Butler's suicide: "the ultimate arbiter, the powerful and impartial referee, the final adjudicator, a kind of human Hansard who knows those tiny little details and interprets them accurately" (*Plays I*: 177–8). Hansard is a reference to the official *verbatim* record of speeches made in the British Parliament. Hansard is a literal notation, used to check what exactly has been said during debates, and often used to confront less-than-honest politicians with their former utterances. Sir is purporting to be able to record the words. It is evident, however, at the end of the play that he has not captured the spirit within the words. The brief final conversation with Anna, Butler's second wife, illustrates this. Sir is reading from his ledger, bringing the audience up to date on the lives of the Butlers. He has just reached Anna herself, and informed the audience that Anna has emigrated to the US, where she lives in Los Angeles:

Anna	That's all?
Sir	That's all I've got here.
Anna	Are you sure?
Sir	Blank pages.
Anna	I see.
Sir	Did you expect there'd be something more?
Anna	I just wondered — that's all.
Sir	Is there something missing?
Anna	No. Not a thing. Not a single thing. (246)

The key to the events is not in the details of the plot. Friel is commenting on the difficulty of decoding and interpreting the words and actions of others. Ultimately, the attempts of the Butler family to understand their situation are unsuccessful. However accurately the words may be transcribed, truth itself lies somewhere beyond the ability of those words to describe it.

Living Quarters is, in common with most of Friel's plays, also driven by memory. In other plays, characters present their individual, conflicting versions of the past. In this case, the entire action is composed of the memories of the characters, forced into a single version by Sir. Ulf Dantanus has described the play as "the formalised memories of people dead or scattered all over the world who in their minds keep turning over the fateful events of this one day" (1985: 160). From a staging point of view, it allows Friel, through Sir, to comment on each of the characters in a way which would normally take much longer.

In contrast to the analytical complexity of the play, the plot is melodramatic, and, on balance, unconvincing. Commandant Frank Butler returns from service in the Middle East. While serving in an outpost called Hari, he and his men came under fire. Butler carried several men to safety and is hailed as "the hero of Hari". His second wife, Anna, whom he had married ten days before his five-month tour has, in his absence, had an affair with his son, Ben, described as a "hesitant, nervous . . . mother's boy". The affair is known to everyone except Butler. As the family gathers to celebrate, old memories and old tensions emerge. At the climax of the play, Anna confesses her infidelity and Butler shoots himself. If this were the progress of the play, then it would be a banal, third-rate drama, but by allowing the characters, including Butler, to be aware that they are re-enacting something that has happened, and by causing them to comment on their own part in the action, the plot becomes the vehicle for an exploration of families, relationships, the effect of the past on the present, and the impossibility of communication.

Early in the play, the three sisters, Helen, Miriam, and Tina, sit in the sunshine, reminiscing. There is a double memory at work here, because the scene in which they are reminiscing is also being remembered, and re-enacted. The word "remember" occurs seven times in one page of text: once as an imperative: "Remember", three times as an interrogative: "Do you remember, Helen?", twice as a negative: "I couldn't remember his name", and, finally, once as an indicative: "Yes. Yes, I remember" (185–6). It is as if Friel is trying to include every parsing of the verb, to interrogate the idea of remembering from every angle. It is only at the end of the interrogation that remembering becomes reluctantly indicative. Before Helen utters the final "I remember", the stage directions state: "*As Helen passes her she hugs her* [Tina] *briefly. Pause.*" It is evident that Helen does not trust this double memory. A little later, she argues the point with Sir: "It's distorted — inaccurate . . .The whole atmosphere — three sisters, relaxed, happy, chatting in their father's garden on a sunny afternoon. There was unease — I *remember* — there were shadows . . ." (188). An insistence on the clarity of her memory is pitted against the collective memory of her sisters and the official version held by Sir. Sir insists that, although the other sisters are aware of the shadows and strains, the events as they have unfolded are "exactly right", creating a tension between external appearances and internal realities. In her subsequent scene with her father, Helen makes the comment: "The past's over, Father. And forgotten" (194). Both she and the audience know, however, that this cannot be true, particularly in the case of the Butlers.

One crucial incident in the attempt to alter the past comes as the family, minus Anna, poses for a photograph, taken by Father Tom. Anna comes downstairs behind them, and calls Frank, who does not hear. At this point, Sir behaves like a stage direction: "She calls Frank twice. But Frank does not hear her. And she goes back to her room and cries" (201). Anna, like Helen, is not content to perform passively, even in a situation she has helped construct. Instead she forces her way into a scene in which she has no part:

> Listen to me, all of you . . . When you were away, all those months I was left alone here . . . I had an affair with your son, Ben — with your brother, Ben! An affair — an affair — d'you hear! (202)

The participants in the scene ignore her. Sir comments: "they won't hear you now". The line is ambiguous enough to leave the reader wondering if the "won't" means, merely, "they will not hear you now", or "they do not want to hear you now". Defeated, she steps back into the plot, having, to paraphrase Sir, shuffled the pages, but changed nothing.

In the next interruption, the characters discuss the choices they could have made. Anna wishes to move on to what she calls, pointedly quoting Sir, "the point of no return". The reason Sir does not allow this is unpleasantly simple:

> Because at the point we've arrived at now, many different conclusions would have been possible if certain things had been said or done or left unsaid and undone . . . And it is the memory of those lost possibilities that has exercised you endlessly . . . (206)

In Sir's control of the drama, he resembles, as Dantanus has stated, the Producer in Pirandello's *Six Characters in Search of an Author*, or the Stage Manager in Wilder's *Our Town*. The Stage Manager, in particular, locates the action in space and time on the bare set, moves chairs and settles props, just as Sir has done, and interprets for the audience the motivations and thoughts of the characters. Where he differs from Sir is that the Stage Manager is a benevolent and avuncular figure, who obviously cares about the town and its people. Sir's concern is verbal accuracy. The fact that the accuracy causes distress to the characters is, apparently, beside the point.

Dantanus maintains that the play relates to Euripides because of the illicit love-affair and the suicide. In *Hippolytus*, Phaedra, realising that she loves Hippolytus, her husband's natural son, kills herself. In *Living Quarters*, Butler, realising he has been cuckolded, kills himself. Dantanus further asserts that the relation is one of opposites. Phaedra kills herself because of her guilt. Frank Butler is innocent, but kills himself while the guilty live "and busy themselves with their torrid and trivial lives" (Dantanus, 1985: 162). Dantanus' evident dislike of the family clouds his judgement. There is no evidence of the rest of the family having anything remotely resembling normal lives. Helen leaves her job because of mental problems, Tina has a dead-end job in an all-night café, Ben is jailed twice for being drunk and disorderly. Anna lives the life of a working singleton in America, and Father Tom is confined to bed in a nursing home. Their lives are certainly trivial, but torrid is not an adjective applicable to any of them. In one way, to live the life of the dispossessed is the punishment meted out to the Butlers. Only Miriam, who is detached from the emotional centre of the play, remains in Ballybeg, married to Charlie, the other observer, who, despite Sir's declaration that there were no spectators, remains steadfastly outside the play's frame of reference.

The dramatic centre of the play is, I believe, the communication between past and present, and how the actions of the past are transmuted and relived in the present. This is a recurrent theme in Friel's work. *Translations* speaks to postcolonial, vaguely anti-British, contemporary Ireland; *Making History* to the myth of the historical hero. *The Gentle Island* looks at the peasant heritage glorified by the fathers of the state and finds it wanting, yet this heritage still permeates modern Irish life. In *Living Quarters*, Friel uses the communication between past and present in one family to highlight the absurdity of the search for absolutes. Sir's ledger captures the words from the past, but not their spirit. One watershed in the Butler family's personal history has scattered them across the world and destroyed their tentative unity, yet a knowledge of the mechanics of that event does not answer the questions they ask about it. The essence of *Living Quarters* is not the certainty it tries to bring to the events of Butler's suicide and the episodes leading up to it, but the uncertainty at the heart of all human interaction, and the difficulty of resolving it.

The play Friel wrote immediately after *Translations* was *The Communication Cord*, and the two, even for Friel himself, are often seen as companion pieces (O'Toole, 1982: 175). According to Friel: "*Translations* . . . was about how this country found a certain shape. This farce is another look at the shape this country is in now" (Comiskey, 1982: 165). It has been pointed out that the themes of *The Communication Cord* are the same as those in *Translations*, but that the former takes them a great deal less seriously. One of the problems seems to be the almost immediate elevation of *Translations* to the status of "Great Play" and the consequent reverence with which it was treated. Because it dealt with the relationship between Ireland and Britain, it was also open to political interpretation of various shades. *The Communication Cord*, on the other hand, deals with modern Ireland in its own terms, not in relation to the British Empire. The country around Ballybeg is still being colonised, but the colonisers are the Irish urban bourgeoisie. It is these who still see the countryside as a rural Eden, and the peasants, in the person of Nora Dan, are reduced to parodying themselves.

In structure, the play contains many of the elements of classic farce: a complicated but trivial plot concerning romantic assignations, concealed and mistaken identity, low verbal humour, repetitive action and the physical discomfiture of pompous characters. Even the mistaken use of language by Barney is taken from the *genre*. In its use of under-wear and darkness as stock theatrical devices, the play is reminiscent of two other short modern farces, *Dirty Linen* (1976) by Tom Stoppard, in which a pair of French knickers appear and re-appear, and Peter Shaffer's *Black Comedy* (1965), which takes place as if the stage were in darkness. Stoppard is a particularly interesting comparison, as will be seen, because as a Czech, English was not his first language. Friel has, on several occasions, lamented the fact that Irish speakers of English will never own the language.

The plot of *The Communication Cord* concerns the at-tempts of Tim, a part-time junior lecturer in English, to per-suade Senator Doctor Donovan to help him acquire tenure. This involves borrowing a renovated Irish cottage from Jack, in order to impress Donovan and his daughter, on whom Tim has romantic designs, with his authentic rural roots. Jack is himself expecting a weekend assignation with Evette, a girl he met at the French consulate. Tim has just over an hour to impress Donovan before Evette arrives. Unknown to both Tim and Jack, Claire is already staying in the cottage. Claire is a friend of Jack's family, and had been previously dating both him and Tim. Unknown to any of them, Evette has been Donovan's mistress. Add to this mix a German with little English who wishes to buy the cottage, the fact that Claire is forced to pretend to be Evette, and that Jack pretends to be the German, both of whom turn up in the middle of the action. In the manner of the farce, the increas-ingly desperate efforts of Tim and Jack to salvage their origi-nal plan lead them into more and more complicated and contradictory stories, until the lies, and the cottage, collapse symbolically around them.

In this play, language is, even more so than in *Transla-tions*, a character in the drama. This is language in the sense of linguistics: Tim is writing a PhD thesis on "Discourse Analysis with Particular Reference to Response Cries". Ac-

cording to Tim's thesis, "Response Cries", the involuntary
exclamations uttered by people in response to others, are
capable of rational analysis. The play also concerns language
in its wider, cultural signification. Tim enunciates one of the
main dramatic points of the play in Act I:

> All social behaviour, the entire social order, depends
> on our communicational structures, on words mutu-
> ally agreed on and mutually understood. Without
> that agreement, without that shared code, you have
> chaos. (*Communication Cord*: 19)

What the play does, essentially, is to sever the agreement: it
cuts the cord, the communicational *umbilicus*, and lets chaos
dominate the stage. English, French and German are confused, and lie builds upon lie, culminating in the fall of the
cottage, itself a refurbished, *bijou* Tower of Babel.

Babel is, perhaps, an apt image for *The Communication
Cord*, for there is a Babel of languages represented in it. English, German, and French are recognisable linguistic markers,
but Irish, Hiberno-English, Anglo-German, pseudo-German
and pseudo-French must also be taken into account. Nora
Dan, the "peasant", speaks what can only be described as
literary-stage-Hiberno-English, a mixture of nineteenth-
century stage-Irish melodrama and the worst imitators of
J.M. Synge. Friel parodies the stage-Irish peasant in her opening lines, calling Tim and Jack "gentlemen" after the manner
of one of Lover's creations in *Handy Andy*. Her use of phatic
phrases such as "Ah sure", "surely", and "Glory be to God",
all of which occur within minutes of her first appearance,
mark her out as a development of a stock character. Nora
Dan also uses Hiberno-English syntax in her speech. Asking a
question negatively is a characteristic of Irish syntax: "Isn't
that grand?" is an almost direct translation of "nach bhfuil sin
go breá?", while the use of the present participle to express
the future in "you'll be staying" corresponds to "beidh tú ag

fanacht". Her speech is laced with dialect words: the girl Jack
had entertained the month before was "a great big stirk
[young heifer] of a girl", who swam naked: "not a stab
[stitch; article of clothing] on her", Barney the Banks
"gulders" [shouts], and has her "deaved" [deafened].

Tim's use of academic English to explain his thesis is impenetrable to any of the other characters. Donovan is confused; Jack has had it explained several times; even Tim himself may not be in a position to finish the thesis. Friel creates
a sliding scale of language and *argot*, in order to convey a
sense of the complexity of communication. He further problematises language for both reader and audience by using the
dialect word "gulder". It comes from the Donegal Irish noun
"guldar", meaning a shout, or a noise (Dineen, 1927: 579). In
this one stroke he makes it clear that, even for native speakers of a language, there are local and dialectical pitfalls. Tim's
thesis provides another level of language, taking it beyond
conscious communication into reflex cries.

When Jack pretends to be Barney the Banks, he speaks
neither German nor English, but rather his idea of what a
German should sound like in English. When the real Barney
the Banks speaks, he is speaking a form of English, but mediated, we are to presume, through his German mother-
tongue. Friel has given himself the task of writing a stage-
German and a bogus stage-German. Their discourse is quite
distinct:

> **Barney** I come here just to talk to you business,
> Herr McNeilis . . .
>
> **Jack**   A million Deutsche mark, Herr Gallagher. I
> hoffer you any monies you hask for. (53, 64)

Jack's version is more exaggerated and grotesque. Interest-
ingly, neither version is based on real German syntax.
Barney's line above would translate "Ich komme hier nur mit

dir Geschäft zu sprechen", where, "sprechen", to speak, gravitates to the end of the sentence. This means that the source for the German accents is not a cultural one, directly, but a theatrical one.

Likewise with Claire's impersonation of Evette, which is limited by Tim to a few phrases. There is little way of telling whether her speech is based on French syntax and grammar, although when looking for her slip she refers to it using the masculine possessive "mon", whereas the French word is the feminine *combinaison*, necessitating "ma" as the possessive. This would lead one to believe that her linguistic genesis is the same as Barney's. In contrast, and by way of theatrical irony, the real Evette speaks perfect English.

Quite apart from linguistic difficulties is the status of the statements made in any language. The premise presented to Donovan, on which the farce is constructed, that Tim owns the cottage, is false. Built on this initial premise are the false identities of Claire, Jack, Barney, and Evette. The untruths spiral out of control until they can only be resolved in a cataclysmic sweeping away of the causes and of the languages. In this structural element, *The Communication Cord* has more than a little in common with tragedy. The idea of sweeping away languages is a serious one. When, in an interview, Fintan O'Toole suggested to Friel that language was a political problem, Friel's response addressed the central concerns of *The Communication Cord*:

> I think that is how the political problem of this island is going to be solved. It's going to be solved by language in some kind of way. Not only the language of negotiations across the table. It's going to be solved by the recognition of what language means for us on this island. (O'Toole, 1982: 176)

In Friel's ideal political world, a language would be found which could accommodate the Babel on the island, be it Nationalist, Unionist, or terrorist.

Much of the comedy is based on verbal misunderstanding, specifically on the reassignment of signifiers. The serious point being made here is that words are, in the Saussurean sense, arbitrary. Saussure divided the linguistic sign, the word, into what he called a two-sided psychological entity, the *signifier*, the sound, and the *signified*, the concept or object. These two together were the *sign* (Saussure, 1981: 67). He pointed out that the connection between the two was contingent, based on convention and consensus, and "united in the brain by an associative bond" (66). There is no necessary connection between the sound {dOg} and the animal, or the sound {galahEr} and Tim.

Jack's renaming of Donovan as "Dr Bollocks" is taken by Barney as a real name, and he greets Susan as "Fräulein Bollocks" (56). His misunderstanding of Tim's instructions leads him to assume that "gulder" means "dresser" and Tim's name, Gallagher, means mad or agitated. As he puts down Claire's underwear, he comments: "I leave them on the gulder for when he is not so gallagher" (57).

The similarity with the work of Stoppard is very strong at this point. In *Dogg's Hamlet, Cahoot's Macbeth*, he begins by teaching the audience a new use for some basic English words. His notes for the play, based on the early sections of Wittgenstein's *Philosophical Investigations*, are useful in the context of Friel's premise:

> A man is building a platform using pieces of wood of different shapes and sizes. These are thrown to him by a second man . . . each time the first man shouts "Plank!" he is thrown a long flat piece . . . "Slab!" and is thrown a piece of a different shape . . . "Block!" and a third shape is thrown. Finally a call for "Cube!"

produces a fourth type of piece. An observer would probably conclude that the different words described different shapes and sizes of the material. But this is not the only possible interpretation. Suppose, for example, the thrower knows in advance which pieces the builder needs, and in what order. In such a case . . . the calls might translate thus: Plank = Ready, Block = Next, Slab = Okay, Cube = Thank You . . . the fact that he on the one hand and the builder on the other are using two different languages need not be apparent to either party. Moreover, it would also be possible that the two builders do not share a language either; and if life for them consisted only of building platforms in this manner, there would be no reason for them to discover that each was using a language unknown to the other. (Stoppard, 1980: 7–8)

In *The Communication Cord*, there are many unshared languages, as the characters grope unsuccessfully for a shared meaning. Friel uses the reassignment technique, but leaves the characters to flounder in the reassigned signifiers.

Donovan's misinterpretation of nicknames is a part of this technique. When told that the swimming figure of Jack was a local fisherman called "Jack the Cod", he indulges in an impromptu, and erroneous, explication of the nickname: "Call a man Jack the Cod and you tell me his name and his profession and that he's not very good at his profession. Concise, accurate and nicely malicious" (46). A cod is not only a fish, but a useless individual or thing in common Irish parlance. Donovan over-explains the name by using more than one interpretation of the noun "cod". Of course, because the name is an untruth, none of the conclusions arising from its interpretation are valid. The same happens in the case of "Nora the Scrambler" and "Barney the Banks". Donovan, at a loss to interpret what he sees as an authentic

Irish soubriquet, pounces on the first association he can think of, scrambled eggs. Having established that Nora Dan has three hens, he is satisfied. Donovan assumes that Barney, so called because his caravan is at the end of the sandbanks, acquired his nickname because of his money. Here, Friel parodies the process in *Translations* by which the places near Baile Beag acquired their new names. Owen, and his real-life counterpart, John O'Donovan, set themselves the task of translating the Irish place names sensitively. O'Donovan's letters show the lengths to which he went to establish the usage and accuracy of the Irish names before he proceeded (Herity, 2000: *passim*). In contrast, Donovan jumps at the most obvious interpretation and pronounces on it authoritatively. The correspondence of names between John O'Donovan and Senator Donovan can hardly be a co-incidence. The dropping of the "O'" (Irish *Ua*, descendant of) removes an immediately recognisable semiotic of Irish-ness. The "O'" was frequently dropped by emigrants and those not wishing to draw attention to their origins. Dono-van's foreshortened patronym undercuts his desire to pay homage to what Kearney calls: "the antique pieties of a lost culture" (1997: 82). Donovan's forenames, Patrick, Mary, and Pious, suggest one who has been steeped in the tradi-tions of the Irish conservative Catholic right-wing. Another index of both Donovan's etymology and Catholic conserva-tism is the brief exchange between him and Tim as he "recreates" the scene in the cottage at the turn of the cen-tury. The cow is brought in and settled with a battle of hay:

> **Donovan** ... An interesting word that — "battle" — it must be Irish, Tim?
>
> **Tim** Scottish. Sixteenth century.
>
> **Donovan** Is it? Anyhow. (60)

Donovan may be forgiven for gliding over another mistake, but the fact that the word is Scottish, and sixteenth century, is important. The word probably entered Irish or Hiberno-English from the early seventeenth century onwards, from the Scots Protestants who were planted in Ulster, especially in Donegal and Tyrone. This is verbal evidence of a non-Irish influence on what Donovan sees as a purely Gaelic civilisation. His real crime is not to acknowledge the contribution of the planters to the language and customs of the area.

There is another communicative code at work in the play, that of communication between past and present, between the reality of the schoolroom in *Translations* and the reconstructed reality of the cottage here. The stage directions at the beginning of Act I are extremely exact: "*The action takes place in a 'traditional' Irish cottage . . . one quickly senses something false about the place. It is too pat, too 'authentic'*" (11). The ironic inverted commas around "traditional" and "authentic" are important. Tradition and authenticity were, and are, very important words in the vocabulary of the Gaelic revivalist. Irish music, for example, was espoused, not only as a traditional pursuit, but as a high art form, and the more inaccessible the performer, the more obscure the venue and the recording, the more authentic it was considered. Flann O'Brien, writing as Myles na gCopaleen, penned a satirical novel in Irish called *An Béal Bocht* (*The Poor Mouth*), in which dirt, discomfort, famine, and bad luck were elevated as authentic Irish traits.

The cottage in *The Communication Cord* satirises the preservation of Irish traditions from the other side — the side which cleans them up and preserves the pleasant aspects, while silently eliding the more pitiable, uncomfortable, and unhygienic practices of the past. Donovan is in the cottage in order to commune, that is to communi*cate*, with his version of the edenic Gaelic past. Because his version of the past, the version represented by the reconstructed, sanitised cottage, has never existed, communication with it is impossible, but the words continue. The repeated phrases — "This is where we all come from. This is our first cathedral. This shaped all our souls. This determined our first pieties" (15) — begin in parody and are taken as a sanctification of place by Donovan, who adds other platitudes: "the restorative power of that landscape . . . the absolute verity . . . You know your heritage . . . Renewal . . . Restoration. Fulfilment. Back to the true centre" (32, 32–3, 34, 46). Lip service is being paid to the past, but to a past distorted by fixed pieties and ideological necessities. It takes the experience of discomfort to make Donovan admit that the cottage is the "greatest dump in all . . ." (75); in all what is never revealed.

Communication surfaces again as the main theme at the end of the play, after Donovan and Susan have left, and Nora Dan is ensconced in the settle bed, and Jack, Tim and Claire remain visible on stage. While he examines the stall where Donovan had been chained, Tim assesses his thesis in the light of the past hours. He defines it as: "Language as a ritualised act between two people . . . The exchange of units of communication through an agreed code . . . Fundamental to any meaningful exchange between individuals" (91). It is an astute summary of the play. The ritual aspect of communication has remained throughout, seen most clearly in "the gesture" used by Barney. In Act I, he mistook Tim's frantic gesturing for a traditional Irish greeting (51), and repeats it at intervals throughout. The difficulty with ritualised behaviour of any kind is that the symbolism needs to be shared; if it is not, the ritual is at best meaningless, at worst ridiculous. The "agreed code" is missing in *The Communication Cord*, not just between speakers of different languages, but among the speakers of English. As a result, there is no meaningful exchange. This leads Tim, and Friel, to conclude that: "Maybe silence is the perfect discourse" (92).

There is certainly a progression beyond words in Friel's work. In *Translations*, the people of Ballybeg are faced with having to learn a new language. In *The Communication Cord*, that language becomes part of a Babel of voices, all speaking but not understood. In *Dancing at Lughnasa*, and, to a lesser extent, *Wonderful Tennessee*, Friel partially abandons verbal communication in favour of music and dance.

As long ago as 1970, Friel made the caustic comment that the direction the Irish Republic had taken was "distressing, very disquieting" (Rushe, 1970: 81). He described the country as becoming "Madison Avenue-ish and slicker in a shabby sort of way". This disquiet continues into the 1990s, as the opening dialogue of *Wonderful Tennessee* shows:

Trish	Help! We're lost!
Berna	Where are we?
Terry	This is it.
Trish	You're lost, Terry; admit it; we're lost.
Frank	It — is — wonderful!
Angela	This can't be it, is it?
Terry	Believe me — this is it.
Trish	Help! (11)

There is a certain Beckettian air about this initial exchange, and although any resemblance to Beckett's style is quickly dispelled, the feeling remains that the play begins in a postmodern uncertainty. The fact that the plot concerns a group of people passing the time waiting for a boat which never arrives is surely a deliberate echo of *Godot*. They pass the time telling stories, singing and reminiscing, and, as they do so, the disillusionment of their lives becomes apparent. As the characters are in early middle age (late thirties, early forties), there is a sense of nostalgia for lost opportunity.

Five of the six characters speak in the opening exchange, but their words barely connect with each other. The instrument of non-verbal expression is George, who has throat cancer, and can barely speak. Instead, George plays the piano-accordion. The other characters sing complete lyrics, verses and snatches of songs drawn from an eclectic number of sources: sacred music ("Jesu, Joy of Man's Desiring"), music hall ("Knees up, Mother Brown"), hymns ("Abide With Me"), Moore's Melodies ("Oft in the Stilly Night"), Wagner ("Wedding March"), Broadway musical ("I Want to be Happy"), American folk music ("Down by the Cane Brake") and German-style cabaret ("Falling in Love Again" as sung by Marlene Dietrich). In many cases, the songs are used to express an emotion that the characters cannot. The opening offstage sound of "Happy Days are Here Again" glides into "O Mother I Could Weep for Mirth" and "I Want to be Happy" in the space of four pages of text. As George's playing performs a further slide into "Jesu, Joy of Man's Desiring", Berna admits to her own desperation: "Have you any idea how desperately unhappy I am?" (15).

The music is a second language behind the dialogue, operating sometimes in parallel and sometimes at odds with the main action. Harry White comments that: "music not only interrupts and halts the action of the play, it also modifies and comments upon the explicit disclosures which are its central preoccupation" (White, 1999: 13). It would appear that the first function of the music in the opening scene is to precipitate the declaration from Berna. "Happy Days are Here Again", despite the jollity of the group, appears to be untrue. Its sentiments are undercut by "O Mother I Could Weep for Mirth", which introduces both religion and uncertainty into the happiness. "I Want to be Happy", which follows, implies an absence of happiness, and the religious force of "Jesu, Joy of Man's Desiring", with its yearning for union with Christ, who is substituted for happiness, further

complicates the emotional matrix. White is correct in claiming that the music is a metalanguage, that is, a language used
to describe or analyse another language. The music in the
opening sequence is describing, however, not the spoken
dialogue, but the emotional language that lies behind it.

In a way, this is a development of the Public/Private dichotomy in *Philadelphia*. There is a greater risk involved in
this technique, because it is one which places demands on an
audience. It presupposes a shared emotional and cultural
access, and response, to the music. If the audience is not
familiar with the music, the play loses some of its impact. Of
course, "I Want to be Happy" and "Happy Birthday" are
almost universally recognised in the West. The impact of
"Jesu, Joy of Man's Desiring", would be less immediate, although the tune is recognisable. The effect of "Regina caeli"
is considerably less now than it would have been when the
liturgy was sung in Latin.

The play quickly establishes that the characters have this
kind of shared access, and that the music and songs are used
as an emotional shorthand, referring, we assume, as much to
other occasions on which the pieces were used as to the
lyrics or to the emotional content. When Angela sings "Falling in Love Again" (28), it is a prelude to the revelation that
she and Terry have an emotional history. The music is, to a
large extent, about history. This is presumably why Friel
chose not to include songs from the characters' formative
years. A group of people in their late thirties and early forties, in 1993, would have been born around 1950. Few of
them would have a memory of Latin hymns, although we
may grant that a musician like George would have some
knowledge of them. But there are no Beatles' numbers, no
showband music, nothing by Status Quo, David Bowie, Marc
Bolan and T-Rex, no glam-rock; no songs, in fact, beyond the
early decades of the century, before any of the group were

born. The music evokes a past that is shared, but at the same time beyond the group on the pier.

In *Dancing at Lughnasa*, the agent of progression beyond words and into music, and the object around which Michael's reminiscences begin, is the wireless set, acquired by the Mundy family in the summer of 1936:

> We got our first wireless set that summer — well, a sort of a set; and it obsessed us. And because it arrived as August was about to begin, my Aunt Maggie . . . wanted to call it Lugh after the old Celtic God of the Harvest. (*Dancing at Lughnasa*: 1)

The wireless is the medium through which the outside world reaches into the isolated cottage. Naming it after a pagan god has connotations of impropriety, of the intrusion of an uncontrollable force into mundanity. The naming is vetoed by Kate, so they name it Marconi, unaware, perhaps that this name is still a foreign influence. Naming as an activity has acquired such great force in Friel's canon (see, for example, Act 2, Scene 1, of *Translations*, where Owen and Yolland debate the place names) that the very fact of giving something a name is a reflexive index of its significance. The rest of the play is seen in relation to Lugh, the pagan god, and Marconi, the foreign inventor. The tension in the communication cord between the past and the present, between the inside and the outside, is evident from the beginning. In the opening narration, Michael, influenced by talk of Lugh, and of Jack's return from East Africa, elides culture and technology in speaking of Marconi's "voodoo" (2).

Friel uses Kate, the schoolteacher, as the agent of repression. She it is who insists that the sisters behave properly. Their discussion on lipstick, hair-colour and dresses can only take place if Kate is not present. In the midst of these discussions, Rose's attempt to dance is a "*gauche, graceless shuffle that defies the rhythm of the song*" (3), as if the spirit of repression denies her the ability. Dancing is, for Kate, emblematic of a lack of respectability. When the possibility of going to the Harvest Dance is mooted, dancing and inappropriate expression become mingled: "This is silly talk. We can't, Agnes. How can we?" (13). Despite the enthusiasm of her sisters, and Agnes' offer to pay for them all, Kate has her way: "No, no, no! We're going nowhere!" (13). She concludes "I don't want it mentioned again" (14). The prohibition on language is balanced by Father Jack, who, since his return from Uganda: "has difficulty finding the English words for what he wants to say" (11).

Chris, the youngest sister, is the mother of a child born out of wedlock. The father, Gerry Evans, visits rarely, and on the occasion of his visit in Act 1, the conversation is at first stilted, and progresses into Gerry's exaggeration and tall tales about his life as a dancing teacher and a gramophone salesman. As he hears the music of "Dancing in the Dark" drift through the window from Marconi, he suddenly takes her in his arms and they begin to dance:

Gerry	Do you know the words?
Chris	I never know any words.
Gerry	Neither do I. Doesn't matter. This is more important. (33)

The dance performed by Gerry and Chris takes the place of the stilted conversation they had been having, and leads Gerry to a proposal of marriage that he cannot mean. When the music stops, they keep dancing.

It is against this background of linguistic repression that the most famous dance in the play breaks out with pagan exuberance. It comes at the end of a sequence in which the sisters had abandoned their plans to attend the Harvest Dance, and had moved on to remember other dances and other boys with whom they had danced. Maggie's story of her prize in the Ardstraw dancing competition had trailed away, and the sisters were returning slowly to the same tasks they performed every day. Chris re-connects the battery to Marconi, and the beat of "The Mason's Apron" emerges: "[v]*ery fast; very heavy beat; a raucous sound. At first we are aware of the beat only*" (21). The beat, the drum, the atavistic pulse, is too much even for the accustomed repression of the Mundy sisters. Friel's description of Maggie is crucial: "*Now her features become animated by a look of defiance, of aggression; a crude mask of happiness*" (21). He is describing the abandon of a primitive ritual, and also suggesting the use of masks that features in such rituals. The mask assumes a life of its own, and hides its wearer, rather in the same way that a theatrical *persona* hides the actor who plays it. Maggie is in the grip of the "voodoo", but she is also taking refuge behind a mask, which becomes an actual mask made of flour seconds later as she "*patterns her face with an instant mask*" (21).

Friel gives more than a page and a half of text to stage-directions, and in doing so he almost returns to his original craft as a short-story writer. First Maggie surrenders herself to the dance, then Rose, then Agnes, Chris, and finally Kate. Chris emphasises the ritual nature of the dance by throwing on Fr Jack's surplice and dancing while wearing it. Kate's dance is described in terms very close to those of Molly in *Molly Sweeney*: "*controlled and frantic; a weave of complex steps . . . ominous of some deep and true emotion . . . Kate makes no sound* (22). Molly dances: "a wild and furious dance round and round that room . . . Mad and wild and frenzied. But so adroit, so efficient. No timidity, no hesitations, no falterings" (*Molly Sweeney*: 31). Friel gives no insight into either the "deep and true emotion" felt by Kate, or the emotional imperatives that drive Molly to dance, unseeing, through a crowded house. One must infer that the emotion is beyond words, and that Friel is striving to make a direct connection, unmediated by words, with the emotional foundations of his characters. The idea of a language beyond words is carried through to the final speech of the play, as Michael summarises the events of the summer, and his central image of it, a memory which has "nothing to do with fact":

> When I remember it, I think of it as dancing . . .
> Dancing as if language had surrendered to movement
> — as if this ritual, this wordless ceremony, was now
> the way to speak . . . Dancing as if language no
> longer existed because words were no longer necessary . . . (*Dancing at Lughnasa*: 71)

Friel, with his passionate interest in words and their ability to shape reality, reaches beyond his passion with an inquiry that results in the emergence of a startlingly new synthesis in *Molly Sweeney*, as will be seen in Chapter Four, "The Grammar of Reality".

Chapter Three

Wonderful Ballybeg

There shall be peace and plenty, the kindly open door,
Blessings on all who come and go — the prosperous and
    the poor —
The misty glens and purple hills a fairer tint shall show,
When your splendid sun shall ride the skies again, Mo
    Chraoibhín Cnó.
                  (Ethna Carbery, *Mo Chraoibhín Cnó!*)

Near the end of *Translations*, Hugh, seeing the Name-Book in which is written the new anglicised place names, muses on his situation: "We must learn where we live. . . . We must make them our new home" (88). In all the plays, the setting is as important and resonant as the words. Whether he deals with urban or rural dwellers, with the past or with the present, one recurring constant is the town of Ballybeg. The name comes from the Irish *Baile Beag*, small town; in *Lovers*, he calls it Ballymore, from *Baile Mór*, a large town. Richard Kearney is of the opinion that Ballybeg is a version of Glenties (1997: 83–4), but even a cursory glance at the stage notes to the plays and the mentions of other, actual locations that occur, lead one to the conclusion that Ballybeg moves and changes according to the dictates of the drama. This is not to say that the town does not reflect something of Glenties, but that it also reflects Buncrana and Derry or many other towns.

Ballybeg first appears in *Philadelphia*, a stagnant, rural backwater, full of people lost in their own delusions because of the meanness of their lives. It is described variously in the notes to the plays. In *Philadelphia*, it is merely "a small village in County Donegal". In *Living Quarters*, it is in "a remote part of County Donegal", and also "in the wilds of County Donegal". In *Aristocrats*, it is "a remote Donegal village". In *Faith Healer*, it is described as "not far from Donegal town". In *Translations*, it is clear that Ballybeg is on or near the coast, and 23 miles from Glenties. The only coastal area at that distance is Bloody Foreland, to the south of which is the island of Inis Meadhon, also mentioned in the play. Other places mentioned as significant — Buncrana, Greencastle, and Burnfoot — are on the Inishowen peninsula. *Wonderful Tennessee* again places it in "north-west Donegal", while in *Aristocrats*, the border is 20 miles away, and Letterkenny is the main telephone exchange.

The point of this is not to attack Friel's knowledge of geography, as historians did his use of history, nor is it to attack his idea of an Irish town. The point is to see Ballybeg, not as a town, or a representation of any particular town. Rather, Ballybeg is an emblem of all Irish towns, and of Ireland itself. Its itinerant tendencies and propensity towards growing and shrinking make this easier. In a sense, Ballybeg is a universal, in the same way that Thornton Wilder's Grover's Corner is in *Our Town*, or Garrison Keillor's Lake Wobegon. Ballybeg is a *locus* for incidents that could have occurred in any small town in Ireland: old men stagnate, young men leave home, families come under strain, social position is invoked to make others inferior, traditional authority declines, lives are shattered by change and tragedy.

The setting of *Philadelphia* is the kitchen behind S.B.'s shop, and Gar's bedroom which opens off it. When the play

opened in 1964, the setting itself must have seemed unremarkable to the audience. Rural kitchen plays were as common in Ireland as "kitchen sink" drama was in Britain at the
same time, although the two had little in common until the
advent of *Philadelphia*. The genre of the rural kitchen play is
still represented in Irish writing. Micheál Ó hAodha attributes
this to the influence of the Abbey Theatre on a generation of
playwrights (Ó hAodha, 1974: 40–59). The Abbey was, in its
inception, an attempt to recapture Irish legend and folklore
for the stage, and still sees part of its role today as "guardian-
ship of the Irish repertoire". Many of John B. Keane's plays,
for example, are set in cottages, or kitchens in small towns,
and concern similar characters: shopkeepers, priests, farmers, local politicians. Friel is taking a stock situation from
1960s Irish drama, and making something new of it. The
kitchen at the centre of *Philadelphia* contains the same elements, but transcends their conventional use. In 1970, Keane
reacted angrily to Friel's suggestion that his plays were "stuck
with the peasants of Kerry" (Murray, 1999: 35).

   Philadelphia is an attempt to broaden the scope of the rural kitchen play, although the repression that characterised
some of Keane's work is still present. The kitchen is described as: "sparsely and comfortlessly furnished — a bachelor's kitchen" (*Plays I*: 26), the table has no table-cloth, the
cups are described as "rough". The implication is that Gar's
mother never had a chance to imprint her personality on the
house, or that the imprint did not last, although from the
time scheme it is possible that she and S.B. were married for
up to two years. The kitchen as the centre of a home is subverted by this initial description. Gar's presence in the
kitchen of his home is subject to S.B.'s rules, as interpreted
by Madge. When his friends call, it is implied that beer-
bottles are frowned upon. Kitchen and bedroom are contrasted as public and private spaces, corresponding to the
two Gars, so the spaces are both naturalistic and symbolic.

Although the Ballybeg hinterland never appears on the stage, enough of it is described to complete a picture of small-town negativity. The offstage presence of the shop appears early in the play as a curb on the development of Gar as an individual. Here, his will is subjected to S.B.'s. His first question to Gar is about coils of barbed wire which he has ordered. The suggestion of entangling imprisonment is carried through into Private's next speech, as he tries to disentangle fact from memory, and recall how many coils he had carried into the shop (*Plays I*: 34). S.B., when he comes in from the shop, carries the keys with him (47). He asks Gar if he has set the rat-trap in the store (48). The shop is synonymous with entrapment and confinement. Other locations in the Ballybeg of *Philadelphia* offer little in the way of comfort. The "boys" stand outside the hotel looking in; Gar is uncomfortable and ill-at-ease in Senator Doogan's house.

The other elements common to this kind of play, returned Americans, frustrated love, and the need to emigrate, are complicated in the interplay of emotions between Gar Public and Gar Private, and by the wall of repression that has built up between Gar and his father. Nothing is resolved in the play, other than the fact that Gar leaves at the end, but the leave-taking is not a liberation; Lizzie and Con, with whom he will live, are childless, a condition with dysfunctional implications in Friel, and, moreover, they are shallow and vulgar. The place that he is leaving for, Philadelphia, is no more home than the place he is leaving. He has been promised a room of his own (59), but this is no more than he already has. Gar is leaving to work in a hotel, which by its nature is a space which is occupied by people in transit; he will still be in the service of others.

Several Friel plays are set in large, old, decaying houses. The "Big House" was the symbol of the English Protestant ascendancy and has its own place in Irish literature, chronicled by Somerville and Ross, Elizabeth Bowen, Jennifer

Johnston, and others. Squiredom was a factor of life in Britain also, but in Ireland there was the added factor that the Big House tended to be emblematic of a dominant alien presence. They were largely Protestant, gentrified, and separated from locals by class and wealth. After independence, the decline of the Big House was seen as an index of the rise of the ordinary citizen. In many cases the land surrounding the houses was acquired by the Land Commission and distributed to local farmers. Those members of the ascendancy who were able to maintain their lifestyle in the new regime watched their influence dwindle in the Republic. For Friel, who considers himself allied neither to the Northern State nor to the Republic, the Big House, especially in its decline, proves a potent symbol of both stagnation and change.

In *Aristocrats*, Friel dramatises the last generation of Big House inhabitants, but chooses as his subject the Catholic gentry. The choice of Catholic over Protestant is important: it absolves Friel of the charge of sectarianism, and removes the possibility that he is attacking traditional upper-class Protestantism or writing a political critique of the consequences of British rule in Ireland. That their class is already obsolete and their time past is evinced by the presence of the American academic, Tom Hoffnung. To him, they are a subject of study, like an endangered species, which, in a way, they are. The title of his study — "Recurring cultural, political and social modes in the upper strata of Roman Catholic society in rural Ireland since the act of Catholic Emancipation" — connects the family with the past and with the countryside, not with the present. A further index of impending extinction is the voice of Father, former District Justice O'Donnell. A bedridden victim of a stroke who appears on stage only for one brief moment, he mutters incoherently, then pronounces loudly on past cases, as if he were still in the courtroom, or accuses Judith, who has had a child out of wedlock, of betraying the family. He is the voice of past authority, a voice without a body, as Uncle George, who wanders silently in and out, is a body without a voice. Both have been dislocated from their environment and exist as vestiges of an earlier way of life.

Hoffnung is a useful character from the point of view of the structure of the play. In Act 1, he, as researcher, can look for information on behalf of the audience. It is his questioning that elicits details about the family and their connections, past and present. He becomes the focus for stories and reminiscences, in a play in which the plot is of secondary interest to the interaction of one culture with another. He is a development on the idea of Sir in *Living Quarters*, because he is integrated into the plot. He does not control the plot in the same way that Sir does, but his questioning guides the responses of the other characters in a similar manner.

More than any other character, Casimir represents the spirit of the house. Although we are told that he lives in Germany and has a job working part-time in a food processing factory, he appears at his first entrance to be the embodiment of the ascendancy. The stage directions give him a number of strange physical mannerisms, in particular his ungainly walk and his facial tics (*Aristocrats*: 12–13). Despite these, Friel insists that Casimir is not disturbed, just "peculiar". His reactions and his mannerisms do not belong in the modern world. Even as a child, Willie recounts that Casimir would walk down the main street of Ballybeg with a gang of children following in a line behind him, imitating his mannerisms. In meeting Willie for the first time in Act 1, he does not remember him, despite their having played together as children. When guessing who Willie might be, he does so in a specifically categorical manner:

> **Casimir**   I have it — it's Deegan, the jarvey! Am I
> right? . . .

Willie	Deegan, the car-man; that's right; he's dead. I'm Diver . . . I used to be about the gate-lodge when my Uncle Johnny was in it. (17)

Willie is from the village, therefore he is placed by Casimir in the category "servant", or, at least, "underclass". Willie slips into the same mode of discourse, defining himself in relation to his uncle the lodge-keeper. Casimir finds this easier to relate to than the story of the two of them in a punt that got taken out by the tide. His idiotic response, "Good Lord! Were we drowned?" (17), separates his discourse from Willie's, and also separates the adult Casimir from this incident in his childhood, by suggesting that the prospect of the boys having been drowned was possible. His memory of his childhood is of the house and of Claire playing Chopin, of sunshine and open windows (14). There is no room in his reminiscences for boys from the village or boating trips with peasants.

In his interview with Hoffnung, Casimir's memories are bound up with those of the house. He shows Tom the items in the study that were associated with the great and the good from Ireland's history who had visited the house in its heyday. It is Alice who casts doubt upon the status of the memories; when asked if she remembered Cardinal O'Donnell, she replies that he has been dead for seventy years (24). Given this *caveat*, Casimir's memories begin to unravel. His claim to remember Yeats is dubious. Friel inserts just enough leeway in the dates to make it possible, but unlikely. It may have the status of an internal joke that Casimir remembers Yeats's cold eyes (68). Yeats's epitaph in Drumcliff churchyard reads "Cast a cold eye / On life, on death. / Horseman, pass by!". Likewise, John McCormack, who died in 1945, might have danced with Casimir's mother in Casimir's lifetime, but it is impossible that Claire, who is now 26, should have played for them. Casimir does not claim to have known Chesterton (d. 1936) personally, but speaks of him in the present tense (24). Three times during the recital of famous family friends, Tom attempts to interrupt in order to note dates; each time, Casimir's flow is unbroken. Tom confronts him in Act 3, on the subject of his story about Balzac's birthday party in Vienna, which, he claims, was gatecrashed by his grandfather. When Tom points out that Grandfather O'Donnell could not have been a contemporary of Balzac (66), Casimir adjusts the story back a generation to his great-grandfather, and continues. In the middle of Act 3, Tom finally lays the ghost of Yeats:

> **Tom**   Well, you were born on April 1, 1939.
>
> **Casimir** Good heavens — don't I know! All Fools Day! Yes?
>
> **Tom**   And Yeats died the same year. Two months earlier. I've double-checked it. (*68*)

As Casimir does not appear to have the puckish sense of humour that would lead him to deliberately misdirect Tom, it is reasonably safe to assume that, at some level, he means what he says. Tom assumes that Casimir is a victim of what has become known as false memory syndrome — that having heard the stories from his earliest memories, he has convinced himself that he was a participant. It is possible that there is more, dramatically, to Casimir's stories than an indication of a flawed character. Friel may be using Casimir as the mouthpiece for Ballybeg Hall itself, articulating the past, real and imagined, of the Big House.

This same attachment to the past is apparent in the beginning of Act 2. Casimir is on his hands and knees, probing in the grass of the lawn for the holes of the croquet hoops. Having found them, he and Claire play an imaginary game. There is a kind of desperate archaeology at work here. Casimir is driving his fingers into the ground in an attempt to find the past. Once he believes he has done so, the game of croquet they play is a phantom one; they have neither balls nor mallets. Instead, it is reconstructed from memories of the game and from other games long over.

Willie's entry into the game is a curious vignette. When Casimir is called to the telephone, he hands him the invisible mallet. Willie is embarrassed by the idea and afraid of ridicule, particularly from Eamon, but is persuaded: "All the same you feel a bit of an eejit — (*to Eamon*) They have me playing croquet now, Eamon! Without balls nor nothin'! Jaysus!" (56). Willie's initial reluctance is expressed in terms of a comic castration motif — he is playing without balls (testicles). He chooses Eamon as his confidant to express surprise at playing croquet, a decidedly aristocratic game, because Eamon is an outsider. Once he decides to enter the game, he does so in plebeian fashion, throwing off his jacket, spitting on his hands, and rubbing them together. In a rather bizarre burlesque of the game of croquet, and of the social and cultural changes in Irish life, Willie quickly comes to terms with the "rules" of the imaginary game, and declares himself the winner by ignoring the rules: "Over! Finished! You're bet! Pack it in! I won, Eamon!" (59). Eamon declares him to be "[a] real insider now". Willie's progress from outsider to insider through learning the rules and changing them to suit himself could be seen as the political development of the Irish Republic in microcosm. When the Republic was originally declared, those who did so had been elected to the parliament at Westminster. Rather than take their seats, they sat in Dublin, with de Valera as president.

Willie's winning of the game is reminiscent of his first appearances in Act 1. Although he defers to Uncle George as "Mister George", an address redolent of class distinctions, Willie is the one who is surreptitiously supporting the family. He wires up the speaker for the baby-alarm, leaves the whiskey for the guests, and has rented the land from Judith, although it is useless for farming. He is quietly infiltrating the

way of life in the Big House, and has replaced it as an economic force. Willie's "new money", earned from low-level
gambling, replaces an economy based on land and tenancy.
Eamon himself has an ambivalent relationship with the ascendancy class, alternatively wondering at them through his
connection with his grandmother, who was a maid in Ballybeg Hall, and sneering at what they represent. Although *Aristocrats* is not an overtly political play, politics, in the sense of
the changing dynamic in the relationships between discrete
social groupings, permeates the play.

Eamon and Willie are two aspects of the peasant response to the ascendancy. While Willie is on the outside and
outwardly respects the traditions of the house, Eamon has
married into the family. He is both protective of the house
and critical of it, and is the one who, at the end of the play, is
most emotional about abandoning it. Friel is not making any
kind of moral judgement as to the respective values of the
social classes. Willie, despite his respect for the house and
his affection for Judith, will not accept her child, who is being
raised in an orphanage. Eamon, despite his humour and
comic commentary, beats Alice, his wife, who is an alcoholic.

Eamon's first entrance is anarchic, designed to contrast
with the restrained conversation of Tom, Casimir, and Alice.
He runs in, wearing Claire's wedding veil, pursued by Claire.
He also contrasts sharply with Alice's picture of him. His
background, Alice tells Tom, was as an Irish Government
observer of the Civil Rights marches in the North in 1968.
When he became embroiled in the conflict on the side of
the marchers, he had lost his job, and was now working as a
probation officer for the Greater London Council. The story
is told in the context of the dissociation of the house from
politics. Eamon had become involved, as had Judith. She had
taken part in the Battle of the Bogside, and had had a child
by a Dutch reporter. It was this engagement with political
activism and sexual nonconformity that had precipitated Fa-

ther's first stroke. Politics, according to Alice, never attracted his attention: "Politics never interested him. Politics are vulgar" (30). The change in tense from past imperfect to present continuous is indicative not only of the former opinions of District Justice O'Donnell, but of the present opinions of Alice, and of her class. Judith's engagement with politics is therefore seen as alien to the spirit of the house. Eamon adds to this theme in his suggestion to Tom that his book should be fiction:

> [A] family without passion, without loyalty, without
> commitments . . . above all wars and famines and civil
> strife and political upheaval; ignored by its Protestant
> counterparts, isolated from the mere Irish, existing
> only in its own concept of itself . . . (53)

According to Eamon's reading of the family, it lacked tribal loyalty. Being neither Protestant ascendancy nor Catholic peasantry, it was removed from both. Its isolation is physical as well as spiritual; the house overlooks Ballybeg; it is not a part of it. It is this isolation from commitment and separation from its context which has led to the entropy of the class represented by the O'Donnell house. The children experienced this isolation early in their lives, and it is Alice, again, who unwittingly articulates it:

Alice	We were sent off to boarding-school when we were seven or eight.
Tom	Casimir, too?
Alice	He went to the Benedictines when he was six . . . Judith and Claire and I went to a convent in Carcassone — a finishing school — and became . . . young ladies. (29–30)

All of the children were removed from their context, and turned into models of an earlier cultural category, one which was becoming extinct in their parents' time. All of this belies Alice's claim to be one of the "local people".

Eamon contrasts with both Willie and Alice in his attitude to the house and the family. His ambivalence, we have noted, comes from his grandmother, who had reared him on stories of dances, receptions, balls, all the grandeur of "the quality": "that's the mythology I was nurtured on all my life . . . not an education — a permanent pigmentation" (34). As an outsider, he is able to appreciate the privilege that was taken for granted by the others. He is, on his own admission, intimidated by the house, and talks too much about it. In some ways, he articulates the unspoken elements of life among the upper classes; he can say what they cannot: "this was always a house of reticence, of things unspoken . . ." (37). He challenges Tom's theory that the Big House had an effect on the cultural and economic life of the country. He considers the political, economic and cultural effect of the house on their co-religionists and on the local peasantry (often the same people) and concludes that Tom's thesis is bogus.

Eamon's disdain for the influence of the house is presumably related to the fact that his family were forced to emigrate, and his grandmother, the servant in the house, brought him up. His memories are not of musical evenings, but of dances in the Corinthian in Derry, dances to which Judith accompanied him. The memory of the dance, in Proustian fashion (he makes a reference to *À la Recherche du Temps Perdu*), reminds him that he had proposed to Judith after one dance, and that she had accepted. An earlier comment, that he had lusted after each of the O'Donnell girls in turn, comes into focus in relation to his fascination with the house and with the ascendancy lifestyle. An inference may be made that Eamon is in love with the ascendancy culture, rather than with Alice, or any of her sisters.

At the end of the play, it is Eamon who protests emotionally against Judith's decision to close up Ballybeg Hall:

"[T]hugs from the village will move in and loot and ravage the place within a couple of hours . . . Oh, your piety is admirable" (77). The choice of the word "piety" is noteworthy. The word occurs in *Translations* and in *The Communication Cord*, but in quite different contexts. In *Translations*, Owen uses it when talking of the origins of the name Tobair Vree, and speaks of keeping piety with the long-dead man (*Translations*: 53). He is unsure whether this is a useful exercise, to cling to the half-forgotten relics of the past. In *The Communication Cord*, the house is referred to, in tones varying from burlesque to irony to distaste, as the place that determined "our first pieties" (15). Clearly, for Friel, "piety" is not a religious sentiment, but a way of keeping faith with the past, or at least with those elements of the past which have shaped the present. It has overtones of loyalty to, and affinity with, the tribe, rather than mere observance. At the end of *Translations*, after recalling his and Jimmy's abortive attempt to take part in the 1798 rebellion, Hugh concludes: "[o]ur pietas, James, was for older, quieter things" (89). The Latin *pietas* means: "dutiful conduct towards . . . gods, country, parents, brothers and sisters . . . (Smith and Lockwood, 1987: 543). In other words, pietas, as used by Hugh, means allegiance to one's tribe. Seen in terms of *Translations*, Eamon's piety for the Big House is a romanticised one, comparable with Yolland's view of peasant Ireland. Although he has burlesqued the life in the house, his feelings at the end of the play are undoubtedly genuine.

The house, as a symbol of authority, is inextricably linked with the unseen figure of Father, particularly because, for most of the play, his voice comes, as it were, from the fabric of the building. It is after his death that we are told of the state of disrepair into which the house has fallen, as if his death has precipitated the fall. In a very real way, of course, it has; the loss of his pension has made the difference between scraping by and having to abandon Ballybeg Hall.

Father's first speech, almost an interrupted monologue, is on the topic of family and betrayal. As patriarch, he demands to know where everyone is, and deals out judgement on Judith for her perceived disloyalty (15). His second speech in Act I is a memory of his courtroom, which he ruled in an old-fashioned, autocratic manner, dismissing a case because of its inconvenience to himself. The stories others tell of Father are stories of power and influence. He arranged for John McCormack to get his papal knighthood; he spent part of his honeymoon with Hillaire Belloc; the house was full of artists and notables. Even Eamon, at his most satirical, does not deny the splendour of Father's reign. Telling a story about Sean O'Casey's attempt to impress Mother, he maintains: "the poor creatur' . . . tripped over the Pope or Plato or Shirley Temple or somebody and smashed his bloody glasses! (54).

Father, the house and the tribal elements of family are brought together in the audio tape made by Anna, the sister who is a nun in Africa. Friel assembles the elements of the scene carefully. The semiotic connotations of "nun" imply, or at least implied in the 1970s, a certain detachment from the operation of the real world, emphasised by the disembodied audio tape. Her physical distance keeps her out of immediate contact with anyone. Friel describes her violin-playing as that of a child (63). Anna is physically and spiritually detached, arrested at an early phase of her development. She is like a living time-capsule, envisioning the house and the family as they used to be:

> [S]itting before a big log fire in the drawing-room —
> Daddy spread out and enjoying his well-earned re-
> laxation after his strenuous day in court and the rest
> of you sitting on the rug or around the Christmas
> tree . . . (62)

Friel has contrived this imagining; it is impossible to envision, however reticent the family may be, that no-one would have mentioned that Alice was married and living in London, or that Father was no longer actively involved in the law. It is a deliberate contrivance, because the tape was sent to Casimir in Hamburg, so Anna must be aware of the diaspora, and the possibility of his not being in Ballybeg Hall at Christmas. Equally, if Anna is unaware of the changes in the circumstances of family members, if she has not been informed (Judith's letters, for example, tell her that Father is in "very good health" (63)), it is because the picture her siblings have of themselves corresponds closely with Anna's memories. Anna's imaginings are the verbal equivalent of the sundial mentioned in the stage notes at the beginning of the play: "Downstage right is a broken sun-dial mounted on a stone plinth" (9). It is never mentioned again, nor is it ever referred to. It stands as an icon of the attempt to arrest time, to preserve it in an era of genteel ascendancy.

The family picture (largely drawn from Friel's earlier short story, *Foundry House*) is of a Victorian or Edwardian Christmas scene: the patriarch on a chair with the family sitting at his feet. Anna's picture is careful to place Father higher than the others. Her tape includes an affectionate enquiry after Nanny, including the trope of the trusted servant; a motif introduced by Eamon in relation his grandmother. Anna's chief address is, however, for Father, as the centre, the *paterfamilias*. This connection with the house is reiterated at the end of the play in Casimir's words: "[s]omehow the hall doesn't exist without him" (70).

This scene with Anna is engineered to provide a sharp contrast with the physical picture of Father that Friel provides as stage notes to the end of the tape: "[a]*n emaciated man; eyes distraught; one arm limp; his mouth pulled down at one corner. A grotesque and frightening figure*" (63). His appearance, with his pyjamas buttoned wrongly and hanging off, is an emblem of the house: he is the antithesis of the dignified and well-connected autocrat of Anna's memories, in the same way that the roof of the once-splendid hall has plastic sheeting over it, and the rain collects in buckets.

In his "Sporadic Diary", written while working on *Aristocrats*, Friel says that the play, in its early stages, was about *"family life"*, with its opportunities for love, affection, and loyalty, and that "[c]lass, politics, social aspiration are the qualifying décor but not the core" (Murray, 1999: 66). By the time the play was finished, it was still about family life, but the love and loyalty were love for and loyalty to an ideal of class affiliation and political distance. Because the family was an unusual one, the chance to use it and Ballybeg Hall to examine a corner of Irishness became a dramatic imperative.

The Big House, in the shape of a manse, appears again in *Give Me Your Answer, Do!*, Friel's look at what McGrath calls the "bourgeois consumerism and materialism of the Irish Republic" (1999: 248). The set is almost a repeat of *Aristocrats*: "*We see the living-room (upstage) and the lawn/garden (downstage) of an old and graceless nineteenth-century house, now badly decayed*" (16). Almost as soon as the set is revealed, the music-guessing game, also used in *Aristocrats*, begins, this time between David Knight and Daisy, Tom's wife. On Tom's entry, the game becomes a quotation-guessing one. Self-conscious scraps of intellectualism float about the stage during the exposition. Tom Connolly, novelist, has published nothing for seven years. His royalties have dried up, and the cost of keeping his daughter, Bridget, in a mental institution is prohibitive. He and Daisy are in debt, and their hope is that David will authorise the purchase of Tom's papers for a Texan university. The exposition itself is run-of-the-mill, in that characters who already know the facts decide to explain them to each other. Friel dresses it up as a disagreement on detail between Tom and Daisy, but the disguise is a transparent one. One detail which does emerge is Daisy's contention that Tom not only wants to be offered money, but that he wants to be offered more than Garret

Fitzmaurice, also a novelist, friend, and rival. Tom's insecurity needs the affirmation of hard cash. Unsurprisingly, at the end of the play, it is Tom who decides not to sell, preferring what Friel called the "Necessary Uncertainty" (Pine, 1999: 308). The phrase: "Give me your answer, do!" is as much an apostrophe to God, or to fate, as it is to Tom or to David, who is referred to as "Mister God" (23).

There is a deal of revisitation of old themes and images in the play. Troubled, childless couples, old houses, mental dysfunction, silence, visiting scholars, promising pianists who were denied chance, lies, uncertainty, ambiguity, and art. Even Jack, who, every so often "improvises a new affectation" (32), has aspects of a cut-down Frank Hardy in *Faith Healer*. It is almost as it Friel has consciously collected those elements of his work which might be called "Frielian" and assembled them into a single, contemporary play, an unflattering extended metaphor of modern Ireland.

Three major themes present themselves. There is the materialism theme, noted by McGrath. There is also the theme of the status and validity of art. Friel wrote: "the play . . . is the play of an elderly/old writer who has got to that selfish and boring, but nevertheless painful, stage where he tells himself he wants an overall assessment of what he has done — a judgement, a final verdict" (Pine: 1999: 308). A number of characters throughout the play comment on the nature of art and artists. Garret, speaking of ageing novelists, says: "[w]e don't formally retire . . . But I hope we have the good sense to know when silence is appropriate" (46). Gráinne, in speaking of the "double act" that she and Garret indulge in, is given a telling comment:

> audiences impose limits on how far we can go. And we're secretly glad of that limitation because we're both still a bit nervous that without that restraint we

might deliver the final thrust, that mortal wound.
(48–9)

It is Daisy, however, who makes the most severe criticism:

> It struck me how wretched you are. You're unhappy
> in the world you inhabit and you're more unhappy
> with the fictional world you create; so you drift
> through life like exiles from both places. (52)

It is tempting to read aspects of Friel's own life into the play,
and, to an extent, his life has reached a point where retro-
spectives are inevitable. Beyond that, it would be dangerous
to extrapolate.

At the heart of the play is the question of the validation
of life, not art. Tom's life, not his art, needs the validation of
money; he needs to be convinced that he has not spent his
life for nothing. Likewise, the other characters are old
enough to be reviewing the past rather than anticipating a
future. Maggie, Daisy's mother, is suffering from degenerative
arthritis, and is distressed by Jack, her husband, a vain liar and
a petty thief. When it is discovered that Jack has stolen Garret's wallet, she echoes *The Communication Cord* in the line:
"That's what shaped my life. Yes . . . whatever deformed con-
tour my life had . . . that's what determined them all — that
little coxcomb piano-player . . ." (67). Her life is shaped, not
by the cathedral of the peasant cottage, but by the grubby
antics of a kleptomaniac husband. A little later in the play,
when Jack has, through his selective amnesia, purged the incident from his mind, he reflects on their life together:

> If she hadn't married the little piano-player, headed
> for a brilliant career in medicine. At least that was
> the expectation. But there's always an expectation,
> isn't there? And they don't always work out, do
> they? So maybe all I did was provide her with a dif-
> ferent set of disappointments. (74)

The play is filled with disappointment, uncertainty, failure, and the embracing of these as necessary parts of life. Acceptance of one's own resources reappears as a minor theme, following on from *Wonderful Tennessee*.

Garret and Gráinne Fitzmaurice resemble Frank and Grace Hardy (Gráinne is the Irish version of Grace) in their attempts to humiliate each other. The materialist theme is played out in their obsession with holidays in Tenerife and visiting the library where Garret's archive will be stored. (It might be added at this point that Friel chose to donate his archive to the Irish National Library in February 2001.)

David Knight has been through a breakdown and needs to deliver to his American masters or be considered, in his words, "sterile" (75). Comfort and affirmation are not offered by the play. In an apostrophe at the end, Daisy outlines what could be Friel's own *credo*:

> But to sell for an affirmation, for an answer, to be free of that grinding uncertainty, that would be so wrong of him and so wrong for his work. Because that uncertainty is necessary. He must live with that uncertainty, that necessary uncertainty. Because there can be no verdicts, no answers. Indeed there *must* be no verdicts. Because being alive is the postponement of verdicts, isn't it? Because verdicts are provided only when it's all over, all concluded. (79–80)

Tom chooses uncertainty, there being, according to Daisy, no alternative for the living. Frank Hardy, in *Faith Healer*, renounced chance by dying. Tom and Daisy reject the offer to buy, not because they are placing art above money, but because they place life above both. At the end of the play, there is a suggestion in Tom's visit to Bridget that he has begun writing again.

As a contrast to the decaying Big House, the restored cottage in *The Communication Cord* has a number of different emblematic functions. The characters are aware that the cottage is more than its bricks and mortar, but they differ as to the symbolism. Jack is caustic about it, treating the idea that the cottage shaped the souls of the Irish nation with scepticism. Tim is obliged to pretend to believe that the cottage, and all others like it, were important in the formation of the national psyche. Donovan is the principal enthusiast for this opinion. He professes an interest in heritage and in authenticity. The semiotics "senator" and "doctor", both of which are signs of power and prestige, help to establish Donovan as a formidable figure, but also as one motivated by political considerations. Politicians fare badly in Friel, from Doogan in *Philadelphia, Here I Come!*, to the caricature cabinet in *The Mundy Scheme*, to Donovan, doctor, senator, and practising hypocrite. Donovan is an antidote to Yolland in *Translations*. Yolland's pastoral vision of the Irish countryside is naïve, even misplaced, but undoubtedly sincere. Donovan, on the other hand, voices pious platitudes about his peasant ancestry: "this . . . transcends all those . . . hucksterings. This is the touchstone. That landscape, that sea, this house — this is the apotheosis . . . this is the absolute verity" (32–3).

In other plays, Friel has used the technique of placing a slightly unsuitable word in the mouth of a character in order to draw attention to a personality trait. In *Philadelphia*, Lizzy used the verb "desist" as an index of her vulgar pretension. Here "apotheosis" and "verity" become twin markers of Donovan's insincerity. The words are not used incorrectly; they are merely unusual in their context. While claiming a Gaelic, Irish, peasant background, his vocabulary becomes more abstruse, distancing him from the very situation he is trying, albeit hypocritically, to embrace. Ironically, the words he uses to describe the cottage are Greek ($\alpha\pi o\theta \epsilon o\upsilon\nu$, to deify) and Latin (*veritas*, truth). In *Translations*, these languages were not incompatible with Gaelic culture. In *The*

Communication Cord, they merely remove Donovan further from his idealised landscape.

The repeated lines also serve to highlight Donovan's hypocrisy. At the beginning of the play, Jack parodies national pieties: "*(In parody)* This is where we all come from. This is our first cathedral. This shaped all our souls. This determined our first pieties" (15). Tim repeats this to Donovan, almost like a mantra or a litany:

Tim   This is where we all come from.

Donovan   Indeed.

Tim   This is our first cathedral.

Donovan   Amen to that. (34)

The recitation breaks down when Donovan finds himself chained in the cow stall, in physical discomfort and mounting distress, concluding that the cottage is a "dump".

Donovan's need to find something in the cottage which feeds his unconscious is not an invention of Friel. Much of Irish political and social thinking is still clouded by Eamon de Valera's vision of "a self-sufficient, bucolic, Gaelic utopia" (Lee, 1989: 187). On St Patrick's Day 1943, de Valera made the radio broadcast to an international audience that has become associated with his vision of Ireland, a speech that has become known as "the dream speech":

> a land whose countryside would be bright with cosy homesteads, whose fields and villages would be joyous with the sounds of industry, with the romping of sturdy children, the contests of athletic youths and the laughter of comely maidens, whose firesides would be forums for the wisdom of serene old age. It would, in a word, be the home of a people living the life that God desires that man should live. (Keogh, 1994: 133–4)

De Valera's vocabulary — *land, countryside, fields, villages, fire-sides* — carefully avoids any mention of cities, factories, or mechanisation. When he uses the word *industry*, he uses it in the sense of "diligence" rather than industrial infrastructure. The country that includes the "laughter of happy maidens" and "the contest of athletic youth", is a country that is sepa-rated and isolated from the contaminating influences of in-dustrial Britain. The invocation of God gives impetus to the imbrication of Irish politics with conservative Catholicism. Michele Dowling has made the point that his vision took root and endured partly because of de Valera's own longevity:

> [b]y the time of his death Ireland was moving away from the image he had worked hard to establish, but his legacy endured nonetheless. His vision is en-shrined in the still extant constitution of 1937. (Dowling, 1997: 41)

She goes on to make the point that de Valera's Ireland had:

> never really existed in the first place. A national im-age does not need to be real to be effective. It merely needs to offer a fixed image of self, a picture of what we like to imagine that self to be rather than what that self is. (41)

The effectiveness of the image may be beyond dispute — it has been used as a selling point by the Irish tourist board for many decades — but is effectiveness to be judged in purely economic terms? This is definitely one of the questions posed by *The Communication Cord*.

De Valera's "dream speech" and the mythology it rein-forced is a definite presence in the play. All the major char-acters are influenced by it, or are reacting to it in various ways. Donovan adheres to the bucolic vision for political reasons. Tim gives lip-service to it, because he wants a job and to secure his relationship with Susan, so his motives are economic as much as romantic. Privately, he feels that the spirit of the house is antagonistic towards him. Jack, whose family owns the cottage, has rejected the vision completely, and treats it with patronising scorn. Barney the Banks, the colonising foreigner, has swallowed it completely. This leaves the peasant, Nora Dan.

Nora Dan is a character almost "left over" from *Translations*. That play dramatised the last gasp of Gaelic Ireland, the surrender of the peasantry to cultural colonisation. Nora Dan is the debased remnant of that peasantry, welcoming colonisation on condition that it brings money. Friel is careful in the notes to distinguish his terms. Nora Dan is "*a country woman who likes to present herself as a peasant*" (22) and not an authentic peasant. The term "peasant" has become one of abuse, and few, if any country people would now describe themselves thus. The phrase, "of peasant stock" is used, but by those who consider themselves safely and comfortably middle-class. It is merely another way of paying lip-service to the rural ideal. Jack's characterisation of Nora Dan is the urban cynic's idea of peasantry: "The quintessential noble peasant — obsessed with curiosity and greed and envy" (21). There is, in Ireland, a deep urban/rural division. This division is the antithesis of Hugh's "spiritual people" in *Translations*, and is a large part of the serious core of Friel's farce. Friel recognised the fact that the word "peasant" is "an emotive word" (Friel, 1972: 52). He identified what he saw as the two dominant characteristics of the peasant: "one is a passion for the land; the other is a paranoiac individualism" (52). Nora Dan's presentation of herself as a peasant is the reduction of her place in the country to theme-park parody, presenting to outsiders the image they expect to see. She is the self-fulfilling prophecy of the Irish rural self-image.

The other relationship of Nora Dan with the cottage in the play is the fact that she believes it to be hers. Jack announces that she is convinced of her legal entitlement. Land

and the ownership of land have an important place in the Irish psyche. Even today, the country has a higher percentage of house ownership than in continental Europe and the US, even in urban areas. At the end of the play, through her injury on Jack's motorbike, she is forced to remain in the cottage. There is a reverse colonisation taking place, the peasants striving against more powerful economic forces and re-capturing their place in the landscape. This is an easy aspect of the play to overlook, given that it is filtered through Jack's disdain at the beginning, and fury by the end, at Nora's obvious and comic opportunism. She attempts to sell her own house to Donovan in order to ensure her tenure in the cottage (87–8), and talks on blithely through Jack's attempts to be offensive.

Dowling also made the point that the national image does not have to be real (1997: 41). To deify something that is not real, indeed to make icons of ideals, or of plays, is something with which Friel appears to have little patience (O'Toole, 1982: 170). Hugh, in *Translations*, warns of the dangers that ensue when a language no longer corresponds with the landscape of fact. Dowling is careful to say, in de Valera's defence, that he never claimed that this was the Ireland that existed, or that it ever had; it was an Ireland that he wanted to bring into being. She also points out that it is just the opening section of a longer speech. This, although a valid defence of de Valera as a visionary politician, is to miss the point. It matters little what de Valera thought about the speech, whether he originated the idea (which he did not), whether he believed it himself, or whether he was appealing to his constituency. The use made of his speech is, perhaps, not de Valera's fault, but he is identified as the architect of the rural idyll. Among its other functions, *The Communication Cord* problematises the relationship of the modern Irish person and the foreign visitor to the rural landscape, and inter-

rogates received notions of belonging by exploring the ideology behind the acceptance of such notions.

One of Friel's most successful investigations into contemporary Irish life is *Wonderful Tennessee*, whose set makes
as clear a statement about the condition of modern Ireland
as anything he has written. In Chapter Two, I noted how the
opening dialogue of the play had a postmodernist ring to it. It
is worth noting that the setting is austere, despite the good
weather: "[a] stone pier at the end of a headland on the remote coast of north-west Donegal" (*Wonderful Tennessee*: 8).
Donegal itself is an extremity; the headland reaches off the
county; and the pier juts into the ocean beyond the headland,
fixed between Ireland and Oileán Draíochta. There is always
an uncertainty about the exact location. Frank, romantically,
it may seem, calls it Arcadia. Trish, throughout the play, is
uncertain whether she is in Donegal or Sligo, and there is
some doubt as to whether they actually are at Ballybeg pier,
and not some other forgotten structure perched at the back
end of nowhere. The physical uncertainty of the play reflects
the insecurity of the characters as they begin to deal with the
problems of early middle age: slowly failing health, difficulties
in personal relationships, financial and career setbacks, and
the final realisation that time is running out on the dreams
and ideals of youth.

The pier, like many of the settings in Friel's plays, is in a
state of dereliction. It has not been in use since the area became depopulated, but still contains emblems of its past:
nets, lobster pots, fish-boxes, iron bollards, rings, and a cru-
ciform lifebelt holder "on which hangs the remnant of a lifebelt" (8). Csilla Bertha draws attention to the Christian
symbolism of the cross-shape (Bertha, 1999: 130). It is, in
fact, more complex than this. The circular lifebelt on the
cross transforms it into a reminiscence of a Celtic cross,
although the fact that it is only the remains of a belt suggests
a fracturing of the perceived association between Irishness

and Christianity. If the lifebelt represents a body, it is still on
the cross, and no immediate resurrection seems likely.

In some ways, as Bertha says, the symbolism of *Wonderful Tennessee* is obvious (1999: 120), and it does appear to
lumber along clumsily. Six characters at a crucial point in
their lives are marooned for a night on a promontory, between a deserted hinterland and a so-called holy island
where, years before, a teenager had been ritually slaugh-
tered. George is dying, Berna has had a nervous breakdown,
Terry is broke. Angela is a classics teacher who can keep the
parallels with Greek mythology before the eyes of the audience at all times. Terry and Berna, and Trish and George,
are childless. Terry was in love with Angela, Berna's sister,
and had married Berna as a second choice when Frank married Angela. Frank is writing a book called *The Measurement
of Time and its Effect on European Civilization*. The six pass the
time on the pier, waiting for Carlin, the ferryman, who never
arrives. In the morning, the bus comes back and their ordeal
ends, each leaving a small votive offering on the pier. The
play is a collection of well-worn motifs, some familiar from
other Friel plays, some new to his canon, but familiar from
other genres. What bind the play together and save it from
being a catechism of cliché are, firstly, the music, discussed
in the previous chapter, and, secondly, the self-conscious
manipulation of the motifs for artistic ends which are other
than those of their original situations.

The classical Greek allusions are ubiquitous, from
Frank's exclamation of "Arcadia" (19), to Friel's description
of the dancing as "*maenadic*" (17); from Angela's description
of the Eleusinian Mysteries, to the persona of Carlin, who
doubles as Charon, ferryman into the Underworld. Blended
with this are pagan Celtic and Christian Irish motifs. The
legend of the appearance of the island every seven years recalls Hy-Brasil, and the landing of the fishermen recalls both
classical and Celtic tales of sailors landing on enchanted is-

lands or the backs of sea-beasts. The many hymns played by George add weight to the religious subtext of the play. It is the motif of the dolphins, however, that binds the past and present, Celtic and Greek together. Oileán Draíochta disappeared and left nothing but dolphins. The sailors who captured Bacchus in Angela's story were turned into dolphins, and Frank has what he sees as an almost mystical experience watching the dolphins dance off the coast of the island.

With so many religious rites and supernatural motifs in the play, one might expect that it had a religious focus. Bertha points out the parallel between the Eleusinian Mysteries and the action of the play: fasting, purification in the sea, initiation rituals, music, dancing, drinking and the offering of sacrifice (1999: 128). Her conclusion is that:

> The search is not for a specified form of worship but for the ability to transcend the material world and rational thinking. And in this broad sense, the spiritual pagan and Christian rituals can all contribute to a non-dogmatic framework for faith. (129)

A significant portion of Bertha's article is a reaction to the unfavourable criticism of David Krause, who thought little of the play (Krause, 1997: *passim*). Krause sees the trip as a futile one, from the spiritual point of view, and dislikes the mixture of Greek and Celtic myth with Christian ritual. Bertha reacts particularly to his comment that "a journey to a holy place, even if unfulfilled, is, by its very intention, good for the soul", and claims that: "[b]y staying near it and meditating on it and on their own lives and failures, they gradually come closer to understanding the island's mysterious and contradictory nature" (Bertha, 1999: 125). While I understand why Bertha would wish to refute an unsympathetic opinion like Krause's, I do think she has forced the religious imagery too far. Such religious experiences as there are in the play are ambiguous: Frank's dawn encounter with the dancing dolphins has a pantheistic, "tree-hugger" quality, and contains elements of stories of UFO encounters — he had used up all his film before the dolphins began their dance. The dance is described in terms very close to both *Dancing at Lughnasa* and *Molly Sweeney*, where the dances represented the momentary release of pent-up anxieties and frustrations of an all-too human nature. Given that this kind of motif appears in Friel in particular ways, one wonders how much of the "deliberate, controlled, exquisite abandon" (70) was anthropomorphically imposed on the creatures by Frank himself, a pattern imposed by the perceiver which then becomes a privileged narrative. This is very much a part of *Making History*.

The music seems to suggest, if not a tension, then a slippage, not only between the sacred and the secular, but also between the past and the present. George switches between sacred and secular music, one to the other, at times quite inappropriately. Just as there is a suggestion of the past intruding on the present in the use of the music noted in Chapter Two, so the sacred intrudes on the secular, and the secular encroaches on the sacred. This is confirmed by the story of the sacrifice on the island, and by Berna's story of the Holy House of Loreto. They are stories from the past, each with a bearing in the present. Each has a religious or ritual centre, but the interpretations of the stories are ambiguous. Equally, the island exists, not so that it can be understood by the six characters, but so that it can be one more element in the means by which they begin to understand their own situations.

I would have difficulty in agreeing with Elmer Andrews, also quoted by Bertha, when he says: "the spirit of rural Ireland may be languishing and deformed, but it hasn't wholly lost its powers to compel and perhaps even to renew" (Andrews, 1995: 260; quoted in Bertha, 1999: 131). This is a very unsafe position to adopt with regard to Friel's work

post-*Communication Cord*. In particular, the position is untenable with regard to *Wonderful Tennessee*, given that towards
the end of Act I, Scene I, Angela sings, to the tune of "Abide
with Me": "That is the place / That shapes our destiny" (35),
a line which has distinct echoes of: "This is our first cathedral. This shaped all our souls. This determined our first pieties" (*Communication Cord*: 15).

The word "wonderful" occurs very frequently, 22 times
in the first scene alone. Krause is dissatisfied with its use,
while Bertha sees it as a signifier of the characters' impoverished use of language. It is perhaps used in the way she suggests, but it has a more fundamental function in the structure of the play, indicated by its use in the title. Many things
are described as wonderful: the pier is wonderful, the island
is wonderful, the sisters are wonderful, Terry is wonderful.
By the second scene, Trish is using "wonderful" wearily (41).
In Act 2, Angela reacts to the story of the ritual killing on
the island with a deeply ironic "wonderful" (75). Two linked
processes are at work here. There is a desperation to find
wonder, and consequently spiritual renewal, in something;
and a debasement of the word by its over-use. It is not that
the language as a whole becomes impoverished, but that the
word itself loses its primary meaning, and, consequently, the
concept behind the word, the signification, is lost. It is the
world that becomes impoverished through the desanctifica-
tion of the language. When "wonderful" means no more
than *pretty*, or *nice*, then the capacity to experience wonder,
and to communicate the experience of wonder, becomes
diminished. This is deliberate on Friel's part, and it is consonant with some of his theories of language, and leads into
the heart of the play. Language, according to Friel, who borrowed the term from fellow Field Day director Tom Paulin,
should form the Fifth Province of Ireland "to which artistic
and cultural loyalty can be offered" (O'Toole, 1982: 169). It
is this Fifth Province of words that is violated by the de-

basement of the language. It was in the same interview that
Friel made his remarks on the centrality of language; that it
is through the recognition of what language "means for us
on this island" (176) that the political problems on the island
can be solved. In *Wonderful Tennessee*, Friel applies this to
human existence. The point of the end of the play is that
there is no *deus ex machina*, no revelation of transcendental
significance; just an abandoned pier and the six middle-aged
friends. Their problems are, if not solved, then certainly
shared through language.

The characters do not find some kind of spiritual renewal, nor even a spiritual experience, by meditation on the
island, or nature, or the Irish countryside. The countryside is
not an agent of spiritual regeneration, it is a *locus* for it. The
characters find that their lives depend on self-reliance, not
on religious aspiration. Angela's crucial, triumphant speech
at the end clarifies this. It is led into by Terry, who is talking
about his financial affairs: "Things will pick up. The tide will
turn. I'll rise again. Oh, yes, I'll rise again" (87). Friel is using
the language of Christianity to emphasise that Terry's recov-
ery is a secular one, owing nothing to supernatural forces,
but to his own efforts and the co-operation of his friends in
keeping his situation a secret. His revelation that he is broke
is followed by an invitation to the others to return to the
same spot again, a year later. Angela responds:

> Yes, we will! Next year — and the year after — and
> the year after that! Because we want to! Not out of
> need — out of desire! Not in expectation — but to
> attest, to affirm, to acknowledge — to shout Yes,
> Yes, Yes! Damn right we will, Terry! Yes — yes —
> yes! (87)

Their return will happen because they want it to, not because they need to, or because they are obliged to. This removes the elements of compulsion which are central to the

tenets of any religion. Even non-aligned spirituality is built on need, albeit that the expectations of particular kinds of worship are removed. Angela's "Yes" is not just to Terry's invitation, but to the concept of life and death that has been revealed on the pier, and recalls Molly Bloom's half-asleep "yes I said yes, I will, Yes", at the end of *Ulysses*. Friel is careful to differentiate between the women. Angela's "yes" is plural, "*we* will", and is said publicly, in the morning, and fully awake. It is an affirmation of faith in the future, not of a memory of the past. The sanctification of the secular is pointed to again by George, the only member of the party who will not return. He finishes playing "Down by the Cane-Brake": "*Still nobody moves. Now George plays in his 'sacred' style*" (88). George, on the cusp of his own death, is transforming a secular folksong into something sacred. The song is one of love and death. "Wonderful Tennessee" achieves the same mythic status as Oileán Draíochta, Hy-Brasil, Atlantis, the Elysian Fields, or Heaven. Ballybeg pier is at once pagan, classical, Celtic, Christian, and post-Christian. In a secular world, it might as well be Tennessee as anywhere else. In an interview, Friel remarked that the working title for the play was *The Imagined Place* (Gussow, 1991: 211).

If it is the case that the play seeks to sanctify the secular, then what is the purpose of the votive offerings at the end of the play, and to whom are they made? Friel is ambiguous about the reason. Angela claims she is leaving the cake in the tin for Carlin, the non-appearing ferryman "to keep him sweet" (77). This seems unlikely, as they have no reason to placate Carlin, never having met him. What it does is to attribute to Carlin the vengeful characteristics of a pagan god. This is nicely counterpointed by Frank when he pours out the cherry brandy on the pier. The action, following Angela, has the quality of a libation, but he comments: "Cherry Brandy. God, that's a sin, isn't it?" (78), contrasting the pagan ideal of sacrifice to the gods with the frugal Irish Catholic idea that to waste food is a serious sin, and thereby confusing the contention that the leaving of items has some kind of religious significance. Frank also refers to the items left on the lifebelt stand as "visiting card[s]" (79). The twice-repeated line "Terry Martin Was Here" (79, 81) is an indication that the items are left as an offering to themselves, rather than to any particular deity. It is perhaps as much to mark their own presence on the pier, and by extension, to mark their immanence. It is Friel who refers to the actions at the end of the play as "votive offerings", and this would seem to suggest that he has a religious practice in mind. This raises a number of issues. A religious action is not necessarily religious in intention; in fact it only becomes religious if the action and the intention have the same end. Furthermore, and significantly, given Angela's speech at the end of the play in which she promises to return (87), a votive offering can merely be an offering made in token of, or in thanks for a vow. The status of the votive offerings is deliberately ambiguous.

Krause states that there is "no need to belabour the link between those who wait for an invisible Carlin and for an invisible Godot" (1997: 364). Perhaps there is a need, because the endings of the two plays are so different. Vladimir and Estragon go nowhere, and exist outside any kind of social *milieu*. The six damaged people in *Wonderful Tennessee* go home, to deal again with the same problems. In 1970, in answer to a question about Harold Pinter, Friel replied:

> What I dislike about him is the complete dehydration of humanity in him. This is also something I don't like in Beckett. There is a complete abnegation of life in both these men. They're really bleak! But life is all we have, you know. (Rushe 1970: 85)

The affirmation of life at the end of the play is testament to the fact that Friel's *credo*, "life is all we have", had not changed in the intervening 23 years. The *Godot* allusions are as deliberate as the religious ones, as Friel attempts to reconstruct a hope based, not on transcendent expectation, but on immanent possibility.

It would be impossible to conclude a survey of settings and characters without looking at the symbolism of place in *The Freedom of the City* and *Volunteers*. In *The Freedom of the City*, Lily, Skinner and Michael find themselves, by accident, in occupation of the mayoral parlour of the Guildhall in Derry. This is one of the few times in his career when Friel has situated a play in an actual location. They have rushed inside to avoid the bullets of a riot in Derry, and the presence of representatives of three very different strands of "republicanism" allows Friel the freedom to compare ideologies both within and without the Guildhall. The political background to the two plays will be discussed in more detail in Chapter Five.

The Guildhall itself dates from 1887, was rebuilt after a fire in 1908, and still dominates the city. Its architecture is Victorian Gothic, with strong ecclesiastical overtones in the façade and the stained glass. Until the mid-1990s, the building was the administrative centre of Derry, and in 1970, when the play is set, was still a symbol of Protestant control. To an extent in this play, Friel was talking to the citizens of Derry, particularly the Catholic citizens, to whom the Guildhall as a semiotic index of imperialism was more highly developed than to others on the Island. The play, with its criticism of British power in Ireland, predictably failed in London. Friel's description of the set is revealing:

> The doors and walls of the parlour are oak-panelled, and at ceiling height the walls are embattled. The furnishings are solid and dated, the atmosphere heavy and staid. . . . On one side . . . a Union Jack flag. On the other side a large portrait of a forgotten civic dig-

> nitary. A grand baroque chair for the Mayor; several
> upright carved chairs for his guests. (*Plays 1*: 105).

The picture Friel conveys is not one of civic continuity and
tradition, but of entrenchment and stagnation. The use of
words like "embattled" is important. It can mean simply,
provided with battlements or crenellations, but it also means
under threat or under pressure. The description of the fur-
nishings as "solid and dated" implies a self-satisfied detachment from the real world, a fixation on the past, as does the
use of "heavy" and "staid". The Mayor's chairs become almost Dickensian in their anthropomorphisation: the Mayor
is "baroque", his guests are "upright".

Ideas of Irishness are explored against the conflicting
ideologies of the three main characters and the array of
voices and official comments on their deaths. All three invaders of the Guildhall are Catholic and poor. Lily works as
a cleaner, and lives with her invalid husband and 11 children
in a condemned building; Michael is unemployed, but has
plans to improve himself; Skinner is a member of the per-
manently unemployed subculture bred in the North through
anti-Catholic discrimination and sectarian business practices.
Although native to Derry, the Guildhall is an alien environment, one in which they do not belong. In the words of
Skinner, "you presumed, boy. Because this is theirs, boy, and
your very presence here is a sacrilege" (140).

In *Volunteers*, the symbolism of the set is as forceful, and
more immediately available. A group of IRA prisoners has
volunteered to take part in an archaeological dig. The dig has
revealed the remains of a clay-and-wattle house and a Viking
skeleton. The volunteers, whose mandate for violent action
against the state is based on their claimed linear descent
from the armed struggle of the past, are brought face-to-face
with the ninth-to-eleventh century Viking occupation of Ireland — an even earlier and more bloodily disputed past.

Keeney, in one of his many burlesques, describes the dig as: "encapsulated history, a tangible précis of the story of Irish man" (36). It is while they are interacting, however obliquely, with the facts of Irish history that a kangaroo court of their fellow political prisoners condemns them to death.

In all the locations in Friel's plays, and in all the interactions between people and the places they inhabit, there is one common trope: the tribe. I do not mean this in a pejorative sense, but much of Friel's output concerns the tensions between different tribal allegiances. Given Friel's background as a member of the Catholic minority in Derry, this is hardly surprising. Even as early as *The Enemy Within*, Columba's tribe was the source of his greatest temptation, and a source of pressure on the life he has chosen. The arrival of Oswald, the novice, marks an attempt by an outsider to penetrate the tribe. In terms of religious communities, this is possible, but in secular communities there are no protocols for acceptance, as Yolland discovers in *Translations*. He elucidates a belief that one might suspect Friel himself of holding, namely, that the private core of the tribe will always be hermetic (48). In an earlier chapter, I discussed the significance of this with regard to language, and the difficulty of translation between cultures. Here, I want to expand on this importance in relation to tribal allegiances.

One of the features of life in the Northern Irish state, particularly before the Civil Rights movement, was the separation of the tribes. Traditionally, Ulster Catholics and Ulster Protestants lived in separate areas, were educated separately, and worked in separate jobs. As a result, myths and misunderstandings flourished in both communities. Protestants saw Catholics as controlled by priests, and by Rome; and as lazy, dirty, indolent and over-fecund. Catholics perceived Protestants as bigoted, imperialist, corrupt foreign oppressors. Sabine Wichert summarises the situation succinctly:

> The political ambitions of the Catholic Church were
> taken for granted, justifying the participation of prot-
> estant clergy in the Orange Order and party politics
> and thus neatly closing the vicious circle that allowed
> catholics to accuse protestants of sectarianism and
> anti-catholicism. (Wichert, 1999: 73)

It is this tribalism which, as we have seen, is at the heart of
Making History.

Several other plays can be read, at least in part, as the
attempt to penetrate the tribe, and the structure of these
attempts gives rise to what Seamus Deane has called the
"Frielian outsider" (1984: 21). Tom Hoffnung in *Aristocrats* is
an obvious example, who is paralleled by David Knight in
Give me Your Answer, Do!. Anna in *Living Quarters*, Peter and
Shane in *The Gentle Island*, Mabel Bagenal in *Making History*,
Frank Hardy in *Faith Healer*, and Yolland and Manus in *Translations* are all outside a tribe, and attempting to understand
the thought-processes and actions of disparate and hermetic
groups. In *The Freedom of the City*, Lily, Michael and Skinner
are plunged in among the ceremonial appurtenances of Un-
ionism, and have to make sense of them, and through them,
of their own tribal allegiances. In *The Communication Cord*
and in *Wonderful Tennessee*, the tribe has dissolved in a
postmodern Babel in one case, and in social and spiritual
dissolution in the other. The problem for *The Communication
Cord* is to establish and maintain contact in the absence of
shared *mores* or even language and tradition, while in *Wonderful Tennessee*, the need is to establish bonds that are personally significant rather than ones which are inherited and
meaningless. In *Wonderful Tennessee*, Friel presents, in the
shape of the Eleusinian mysteries, the ultimate impenetrable,
undecodable tribe.

Chapter Four

The Grammar of Reality

> for language being accommodated to the common
> notions and prejudices of men, it is scarce possible
> to deliver the naked and precise truth without great
> circumlocution, impropriety, and . . . contradictions.
> . . . (George Berkeley, *A New Theory of Vision* §120)

In 1971, Friel broadcast a "self-portrait" for BBC Northern
Ireland. In it, he gently parodies both himself and the inter-
viewers who had prodded him with questions about his life
and work, and speaks about the years he spent teaching,
during which he began to write and to explore the *mores* of
the community in which he lived:

> I began to survey and analyse the mixed holding I had
> inherited — the personal, traditional and acquired
> knowledge that cocooned me: an Irish Catholic
> teacher with a nationalist background, living in a
> schizophrenic community. . . . (Friel, 1971: 103)

There are two crucial phrases to be taken from this passage.
The first is the characterisation of his cultural inheritance as a
"mixed holding", a phrase used to describe small farms in
which more than one type of agriculture is practised, as if the

heritage was something that was not just passed on, but needed to be constantly husbanded, replanted, and restocked. The other is his description of Derry in the 1950s and 1960s as "schizophrenic", meaning split, or characterised by mutual inconsistency and contradiction. The definition certainly fits Northern Ireland, now as then. The divide between the communities has long transcended race, religion or politics, and appears to have become a way of living. Politically, the same set of facts can be given two breathtakingly different interpretations, and the stances taken by extremists on both sides are mutually exclusive. Living in a community such as this, it is unsurprising that Friel became interested in the gaps between word and deed, between thought and feeling, between action and memory, and between the heart and the head. Facts, in this world, become fluid; they become whatever they can be reconstructed to be.

In *Faith Healer*, *Dancing at Lughnasa* and *Molly Sweeney*, Friel teases out the details of what might be called self-representation. By this I mean that Friel explores the way in which individuals construct themselves, and thus respond to an external reality. He does this without recourse to the overt visions of Irishness that permeate *Translations* or *The Communication Cord*, but his ruminations still illuminate some of the darker corners of the Irish psyche. In *Performances*, he extends the thesis still further, blurring the boundaries between the construction of self and the construction of others. The gap between word and deed becomes the gap between word and meaning, between word and music, and between word and true expression.

Frank Hardy in *Faith Healer* is confronted by a gift which, if it exists at all, defies explanation, and all attempts to encompass it rationally. The repeated self-reconstruction he indulges in throughout the play is a misguided attempt to comprehend his gift, an attempt that leads to the disintegration of his life, and his violent death. In *Dancing at Lughnasa*,

the reality of the Mundys' existence is challenged by the atavistic, wordless dances that erupt into the action. Mundy is
cognate with "mundane", and it is this very mundanity which
is under threat. *Molly Sweeney* raises the questions to a new
height, challenging not only perceptions of reality, but problematising the very nature of reality itself. However, the
roots of this theme in Friel's drama go right back to some of
his earliest work, and a line of development can be traced.

In *Philadelphia, Here I Come!*, Friel constructs a scene in
which Gar and his friends sit around the kitchen table and lie
about their sexual exploits. To some extent, this is not untypical of young males anywhere, albeit that these males are
less young than they might be to indulge in such practices.
The lies are exposed by Private, at his most coruscating. We
see also Master Boyle, fantasising about a high-status job in
America.

In *The Loves of Cass McGuire*, the play which followed
Philadelphia, the simple lies and harmless fantasies have developed a step further into something more fundamental.
The reality of Cass's situation, that she has been dumped
into a retirement home, and belongs nowhere, is contrasted
with the rich fantasy life of Trilbe Costello and Mr Ingram.
Here the fantasy is taking over at a much more fundamental
level, with the construction of elaborate alternative realities.
Cass, through her apostrophes to the audience, and her admission of her hard life, appears to be a hard-nosed realist:
"For fifty-two years I work one block away from Skid Row
— deadbeats, drags, washouts, living in the past. . . . The
past's gone. Good luck to it. And Gawd bless it" (*Cass
McGuire*: 19). In contrast, Trilbe's first entrance has all the
hallmarks of senile dementia. She speaks as though she were
an adjudicator addressing the audience of an elocution competition. Mr Ingram trots after her, feeding the fantasy.
When they return, Mr Ingram is reading the story of Tristan
and Isolde. Trilbe remarks "It's the part about the exile I like

best" (28), betraying not just a romantic sentiment, but the fact that she is exiled from her real past: "The Costellos from Ardbeg. . . . All high-falutin' chat and not a penny to scratch themselves with" (23).

Cass reacts nervously as Trilbe settles herself in the winged chair for the first time and begins to tell her story. It is a penny-romance story of love at first sight, wealthy marriage and exotic foreign travel. Cass gapes after them "*in naked astonishment*" (31). She finds, however, that she is drawn into the fantasies. In the beginning of Act 2, she recounts the story of Mr Ingram's marriage to the showgirl as though it were true. She appears to believe it, although Ingram contradicts it with a slightly different story some time later. The family situation contributes to Cass's slide into fantasy. Her brother's rejection of her money, which she had sent every week, angers her. He has kept and invested the money, which he proposes to return to Cass as a fund for her old age, but she is angered by the fact that she had deprived herself for 52 years in the belief that her money was needed in Ireland. She retaliates by telling unsuitable stories at the dinner table. Possibly it is the fact that her vision of family and home in Ireland were illusory that precipitates her descent into the fantasy world of Eden House.

Early in Act 3, there is an exchange between Trilbe and Mr Ingram which is, perhaps, emblematic of the way in which the play as a whole works. Trilbe is reading the obituaries from the newspaper:

Trilbe	I told you about him yesterday. Principal of Fairhill Secondary School. A Kerryman. A very . . . athletic principal.
Ingram	I remember.
Trilbe	"He is survived by three sisters and three broth–" Surely that's a misprint!

Ingram	Hm?
Trilbe	I presume it should read three sisters and three brothers. He would never have left three brothels, would he? (52)

Here, the text itself indulges in fantastic speculation. Even Trilbe's pause before "athletic" suggests other possibilities in the narrative.

The play ends with the fantasy engulfing Cass. She sits in the winged armchair and takes flight. Mrs Butcher, true to her name, attempts to undercut the fantasies, much as Cass herself did at the beginning of the play. The inference is that she too will succumb, as even Tessa, the maid, has done.

In comparison to Friel's later plays, the structure and premise of *Cass* are unsubtle. It becomes obvious at an early stage in the play that Cass the realist, who had no time for sentimental memories, is going to be subsumed into a kind of *Gotterdammerung* for the elderly. Trilbe's injunction to: "[j]oin with us, Catherine, join with *us*", (47) is a little too obvious. The fact that both Trilbe and Ingram know that their world is one of make-believe is difficult to accept. The lines:

Trilbe	Never mind, Catherine, you have us. Our world is real, too.
Ingram	Our world is just as real. (60)

fail to convince us that they are doing anything more serious than spinning stories to while away the time. Yet we are expected to believe that this is an alternative to facing the cold and uncomfortable facts of their real lives.

In *Lovers*, the alternative to the reality of the life that Joe and Mag live, and to Mag's pregnancy, is death, although whether by accident or suicide is not clear. Ironically, Friel named that section *Winners*. In *Losers*, the companion piece, Andy disillusions Mrs Wilson and Cissy, by telling them that

Saint Philomena had been removed from the canon of saints. The result is not a clearing away of the debris of illusion and the beginning of a new life. Instead, the women close ranks, and choose another saint. As Cissy tells Andy:

> Aha, that's something you'll never know. . . . Wild horses wouldn't drag that out of us. You robbed us of Saint Philomena but you'll never rob us of this one, for you'll never be told who it is! (*Lovers*: 76)

One illusion is replaced with another, with one which cannot be attacked because it remains secret. Because of his brutal assault on the interior life of the women, Andy is excluded from even the physical life of Hanna, his wife, who now sleeps with her mother.

Fox Melarkey is a professional purveyor of illusions in *Crystal and Fox*. Friel has found an apt image in a run-down theatrical manager, from whom one would expect a degree of theatricality and posturing. Even his name suggests unreality; "malarkey" is slang for nonsense, foolishness, silly talk. At the opening of the play, his ability to weave illusions is on the wane. His travelling troupe, once one of the best in the country, has become shabby, and his best acts are deserting to other companies. Fox himself treads the fine line between creating illusions and believing in them himself. He is weary of creating second-rate illusions for other people, at a time when Ireland had just discovered television. He has had a dream: "I want to live like a child. I want to die and wake up in heaven with Crystal" (*Crystal and Fox*: 36). His vision of a simpler and more carefree existence is summarised in his memories of the past, a past he believes he can recreate:

> And when I do there'll just be you and me and the old accordion and the old rickety wheel — all we had thirty years ago, remember? You and me. And

> we'll laugh again at silly things and I'll plait seaweed
> into your hair again. (55)

In pursuit of this vision, he drives away the rest of the troupe. Billy Hercules and the Fritter twins have left before the play opens; he rows with Tanya and Cid over the order of the curtain-call, and poisons Pedro's dog. The pursuit is so single-minded that he cannot stop himself lying to Crystal, telling her that it was he who informed on their son, Gabriel, wanted by the English police for attempted manslaughter. In point of fact, it was Papa, who was in hospital, and whom Gabriel refused to visit, who had informed. Dantanus points out the parallel between the conventional emotions of the play-within-the-play, "The Doctor's Story", and the emotional complexity in Fox's life (1985: 139). The happy ending, which is "[a]ll the hoors want" (13), is unavailable to the purveyor of that ending for others.

The plotting is heavy-handed, and the end overly melodramatic, but the threads of illusion and of story that run through Friel's work are clearly discernible. Ultimately, Fox's character fails to convince us that his self-destructive streak is rooted in a realistically created character. Although characters motivated by self-destruction appear in *The Gentle Island* and *Volunteers*, it is not until *Faith Healer* that Friel succeeds in creating a character whose search for extinction is chillingly believable: Frank Hardy, the faith healer.

Faith Healer opened in New York in April 1979, and closed after a week. Despite the cool reception, the play is now acknowledged as one of his masterworks. It consists of four monologues, spoken in turn by three characters: Frank, the eponymous faith healer; Grace, his wife; Teddy, his manager; and Frank again. In this play, we begin to see that what began as an exploration of the illusions that people create for themselves is giving way to something more fundamental. The monologues in *Faith Healer* contradict each other in many fundamental details. It is evident that Frank was, observed from without, prone to exaggeration and lies. When we listen to Frank himself, with his relentless interrogation of his own motives, of his gift, of his relationships, and of his decision to attempt a cure that would cost him his life, the lies become more than untruths. They become alternative truths. Not empty boasting like Gar's friends in *Philadelphia*; not fantasies knowingly shored against the ruins of a life, like Trilbe, or, ultimately, Cass; not part of a profession of illusion and the suspension of disbelief, like Fox, but elements of a life absorbed into the ontology of the character at a fundamental level, reconstructed and transmuted, and necessary for that character's existence.

In his monologues, Friel returns to a native Irish tradition of storytelling. For most of his work, he is never far away from it; one thinks of Manus in *The Gentle Island*; the narration by Michael in *Dancing at Lughnasa*; Cass's apostrophes to the audience; or the Commentators in *Lovers*. In *Faith Healer*, however, the three characters speak for themselves. There appears to be little of what could be termed dramatic in the play; the set is minimal: some chairs for Frank; a chair and table for Grace; the same table, a different chair, and a small locker for Teddy. Behind the first three scenes hangs the tattered poster advertising: "The Fantastic Francis Hardy, Faith Healer, One Night Only" (*Plays I*: 331). There are no entrances, no exits, no major lighting changes, no fight scenes, no voice-overs, no exotic props. There is one sound cue, the recording of "The Way You Look Tonight". All of these elements would appear to point towards a dull evening in the theatre.

What Friel has done, in fact, is to produce a theatrical piece in which the drama, in the sense of conflict, is transferred almost in its entirely to the language. One thinks almost of bardic recitation of heroic epic poetry. The presence of an actor is still necessary, but it is a *presence*, almost in the uncanny sense in which we speak of an actor "having presence". In a conventional play, the action unfolds before an audience. In the monologues in *Faith Healer*, each member of the audience must feel that they, personally, are being told the story, almost in the manner of the Ancient Mariner; they are confronted with the story whether they like it or not. This drama of language puts enormous strain on the craft of acting, and on the listening abilities of the audience.

Because it is a drama of language, the conflict is on the level of language, and it is the *discourses* of the three characters which come into conflict, rather than the characters themselves, who are never on the stage at the same time. If the drama is looked at in this way, then it is more than just three contradictory stories, but three contradictory languages, three contradictory ways of perceiving reality.

Saussurean semiotics asserts that language does not describe pre-existing categories in the world. According to Saussure, language is "a system of interdependent terms in which the value of each term results solely from the simultaneous presence of the others" (1981: 114). In this way, language *creates* the categories, thereby forcing the speaker to see the world in a particular way. A simple example is the way in which languages divide the colour spectrum. In Irish, "glas" usually translates as "green", but can also be used to describe clouds which in English would be described as grey. In the perceptions of the Irish speaker, the differences which English speakers perceive between green and grey are elided. It does not mean that the Irish are colour-blind. It means that the divisions of the spectrum are different. Put another way, each individual may, using his or her own *langue*, perceive, or more correctly, construct, external "reality" in a different way. This is true of schizophrenics, and of other categories of mental dysfunction; where there is a discontinuity between the patient's perception and that of the rest of society.

In *Faith Healer*, Friel exploits this discontinuity in the shifting litany of place names, the alternative identities Frank gives himself, his father, and his wife. George O'Brien remarked that "[v]irtually every circumstance in the play is subject to different interpretations" (O'Brien, 1989: 98). Even the status of the three speakers is suspect. Frank describes his own death; Teddy tells us that Grace has been dead for some time. So what is their status on the stage? Are they phantoms haunting the audience, or suspended in some way beyond reality. The solid squalor of their lives appears to counter any ideas we have of transcendence. Where is the play set? There are suggestions of a village hall, or a room in a bedsit, but these are suggestions of the language as much as iconic stage representations. The answers to all of these questions are unavailable, either to the audience or to the characters themselves.

Like Fox, Frank Hardy is a run-down showman, living out of his van and existing from day to day. Friel's description of his coat could equally be applied to the rest of him: "*shabby, stained, slept-in*" (331). He begins with a recitation of place names, Welsh and Scots villages that they had passed through, so despite the fact that Frank is standing relatively still, the play begins in motion, criss-crossing Scotland and Wales. Both he and Grace lapse into this chanted mantra at intervals, and the effect is to give the play a rootlessness, like its characters, and a shifting quality, like Frank himself.

Many critics and, indeed, Friel himself, have noted that the play functions as a metaphor for the craft of the playwright, or, indeed, of any artist. He describes the play as:

> some kind of metaphor for the art, the craft of writing, or whatever it is. And the great confusion we all have about it. . . . So there's an exploration of . . . the element of the charlatan that there is in all creative work. (O'Toole, 1982: 173)

In his 1971 broadcast, Friel described his entry into the craft
of playwright in terms of being:

> ignorant of the mechanics of playwriting and play
> production, apart from a modest intuitive knowledge
> . . . like a painter who has never studied anatomy or
> like a composer with no training in harmony. (Friel
> 1971: 103–4)

Likewise, Frank describes faith healing as "[a] craft without
an apprenticeship, a ministry without responsibility, a vocation without a ministry" (333).

The means by which one comes to one's craft, and the
mastery one exercises over it, or the mastery it exerts over
its practitioners, is the subject of a significant section of the
play. Frank's introduction into the world of faith healing
sounds plausible, particularly as he contradicts himself: "As a
young man, I chanced to flirt with it and it possessed me . . .
No; let's say I did it . . . because I could do it" (333). He is
conscious that his craft works only occasionally, and that he
has no control over it, nor any grasp of its mechanism.

During the 1971 broadcast, Friel describes autobiogra-
phy as having elements of exhibitionism, exorcism and expiation (Friel, 1971: 108). In the immediate context, he was referring to himself. By association, he was talking about the
craft of the playwright, but the words describe the progress
of *Faith Healer* flawlessly, although it did not come to be
written for another seven or so years.

To the extent that he is a showman, Frank Hardy is an
exhibitionist. He exhibits his talent to heal, when it works.
He also exhibits sociopathic tendencies. He treats others as
ciphers, to be deployed as he wishes. Those he cured were
not people, but "his fictions, extensions of himself that came
into being only because of him" (345). Grace remembers
with bitterness how he continually changed her name:

> One of his mean tricks was to humiliate me by al-
> ways changing my surname . . . and we weren't mar-
> ried — I was his mistress — always that — that was
> the one constant: "You haven't met Gracie McClure,
> have you? She's my mistress," knowing so well that
> that would wound me and it always did. (345)

Frank's wish to be unconnected with anyone is associated
with his uncertainty about his faith healing. To be connected
to anyone is to be anchored and fixed. His reduction of
Grace to mistress gives her a degree of disposable imper-
manence, while the constant change of names is a means of
re-inventing her at a whim. Naming and renaming is an important theme in Friel. In *Translations*, Owen can exclaim:
"We name a thing and — bang! it leaps into existence"
(*Translations*: 56). Frank's compulsion to treat those who are
devoted to him badly is a test of their faith. Paradoxically, he
has no faith in himself, and the thought devours him, slowly.

The exorcism aspect of the play is more complex than
the showmanship. The monologue form is confessional, as if
telling the story was cathartic, like a session on a psychia-
trist's couch. What is being exorcised is the gap between
the belief that others have in Frank, and his lack of belief in
himself. He is never quite convinced that he is not a conman:

> *Am I endowed with a unique and awesome gift?* my
> God, yes, I'm afraid so. And I suppose the other ex-
> treme was *Am I a con man?* — which of course was
> nonsense, I think. And between those absurd exag-
> gerations the possibilities were legion. Was it all
> chance? — or skill? — or illusion? — or delusion?
> (333)

Frank wishes to exorcise uncertainty. At the very end of the
play, as he walks to his death in Ballybeg, he is "renouncing
chance" (376). His expiation is his attempt to atone for the

lives that Grace and Teddy have led. Ultimately, it is only Teddy who remains alive, as Grace commits suicide. Towards the end of Teddy's monologue, as they sit in the lounge bar, Teddy looks at Frank: "the way he's gazing at me and the look he has on his face is exactly the way he looks into somebody he knows he's going to cure" (368). He then turns to look at Grace. It has become obvious in the course of the monologues that the affliction suffered by Teddy and Grace is Frank himself.

In a major section of his monologue, Teddy expands the idea of an artistic gift. In talking about one of his earlier acts, Rob Roy the Piping Dog, Teddy explains:

> apart from his musical genius that whippet in human terms was educationally subnormal. A retarded whippet, in fact. I'd stub my toe against something, and I'd say "God!", and who'd come running to me, wagging his tail? (356)

Similarly, Miss Mulatto, although talented, was devoid of intellectual activity: "Nothing. Empty. But what a talent" (356). In contrast to these, Frank's brain is a disadvantage: "those bloody brains? They bloody castrated him — that's what they done for him — bloody knackered him" (357). Intelligence is not only unnecessary for the creative process, but is seen as an impediment to it. According to Teddy, Frank was fine "when his brain left him alone" (358). Friel is undoubtedly making a comment, not just about the craft of writing, but about the craft of acting.

Ultimately, however, the play is not an extended metaphor on the craft of the playwright, nor of the actor. If it were, it would be merely pretentious. *Faith Healer* is a play about faith, and about the power of words in the creative process, particularly in the creation of self. It is about the necessity of faith in something, not necessarily a deity, but in a person, a variety act, a mysterious gift. Frank dies when he can no longer sustain his lack of faith in himself. His pilgrimage to Ireland is an attempt to restore that faith, much as the three couples in *Wonderful Tennessee* travel to Ballybeg Pier to try to draw from some well of spiritual forces in the Irish countryside. Frank is no more successful than they are.

The play is also about the creative power of the Word. It is almost a return to the idea of the Logos, the Word that was made Flesh, in the Gospel of John. In this, it is the Word of God that becomes incarnate as Christ. In *Faith Healer*, the creative power is used to deceive, to reconstruct and to negotiate selfhood. Both Grace and Teddy contradict Frank's account of the incident at Kinlochbervie. Grace and Teddy maintain that she had her baby there, and that it died, and was buried in a field. Of course, their stories are not entirely the same. In Grace's version, it is Frank who makes the cross for the grave. In Teddy's version, Frank walked away as soon as Grace went into labour, and did not return until just before dark. Frank's version is that in Kinlochbervie he received news of his mother's heart attack, and describes in detail his return to Ireland, just too late, and how he cried with his father. All three versions of the story are about death, and a release of grief, but Frank has transformed the squalid death of his infant into a story that exculpates himself. As there is no outside commentary in the play, the audience cannot decide between the stories, assuming that one is correct and the others are not, which is not a safe assumption. McGrath points out that each recounts the story according to his/her own pathology:

> Teddy's version preserved both the illusory separation of his personal and professional lives and the courtly love romance. . . . Grace's version . . . gave Frank much of the prominence in the incident. . . . Frank's memory erased the incident altogether and

> displaced it with an egocentric crisis that ostensibly
> had nothing to do with Grace. . . . (1999: 165–6)

McGrath compellingly details the crucial changes in the incidents in the play, and illustrates how the "shaping of memory" (1999: 172) is explained by the desires of the individual characters. The invocation of desire recalls the analytical theories of the French psychoanalyst Jacques Lacan, which are useful in describing *Faith Healer*.

Lacan, who began as a Freudian, proposes that the human "self" is an illusion created by the Unconscious. In order to become aware of this illusion, a developing child passes through what Lacan calls "the mirror stage". The child sees itself in a mirror, and is told "that's you". Of course, the image is not the child, so the recognition of self is a misrecognition. It is not the self, but "other". For Lacan, the illusion of selfhood is created through the ability to recognise objects in the world as "other". As others are also involved in this process, any stability in the idea of self is illusory, as what is involved is a system of negotiations without a stable centre. Desire, as a concept, is the desire to be the centre, to be the centre of the system, the centre of the symbolic order, the centre of language itself, and to be the other. By definition, this desire can never be fulfilled.

The monologues in *Faith Healer* are an illustration of the negotiation between the past and the present, and between the self and other, in the construction, and ultimate deconstruction, of a personality. All of Friel's plays are concerned with memory, and with the means by which even a false memory can become a cherished moment. In recalling a fishing trip with his father, Friel realises it could not have happened. He acknowledges, however, that the memory is a part of him: "because *I* acknowledge its peculiar veracity, it becomes a layer in my subsoil. It becomes part of me; ultimately it becomes me" (Friel, 1971: 101). In like manner, an

image we may have of somebody else, and of their relation
to us, ultimately becomes part of how we define ourselves.
Frank's assessment of Grace as his loyal drudge (to use
McGrath's phrase) is one of the negotiations he uses in order to define himself. While Teddy accepts his role as "acolyte to the holy man" (345), Grace is attempting to redefine
herself as wife, something Frank will not allow. Grace certainly defines herself in relation to Frank, to the extent that
she can see, and resent, his constant redefining of her to suit
a particular situation or mood. The rows that ensue appear
to be about nothing, certainly nothing that Teddy can define:

> [Y]ou could say it was because the only thing that fi-
> nally mattered to him was his work. . . . Or you
> could say it was because the only thing that finally
> mattered to her was him . . . But when you put the
> two propositions together like that . . . somehow
> they both become only half-truths. . . . (360)

The rows occur because neither can accept the definition of
themselves negotiated by the other. In Lacanian terms, both
Frank and Grace are struggling to define themselves with
relation to the other, while dealing with Frank's desire to
possess the other.

The need to see the self as other can be carried over
into the interpretation of the play advanced by Anthony
Roche. He proposes a political allegory: that Teddy represents England; Grace, Northern Ireland; and Frank, the Republic. As the main action takes place in Scotland and Wales,
the "British Isles" are inscribed in the play. He describes
their conflicting stories as "contending, conflicting dramas of
national identity" (quoted in McGrath, 1999: 174). To the
extent that national identity, as much as individual identity, is
based on the identification and categorisation of "Other",
then this is true. According to Eugene O'Brien:

> Every culture defines itself through a process of nar-
> rative imagination, a re-telling of stories about its
> own past which reaffirms the ritual unities of the cul-
> ture in question. For example, Irish people remem-
> ber the 1916 Easter rebellion as a nodal point in the
> political and cultural reaffirmation of Irishness *per se*.
> (O'Brien, 2001: 15)

Irishness is defined, to a very large extent, as "not English", as we have seen from Chapter One; hence the continued power of Irish language pressure groups. Certainly, the constant re-telling of stories by Frank, and the relentless alterities he produces are consistent with the process of narrative imagination as defined by O'Brien.

It is to Friel's credit as an artist, and as a craftsman, that, even when the themes of the play include the decentered-ness of the modern psyche, he can approach them in such a way as to make the play accessible. One of the ways in which he secures his shifting texts is the use of the repeated lines. One of these is the litany of place names. Although it changes in detail, the rhythm it creates is constant. More important are the descriptions of Kinlochbervie and Bally-beg. Each monologue introduces the Kinlochbervie episode with almost the same words: "a village called Kinlochbervie, in Sutherland, about as far north as you can go in Scotland" (337, 344, 362, 370). Similarly, the final episode, the return to Ireland, is linked to a repeated line:

> So on the last day of August we crossed from Stran-
> raer to Larne and drove through the night to
> County Donegal. And there we got lodgings in a pub,
> a lounge bar, really, outside a village called Ballybeg,
> not far from Donegal town. (338, 351, 367)

These function as linguistic anchors in the text, the nearest thing an audience gets to proof of the truth of any of the monologues. They also alert an audience to the impending alternative version of the story; they act as warning buoys of consensus in the sea of the negotiated self.

In *Molly Sweeney*, Friel continues where he left off in *Faith Healer*, a fact signalled by the similarity in structure. Again we are presented with three monologues, two male, one female. Again, they present different aspects of a story; however, this time they are interwoven rather than staged separately, but at no time does any character address any other.

Molly Sweeney is a woman of 41 who has been blind since she was ten months old. She is not totally blind; we are told that she could tell light from dark, see the direction from which the light came, and see shadows of objects (*Molly Sweeney*: 17). Her husband, Frank, is sighted, and an enthusiastic autodidact, although one who has spent his life hopping from project to project, without the stamina to finish. He persuades her to consult a specialist, Mr Rice, once a leading ophthalmic surgeon, but now relegated to working in Ballybeg Hospital, after a breakdown which led to alcoholism, or at least chronic drinking. Rice has lost faith with himself. Both men pin their hopes on Molly: Frank, because she is his current project, and Rice because he believes that achieving a miracle cure will re-establish his reputation. Molly is persuaded to have an operation, which is, in its own way, successful. Thick cataracts are removed from her eyes, and new lenses inserted. Her damaged retinas can again carry messages, however imperfect, to her brain. But, having sight thrust suddenly upon her, Molly is unable to comprehend what she sees. The world of sight makes no sense to her. Frustrated, and unnerved, she retreats into a condition called "blindsight". Mr Rice describes this as a physiological condition, not psychological:

> She *was* indeed receiving visual signals and she was indeed responding to them. But because of a mal-

function in part of the cerebral cortex none of this
perception reached her consciousness. She was unconscious of seeing anything at all. (56)

After a period of uncertainty, Molly withdraws from the external world, and becomes confined to the same psychiatric
hospital that once treated her mother. At the end of the
play, her death appears imminent.

Blindness as an image has many powerful associations,
both from classical antiquity and Irish cultural history: Oedi-
pus, blinded for incest; Homer, blind poet of the *Odyssey* and
the *Iliad*; Tiresias, blind prophet, who had been both male and
female; and Gloucester, in Shakespeare's *King Lear*, whose
blindness is not just physical, but political and psychic. In Irish
tradition, many musicians and poets have been blind: Tur-
lough O'Carolan, the eighteenth-century harper, Seamas Dall
Mac Cuarta, and Blind Raftery. Blindness in literature can be
associated with punishment; or with innocence; with foolishness or inability to comprehend; or with compensatory gifts,
perhaps other kinds of sight, be it poetry, prophecy, music or
simply, insight. While Friel does not draw directly on most of
these traditions, they are gathered silently behind and below
the symbolism of *Molly Sweeney*. There is an expectation that,
because she is blind, she will "see" differently.

There are a number of useful ways of approaching this
play, the first of which is the idea of Molly herself as a contested body. In her opening speech, we are told of the
teaching methods used by her father. In the course of this
speech, two things become evident: that her mother is men-
tally fragile; and that her father drinks. She specifically mentions liking the whiskey on his breath, a factor which becomes significant in her dealing with Rice, who also drinks. It
is also apparent that her parents argue a lot: she mentions
listening to them "fighting their weary war downstairs" (15).
As the play progresses, it emerges in her various reminis-

cences that she is the cause of the conflict between her parents. In Act 2, she remembers one of the few visits she paid to her mother in hospital. She is confined outside the screen, while her parents argue inside. Her mother is screaming at her father:

> She should be at a blind school! You know she should! But you know the real reason you won't send her? Not because you haven't the money. Because you want to punish me. (58)

The war between her parents is a territorial one, with Molly as the contested territory. She herself prefers to see it as her father's meanness (67), but the theme is confirmed by its reiteration in the contesting claims of Frank and Rice.

Friel constructs Frank as a character full of enthusiasm. He has worked for a charity in Nigeria, he has kept goats with the notion of making cheese, he has, at one stage, bought beehives with a friend, toyed with the idea of introducing blueback salmon to Irish fish farms, and, at the very end of the play, develops an enthusiasm for African bees, which he is sure would thrive in County Leitrim. The point of these enthusiasms is that none of them has amounted to anything, and most have ended either in failure, or in their replacement by the next enthusiasm. Molly's friend, Rita, makes it plain: "All part of the same pattern, sweetie: bees — whales — Iranian goats — Molly Sweeney" (38).

Rice, on the other hand, is a man whose enthusiasms have been burned out. His wife has left him for a colleague, taking their two daughters, who now live in Geneva with their grandparents. It was this incident which precipitated the breakdown and the drinking. He immediately perceives Molly as: "the chance of a lifetime, the one-in-a-thousand opportunity that can rescue a career — no, no, transform a career — dare I say it, restore a reputation?" (18).

Both men make an emotional investment in Molly's operation, and, she finds herself in the position of undergoing life-altering surgery for their reasons:

> And then with sudden anger I thought: Why am I going for this operation? None of this is my choosing. Then why is this happening to me? I am being used.
> (31)

It is this anger which causes Molly to erupt into her furious dance, a dance of frustration and fury, but also one of adeptness and hubris. Molly is expressing something beyond words, but also demonstrating before the audience of neighbours and friends that her mastery of her world is quite as complete as their casual acceptance of theirs. Richard Pine takes the idea of the contested body further, and interprets the play as an allegory of colonisation (Pine 1999: 288). To the extent that the play is about the invasion and destruction of Molly's world, then this is true, and to the extent that one can build on Anthony Roche's work in relation to *Faith Healer*, Molly can be seen as colonised.

Allied to the theme of Molly's body as a contested site of conflict, there is a theme of authority running through the play. Frank's autodidacticism is the key to this theme. From the file he presents to Rice, to his own words in his monologues, Frank presents an eclectic selection of authorities to validate his ideas. The list Rice recites disdainfully contains results of tests, certificates of proficiency in physiotherapy, photographs, certificates for swimming, selections from philosophers, and magazine articles on miracle cures for blindness in Tibet. There is no discrimination of status made between them. Throughout the play Frank makes reference to articles on philosophy he has found in DIY magazines, television lectures on psychology, *The National Geographic*, and the local library. It is partly the manner in which Frank parades his knowledge, gleaned from such an uneven variety of sources, that irritates Rice, whose own education was conventionally brilliant. His monologues are littered with professors and colleagues, prestigious hospitals, conventions and lectures, a "glowing, soaring" career (32).

Molly's authority is very much her own. True, she has had her father's tutelage, and more will have to be said about that, but, until the advent of Frank, we know little of how she learned. We know that she has certificates for swimming and physiotherapy, but are never told how she came by them. Her description of one of those activities, swimming, is unconnected to anything but herself:

> every pore open and eager for that world of pure sensation, of sensation alone — sensation that could not have been enhanced by sight — experience that existed only by touch and feel; and moving swiftly and rhythmically through that unfolding world; and the sense of such assurance, such liberation, such concordance with it . . . (24)

The passage is full of words such as sensation, sense, touch, feel. Friel is attempting to evoke a non-sighted world, but he is also describing one that is reflexive, almost hermetic.

Thus, the conflict of authority that takes place is between the undisciplined self-taught mind, the disciplined but disillusioned one, and the mind that is not shared with anyone else. Molly is a party to the conflict, the site of the conflict, and the prize for the victor in a contest that is ultimately lost by all three.

Part of the conflict of authority is paternal. Molly trusts Rice for exactly the same reason that Frank does not: he smells of whiskey. Speaking of the way her father used to kiss her, Molly explains: "I loved that because his whiskey breath made my head giddy for a second" (14–15). This attribute outrages Frank on their first visit to Rice's house:

"there was a smell of fresh whiskey off Rice's breath . . . and I could barely stop myself from saying to Molly, 'Do you not smell the whiskey off his breath? The man's reeking of whiskey!' Ridiculous!" (26). Friel presses the point home after the bandages are removed from Molly's eyes following the first operation. Rice exclaims, "You are a clever lady" (42), recalling her father's use of the identical phrase (14). In response, her head becomes "suddenly giddy" as it did when she was a child. As both men are attempting to use Molly to further their own agendas, the paternalistic element forces her into the role of feminist heroine, or the classic female roles as both the site of the struggle and the passive prize.

Following Friel's investigation into the problems of communication in almost every line he has written, and his interrogation of ontology in *Faith Healer*, we should not be surprised to see him visit those themes again in *Molly Sweeney*. In *Faith Healer*, we saw how Frank and Grace objectified Lacan's mirror stage, each attempting to identify the self in terms of the other, while at the same time attempting to possess the other. In *Molly Sweeney*, Friel broadens his canvas and attempts to interrogate the nature and construction of reality. The conflict goes beyond the realm of language, because, unlike *Faith Healer*, none of the three versions of the story substantially contradicts what the others have said. Where the stories overlap, it is diverse details that are remembered, rather than conflicting incidents.

The epigraphs to the play are of particular use here. The second, shorter one by Denis Diderot alerts us to the fact that the play is about language: "Learning to see is not like learning a new language. It's like learning language for the first time" (11). The language dealt with in *Molly Sweeney* is not only verbal language, not just the Lacanian construction of alternative realities, but a language which operates without words: the grammar of reality. The difficulty is that this must be expressed in words, but it is a language rich in images — the dance, the struggle of the badgers, swimming, the engrams of the Iranian goats — while the language struggles to transcend itself. The relationship between blindness and sight, between the tactile world and the visual world, is used as a metaphor of the relationship between language and reality. The difficulty Molly experiences in coping with a sighted world is analogous to the difficulty suffered in the poststructuralist world. If the connection between the sound, the signifier, and the object, the signified, is an arbitrary one, then the connection between language and reality is similarly arbitrary and conventional, subject to slippage and change. As Frank informs us, according to Bishop Berkeley: "there was no necessary connection *at all* between the tactile world — the world of touch — and the world of sight . . ." (21).

Molly's world is, Frank tells us, a sequential one, unfolding in time. She feels the handle, the blade, the sharp edge, and realises that what she is holding is a knife (35). This is consonant with the longer epigraph, a poem from c. 1868 by Emily Dickinson:

> Tell all the Truth, but tell it slant —
> Success in Circuit lies
> Too bright for our infirm Delight
> The Truth's superb surprise
> As Lightning to the Children eased
> With explanation kind
> The Truth must dazzle gradually
> Or every man be blind — (10)

Truth, or reality, for Dickinson, is something gradually and obliquely revealed, or it will overwhelm. Molly is confronted with a truth to which the others have no access: that the connection between the interior and exterior worlds is contingent and conventional. Since she is unschooled in the conventions, what she sees becomes more and more chaotic, leading to the visions/hallucinations of the dead who visit her in hospital at the end of the play. This is explored by Friel in the pun on the word "gnosis", used by Rice and looked up in the dictionary by Frank. Rice condescendingly tells Frank that "g-n-o-s-i-s" means "a condition of impaired vision". Frank's own research reveals that the word means: "a mystical knowledge, a knowledge of spiritual things" (54). Gnosticism was, in fact, a second-century heresy against the Christian church, which proposed the replacement of faith with knowledge, the *gnosis*. According to Copleston: "Characteristic of Gnosticism in general was a dualism between God and matter . . ." (Copleston, 1962: 34).

The dualism is further exploited by Friel in his reference to Molyneaux, Locke and Berkeley, who believed, along with Mill and others, that external reality was merely what it was perceived to be. In *A New Theory of Vision*, Berkeley attempts to show that it is irrational to believe in the existence of an external reality existing independently of the mind. This makes the reference to the philosophers more fundamental than O'Toole, Pine, or McGrath recognise. O'Toole, quoted by Pine, says the play is "buttressed with philosophy" (1999: 298). Pine, in defending Friel, sees the importance of the philosophers in their contribution to the colonial and post-colonial debate about the location of authority and the location of culture. McGrath recognises the fundamental importance of the reference to Friel's canon, noting that in other Friel plays such as *Aristocrats*, *Faith Healer*, *Translations*, *The Communication Cord* and *The Freedom of the City*: "various language worlds or worlds of discourse collide, always with destructive results" (254). His claim, however, that there are "two different worlds, each with its own distinct vocabulary and syntax, its own principles of organization, selection, and orientation, its own biases, reference points, and master narratives" (254) in *Molly Sweeney*, is true as far as it goes, but it fails to take sufficient account of Berkeley's position, which is that knowledge cannot extend beyond the state of consciousness of the knower. The world is what it is perceived to be. It is not just Molly and the sighted world who are in conflict. The same conflict pertains between Frank and Rice. Frank's perception is made up of the detritus of popular magazines, Rice's of the smooth intellectualism of professional learning. Their perception coincides at many points, but at many others it does not.

In a very real sense, Friel has been groping towards this point since *Cass Maguire*. We might even push the date back further, to *Philadelphia*, *Making History*, or even *The Enemy Within*, where the perceptions of a monk focused on heaven and those of an earthly prince construct very different world-pictures. In *The Communication Cord*, the constructs were exploited for comic ends, and based on linguistic misunderstandings. *Faith Healer* deepens linguistic misunderstandings into postmodernist slippage of the signifier and the signified. In *Molly Sweeney*, Friel has pushed the boundaries of epistemology beyond the demands of contesting languages, or discourses. In *Molly Sweeney*, the battle has retreated into the minds of every individual, and it is suggested that the conflict is ubiquitous and unending.

Molly Sweeney is the apotheosis of Friel's attempt to locate perception somewhere beyond language, but, as we have seen, it was neither the first, nor the best received. *Dancing at Lughnasa* opened at the Abbey Theatre, Dublin in April 1990, and transferred to the National Theatre in London in October of the same year.

The household that Friel assembles in *Dancing at Lughnasa* is a familiar one from his other work. Kate, the schoolteacher, is the embodiment of conservative repression, recalling the claustrophobic atmosphere of *Philadelphia, Here I Come*, and life-denying characters such as S.B. O'Donnell. Michael, the narrator, also speaks the lines of the child, who is himself in 1936. This is an interesting adaptation of the conceit used in *Philadelphia*, but the divide is between past and present, rather than public and private. Chris, with her child born out of wedlock, is like Judith in *Aristocrats*. Rose, with her mild mental handicap and disappearance in Act 2, recalls Smiler in *Volunteers*. Even Father Jack, returned after 25 years in Africa, is a literary descendant of Father Chris Carroll in *The Blind Mice*, who is allowed to return to Ireland from a Chinese communist prison only because he has abandoned his faith. The domestic background, a child living with his aunts, appeared in an early short story, "A Man's World".

The year is 1936, the year of the Spanish Civil War, in which Irish soldiers fought on both sides. The outside world is on the brink of the catastrophic change that was the Second World War, while Ireland closed its borders and remained neutral. According to F.S.L. Lyons, Ireland lost more than it gained:

> It was as if an entire people had been condemned to live in Plato's cave, backs to the fire of life and deriving their only knowledge of what went on outside from the flickering shadows thrown on the wall. . . . When after six years they emerged, dazzled, from the cave and into the light of day, it was to a new and vastly different world. (Lyons, 1971, quoted in Lee, 1989: 258)

This is the setting for one of Friel's masterworks, which, like *Translations*, was acknowledged as such from its first performance.

The most pervasive image in the play is the dance, or rather, the dances, as there are several, and their meaning, as one expects of Friel, shifts. All of the dances represent some shift in the order of things, some intrusion into mundanity. The Irish dance early in the play is the most potentially subversive, as it appears to come from within. Elmer Andrews sees it as "a break in the acknowledged order, an

irruption of the inadmissible within the usual routine, a ritualised suspension of everyday law and order" (Andrews,
1995: 223). This is true, but the dance must also be seen in
the context of three other potentially disruptive dances:
Chris's dance with Gerry, Jack's description of the Ugandan
festivities, and the Festival of Lugh, in the back hills.

Thus far in this chapter, we have been examining the
manner in which language, be it verbal or otherwise, shapes
the reality of the perceiver; specifically, the manner in which,
far from being a passive describer of an unchanging actuality,
language creates the categories and forms the impressions.
Because of its realistic details, *Dancing at Lughnasa* hides this
theme in its deeper structure, and the concern with the
perception of reality emerges in the dances and in the character of Father Jack.

Jack has spent his adult life in Africa, in the leper colony
of the Ryangans in Uganda. During that time he spoke Swahili, apart from those occasions when Europeans were received in the village, and a brief sojourn in the British Army
during the Great War. An interesting colonial side-issue is
the refusal of the English District Commissioner to speak
Swahili at all, presumably to keep his perceptions pure. Returned to Ireland, Jack has difficulty in adjusting his language.
Kate refers to this difficulty early in the play:

> the doctor says we must remember how strange
> everything here must be to him after so long. And
> on top of that Swahili has been his language for
> twenty-five years; so it's not that his mind is con-
> fused — it's just that he has difficulty finding the Eng-
> lish words for what he wants to say. (11)

Given Friel's interest in language as the creator of realities
and illusions, the language difficulty is not, despite what Kate
says, "on top of" the other difficulties, but is the cause of
them. Chris, however, can only conclude that the failure to

adapt to English-language perceptions is evidence of confusion: "Sometimes he doesn't know the difference between
us. I've heard him calling you Rose and he keeps calling me
some strange name . . ." (12). Jack further compounds the
picture by being unable to recall the layout of the house
(17), and by referring to Rose's pet rooster as "a strange
white bird" (39), despite the fact that there are roosters in
Uganda. Almost immediately he refers to the beginning of
the Ryangan ritual to appease the gods, in which a young
rooster is sacrificed. One would expect him, under normal
circumstances, to retain the concept, or the Swahili word.
Obviously, what is happening to Jack is more fundamental
than a shift between words; it is a shift between worlds. Jack
is experiencing, in embryo, the transition that becomes the
main theme in *Molly Sweeney*: the virtual impossibility of
transference between one set of perceptions and another.
From this point of view, the idea that Jack has "gone native"
(39), with the pejorative associations that implies, is no
longer an adequate explanation. He has exchanged the world
view created by one language for that of another without
realising it, and, not knowing what has happened, he is unable to find his way back. Fintan O'Toole invokes Berkeley
again in relation to *Dancing at Lughnasa*:

> The play often seems to operate on Berkeley's *Esse
> est percepi* principle: to be is to be perceived. The
> young Michael exists because he is perceived by the
> others, and in a daring extension of the theme, the
> perceived Michael himself becomes the eye which
> perceives Chris and Gerry from behind the bushes
> and gives their loves existence. (O'Toole, 1993: 213)

As we have seen in relation to *Molly Sweeney* and *Faith
Healer*, the idea of perception as a creative force goes further than this. Kate's version of Ballybeg is the nearest we
can get to a basic position. She embodies the inward-looking

Ireland of the 1930s and 1940s: detached, Catholic, morally superior in attitude, clinging to respectability, attached to an idealised past, repressing or denying those aspects of life which do not fit their model. This situation had already appeared in *Aristocrats*, where the morally and socially isolated O'Donnells lived "overlooking the village of Ballybeg" (*Aristocrats*: 9). The Mundys likewise live "two miles outside the village of Ballybeg" (*Dancing at Lughnasa*, before p. 1), implying a separation between them and their immediate world. Kate is the one who voices the fear that their world is coming to an end:

> You try to keep the home together. You perform
> your duties as best you can — because you believe
> in responsibilities and obligations and good order.
> And then suddenly, suddenly you realize that hair
> cracks are appearing everywhere; that control is
> slipping away; that the whole thing is so fragile it
> can't be held together much longer. It's all about to
> collapse, Maggie. (35)

For Kate, the partial remedy is to be found, as is her perception of reality, in a form of words. Jack's alternative perception is reduced to his "own distinctive spiritual search" (60).

Swahili is not the only discourse attempting to colonise Ballybeg in 1936. Marconi is capable of emitting Irish discourse, like the "Mason's Apron", but more frequently its discourse is alien. When Gerry Evans arrives for the first time, the radio plays "Dancing in the Dark", a suitable metaphor for what Chris and Gerry are doing. She is unaware of his family in Wales, he is unaware of what to do with his life, and is looking for a romantic cause. On his second visit, the music is Cole Porter's "Anything Goes", this time with lyrics. Again, as an emblem of the changes being forced on the community, Marconi is either prophesying or commenting ironically.

Even the Irish dance music can be read as an atavistic intrusion into the discourse of Catholic respectability. The reaction of the sisters to the music is not at all what one would expect. Claudia Harris has noted that in the original production, the traditional group was required to add a heavy bodhrán beat to the tune, thus emphasising the connection to Jack's primitive rhythm on the kite-sticks later in the play (1997: 72, n. 1). This music, as has been well-documented, represents the extrusion of underlying paganism into the lives of the sisters. Behind the façade of genteel respectability is the Festival of Lugh, held with bonfires and purification rites in the back hills, a dance and a music older than Christianity. It is represented as dark, threatening, and primitive. It has injured people, the Sweeney boy in particular, but to what extent and in what way is unclear.

The opening of the knitting factory is frequently interpreted as the intrusion of the industrial revolution on rural Ireland, and so it is. It is also a different discourse, an urban discourse in which soulless repetition and unit-production takes the place of husbandry. It intrudes in a very destructive way, as it is the reason for Agnes and Rose leaving Ballybeg, again for the anonymity of the urban landscape.

Tensions also exist between the discourses of the present and the past. Michael, as narrator, evokes, in his opening speech, a golden past, but this is undercut quickly by the anxieties in the situation. Rose is being pursued by Danny Bradley, a man with a wife and children, who is trying, we may assume, to take advantage of her simplicity; Chris's child is fatherless; Kate is about to lose her job, as are Agnes and Rose. Maggie's most exciting days are behind her, in her memories of dancehalls and the boys of her youth. Jack is under a cloud, as the discourse of the Catholic church will not be contradicted by one of its priests. Friel evokes this tension very well; the tableaux at the beginning and end of the play give a nostalgic unreality to even the most unpleasant revelations. In a way, the separation of Michael from the action of the play places him in the role of chronicler, or even researcher into his own past. This role allies him with other chroniclers and scholars in Friel's work, such as Sir in *Living Quarters*, Tom Hoffnung in *Aristocrats*, Lombard in *Making History*, or David Knight in *Give Me Your Answer, Do!* One aspect that all of these have in common is that their research, or investigations, or comments are, in the final analysis, inadequate. Michael's ruminations are clouded by nostalgia, and, although he is aware of the details of the plot, he is also aware that his strongest memory of that time owes nothing to fact: "In that memory atmosphere is more real than incident and everything is simultaneously actual and illusory" (71). Friel is at the same time evoking marvellously a sense of a Golden Age, a sensuous Keatsian autumn, and questioning its existence. The ambiguity at the heart of Michael's reminiscences is what gives the play its bittersweet flavour; we are able to savour the memories for themselves, and for the rich quality of the crafted language, while recognising that their truth is, to say the least, questionable.

Seen from another perspective, all the discourses we have examined are forceful masculine penetrations into an almost exclusively female world, resulting in the disintegration of what appeared to be a unified system. The idea of rape is useful in a number of ways, as it allows us to generate a feminist interpretation of the play, and at the same time to focus on the position of unmarried women in the first third of the century in Ireland. The external discourses are almost entirely masculine. The radio is given a male *persona*, and its music penetrates not only the household, but the garden, and the memories Michael holds from childhood. Jack is a male, nominally celibate, but we may infer from the "revelations" in the text that he was not so (60). Gerry Evans disrupts the household, and has fathered a child on Chris. Danny Bradley may have had sexual intercourse with

Rose, which, given her mental disability, would be technically rape. The setting up of the knitting factory establishes a male hegemony over a traditionally female activity. Given that Friel interrogates the idea of the female body as a contested site in *Molly Sweeney*, this is a reasonable reading of the play.

The Irish Constitution was in the process of being drafted in the summer of 1936. Article 41.2.1 was particularly concerned with women: "In particular, the State recognises that by her life within the home, woman gives to the State a support without which the common good cannot be achieved." Article 41.2.2 continues: "The State shall, therefore, endeavour to ensure that mothers shall not be obliged by economic necessity to engage in labour to the neglect of their duties in the home" (*Dréacht Bunreacht*: 88). The word "mothers" is a less emphatic translation of the Irish "máithreachaibh cloinne", mothers of a family. The Constitution, then, in both articles, considers women only when they are married and looking after a home, and in particular when they have produced offspring. The irony was, according to Lee, that: "social values prevented a higher proportion of women from becoming mothers than in any other European country" (Lee: 1989: 207). Nonetheless, the position of the unmarried mature woman was a social embarrassment. A house full of them would have been even more so. The prevailing emotion directed towards them, in normal circumstances, would have been a slightly condescending pity. Kate obviously feels this in her dealings with the inhabitants of Ballybeg village, and it informs her decision to forbid attendance at the harvest dance: "Do you want the whole countryside to be laughing at us? — women of our years — mature women, *dancing*?" (13). The lack of men that they all experience is a socially conditioned response; even Rose teases Kate over her attraction to Austin Morgan, while she herself feels the necessity to visit the back hills with Danny Bradley. Chris's man is absent, leaving her "sobbing and la-

menting" (35). Maggie subsumes her sexuality into a passion
for "Wonderful Wild Woodbine[s]" (23) and slushy romantic songs, and Agnes into protection for Rose. All of these
strategies are bound to fail, and, indeed, do, in the face of
both social convention and social change.

Performances is a play which could only have been written by one who had spent a lifetime in the theatre. It compares with Beethoven's *Late Quartets*, in which the four in-
struments were induced to play music that is deceptively
simple, yet deeply complex in its interactions. It bears comparison with the late Yeats returning to the ballad form to
find in its seemingly simple rhymes and rhythmic structures a
power and control achieved after a lifelong apprenticeship.
Likewise, Leoš Janáček himself, after a lifetime of writing op-
eras, composed the *Intimate Letters* quartet in the year of his
death, and it is this period in the composer's life which provides the historical context for Friel's *Performances*. Friel has
created in *Performances* a rich and elusive play about the nature of language and of artistic creation and the function of
both in creating the image of the artist.

In this short play, Friel has carried his fascination with
musical structure further than in any other work. It is a play
which is impossible to stage without the services of a string
quartet whose members can also make some attempt at acting. Janáček's *Second String Quartet* is wound around the play
and inseparable from it. Without the music, the play, given
its topic, makes little sense. Without the words, the quartet
still stands as a discrete object. One must assume therefore
that Friel has chosen to structure his play so that it is almost
entirely dependent on the music. Yet Friel has not made
himself a librettist or a lyricist. The play has its own life, but
it is a symbiotic, indeed almost parasitic life. Given that one
of the main themes of the play is the instability of words at
the boundaries of language, this is a very adroit artistic and
theatrical conceit. The characters speak of music, they speak

about the creation of music and the process by which this is accomplished, but at the end of the play it is the music that takes over, speaking, as it were, directly, rather than mediated through words.

Performances takes Friel's obsession with communication out of a specifically Irish framework, and situates it outside a social and political context. The play is set somewhere beyond the grave. It is, in fact, vintage Friel — neither in this world nor in the next, but in some rationally impossible but theatrically viable space in which the dead and the living, and those of uncertain status, can commune with each other and with the audience. The experiment is destined to fail, and Friel knows this, indeed, it is part of the meaning of the play that there can be no text without context, and that the relationship between them is more a constant negotiation than a verifiable *status quo*. The plot is simply an interview between the now long-dead composer Leoš Janáček and an enthusiastic doctoral candidate named Anezka Ungrova. While they speak, a string quartet rehearses and later plays Janáček's *Second String Quartet* called, by him, *Intimate Letters*.

The intimate letters of the piece's title are a series of over 700 pieces of correspondence between Janáček and a much younger married woman, Kamila Stösslová. He met her in 1917 in Luhačovice, a spa town where he stayed for a period after his divorce. She was the wife of an antique dealer from Písek, and half his age. Most of the letters which remain are from Janáček to her. In these letters, it becomes clear that Janáček considered her the muse of his later work. That he was in love with her there is no doubt; that the love was never consummated appears to be equally certain. What information remains about Kamila herself indicates that she was a simple woman, who warmly enjoyed Janáček's attentions, but who would have been incapable of understanding his music, or her status as the muse of a famous artist. Friel exploits this dichotomy too, between the actual person and her elevation as Muse.

Despite the fact that we are told in the notes that "it becomes apparent very early that Janáček is long dead" (*Performances*, 2003: 11) the setting appears to be a real place — Janáček's work-room in Brno, Moravia. The musicians and Anezka appear to be very much alive, and have no difficulty accepting a figure who is dead and very much aware of it, but who also inhabits a space in which he can eat, converse, and play music. The conceit is useful in that it gives Janáček what living beings cannot achieve — a perspective on the whole of his own life. The musicians, we are told, are "fully at ease in this house" (13), a symbol for the co-existence of composer and musician. Anezka, on the other hand, is an outsider, as are all academics in Friel.

The play begins and ends with musical performances. As the play opens, Janáček is playing the piano, and challenges Anezka by playing several pieces in rapid succession (14). Friel has constructed his character in such a way as to give himself the ability to move from topic to topic without providing connective material: "He [Janáček] speaks rapidly, his mind leaping impatiently and with seeming illogic from one idea to the next" (13). This allows Friel both the freedom to explore his twin themes of art and artists and of the limits of the spoken language, and the dramatic shorthand to accomplish it with a minimum of fuss.

The theme of artistry and artistic creation provides the dynamic for such plot as there is. Anezka, the academic, is exploring the last year of Janáček's life, using the texts of his letters to Stösslová. Despite being established as one who knows a great deal about Janáček and his music, she succumbs to the temptation to read the author into his work. When he reveals the extent of his exploitation of the relationship between himself and Stösslová, Anezka is shocked, and leaves. The play ends with the third and fourth movements of the quartet played on stage.

Quite early in the play, Anezka is seen attempting to force a context, the letters, upon a text, the quartet. Ruth, the first violinist, warms up by playing the first nine bars of the first movement:

Ruth	(*Sings*) Ta-ra-ra-ra — Ta-ra-ra-ra. "I'm my own man", that's what it says to me.
Anezka	(*Reads from the green folder*) "I've just completed the opening movement and it is all about our first fateful encounter and how you instantly enslaved me —" Mr Janáček's letter to Kamila, February 1, 1928.
Ruth	(*Indifferently*) Bang goes my little theory then, doesn't it?

The stage directions are noteworthy. Ruth *sings*, and speaks only of what the music says to her. Anezka *reads*, and attempts to formulate an unchanging theory behind the music. Ruth then abandons her own idea *indifferently*. The suggestion is that what music *says*, when translated into words, can never be of any real consequence. An explanation of how the music came about is not an interpretation of the music. Anezka's excerpt is the beginning of a trope in which she attempts to pin down the Quartet using what Janáček calls "these ridiculous quotations" (20). Ruth, possibly irritated by Anezka, plays a section of the Third Movement. Anezka produces a quote from the letters to explain it, but fails to see the irony in what she reads: "'A slave, yes, but such a happy, divinely happy slave. But there are no words to talk of a meeting like that. So I talk about it in the andante'" (20). Where words fail, music takes over. Friel has approached this topic repeatedly, most notably in *Dancing at Lughnasa* and *Wonderful Tennessee*. In *Performances* the music gestures, in the absence of words, towards a world of true emotion and absolute clarity of expression, which can only be reported on by "people who huckster in words" (31). Throughout the play, Janáček denies the quotations from the letters, ridicules them, and accuses Anezka of making them up. He reminds her severely that his "first language" was music (31).

It is interesting to speculate to what extent Friel had his tongue in his cheek when he wrote this play. While he has produced a meditation on the artistic process unparalleled since *Faith Healer*, it is still possible to read it as an elaborate theatrical joke. He has written a play in words about the inadequacies of words, to be commented on in more inadequate words while, through the fabric of the verbiage, the music drips and leaks, becoming at the end a torrent of pure emotion which silences the stage. The irony is further compounded by the subject-matter of the words: the connection between an author and his life.

Anezka is convinced that the facts of Janáček's relationship, as evinced in his letters to her, are responsible for the creative burst at the end of his life which produced the *Intimate Letters* quartet. She sees them as love-letters, and is convinced that Janáček's passion for Kamila Stösslová fired his creativity. As a critical position, mining the artist's life for information about the works has never gone entirely out of fashion, although it was intensely opposed by Eliot and the modernist movement. Although Stösslová was undoubtedly Janáček's inspiration, the play insists on the fact that it is the remembered and reconstructed Kamila, rather than the factual woman who becomes the muse. Anezka acknowledges this as she reads from one of the few extant letters from Kamila to Janáček: "maybe she's suggesting . . . that perhaps you're not in love with her but with an imagined Kamila, an image of her you've fashioned yourself" (33). Janáček takes the process one step further. In the throes of the creative

process, he claims to have transferred his aspirations on to
Kamila, deliberately manipulating both her and his feelings,
so that she became, for him, the music made flesh: "so that
in his head she was transformed into something immeasura-
bly greater — of infinitely more importance — than the
quite modest young woman she was . . ." (35). Janáček slides
into the third person when describing how he had "invented" Kamila as an expression of the best of himself. This
is a version of events which Anezka finds unpalatable, again
missing the irony that it is she herself who has created this
version of Janáček from the letters, a version which may
have little connection with the real individual.

Friel has given comparatively few interviews, and those
he has given have been seized upon by critics, including myself, and used to formulate theories of "Frielian" composition. When Anezka produces her critical apparatus, it is
dismissed, denied and rubbished by the subject of the criticism. What currency are we left with, then, to approach the
elusive Brian Friel? The short answer is, of course, none.
The relationship between author and critic, always treated
with some suspicion in Friel, is as much at the mercy of the
text/context negotiation as any other form of discourse. It is
the victim of the deficiency of words and, ultimately, futile in
any absolute sense. Anezka's untimely exit towards the end
of the play is pointed: she does not hear the music to its
conclusion; she leaves her green folder behind. She cannot
reconcile her version of Janáček with the version produced
by the figure before her. I say produced, because Janáček's
performance as himself is also a version, negotiated between
the long-dead composer and his life. It is, furthermore, re-
negotiated by both Friel as playwright and an actor interpreting the role. While insisting her reading of his letters is
more "true", Anezka does elicit an admission from Janáček
that "both readings can coexist . . . in a kind of equilibrium",

but he still insists that everything, meaning the facts of his life, is subservient to the work.

The epiphany of the play has a strong Chekhovian influence: it is neither earth-shattering nor life-changing, but sufficiently unsettling to alter the relationship between the characters. Anezka cannot bear to be near the new version of Janáček, but will write him: "a very punctilious thank-you letter" (38). It is a small irony in the play that she herself cannot escape words. Her effect on Janáček's household is neatly summed up by the exchange as she leaves:

Judith	Nice lady.
Miriam	Lovely lady.
John (*To Miriam*)	What about another vodka?
Ruth	Come on, you can chat later. Work work — work!
Judith	Play — play — play!

She is politely dismissed, leaving hardly a ripple on the work, and play, of the household. Janáček glances at the abandoned folder, then leans back and listens to his music.

As with the competing interpretations of the opening of the quartet, Friel has given no insight into a privileged reading of Janáček's life. Whether he is a man spurred on by love or an egomaniac who used those around him for artistic ends will not be revealed. Instead, it is one more layer of uncertainty, one more situation in which words prove inadequate, and which makes *Performances* an elusive minor masterpiece.

Faith Healer and *Molly Sweeney* are primarily about perceptions of reality, a fact emphasised by their relatively simple dramatic structure. *Dancing at Lughnasa* is, structurally and thematically, far more complex and rich than either of the other plays. It would be easy to allow its setting and narrative to obscure the fact that memory is a perception. *Per-*

formances, while problematising the function of verbal language, prioritises the reality of artistic creation, and is dismissive of the memories of a life already lived. Stories that are told in *Faith Healer* and *Molly Sweeney* are enacted in *Dancing at Lughnasa*, and the very enactment gives weight to what is still a version of reality told by one of the participants, years later. What we see on the stage is not merely what happened, but a version of it.

Chapter Five

The Schizophrenic Community

If you think you understand the situation, then you haven't been properly briefed. (*Comment on Northern Ireland attributed to a British Civil Servant*)

The Mundy Scheme, written in 1969, was an early attempt to write a satire on the state of Ireland. Dantanus describes the mood of the play as "an expression of bitter disappointment released through cynical satire" (1985: 142). It is this cynicism which deprives the play of its artistic edge, and led to Friel's description of it as "bad just because it wasn't half good enough" (Boland, 1973: 114). The plot concerns an attempt by the government to stimulate the economy by converting Connaught into a cemetery, with a view to attracting American clients. According to Patrick Burke: "Ryan [the Taoiseach] is a fifty-year-old bachelor whose love-hate relationship with his mother reflects his sexual immaturity. . . . Friel skilfully implies . . . the deleterious consequences of public policy being informed by emotionally arrested men . . ." (Burke, 1999: 44). Significantly in this sell-off of the national resources, the Taoiseach is an ex-auctioneer. Critics in Dublin and New York savaged the play.

The idea for *The Mundy Scheme* was not a bad one, but rather too thin to spread over a full-length play. It grew out of Friel's disappointment with the way in which the state had developed, and the way in which cultural values were eroded by what Friel had called "Madison Avenue-ish" ethics. His next attempt at writing a political play, *The Freedom of the City*, was more successful artistically, but attracted a great deal of criticism, both for the play and the author, because of its subject matter: the Bloody Sunday shootings.

In the late 1960s and early 1970s, the Civil Rights movement in Northern Ireland had developed in an attempt to wrest from the authorities the same rights for Catholics in Northern Ireland as were enjoyed by the majority of Protestants. By 1972, such marches had become commonplace, almost always attracting the violent attention of loyalist protesters or the RUC (Royal Ulster Constabulary). On Sunday, 30 January of that year, an illegal anti-internment march was organised in Derry. A section of the crowd confronted the British Army at a barricade, and a riot developed. Soldiers of the First Parachute Regiment opened fire from a derelict building (CAIN: 1968). By the time the shooting ended, 13 civilians had been killed by army fire. The soldiers claimed that they had been fired on first, but no proof of this could be produced.

The tribunal set up by the British Government to investigate the incident reported in April. Lord Widgery, the Lord Chief Justice, caused fury among the people of Derry by concluding, among other things, that there was "no reason to suppose that the soldiers would have opened fire if they had not been fired upon first" (CAIN: Widgery). This is still a matter of dispute, almost 30 years later.

Friel himself had actually taken part in the march, but claims that the play was not a direct response to Bloody Sunday, and that he had been working on the play that became *The Freedom of the City* for ten months before the events of 30 January. It was to be called "John Butt's Bothy", was set in the eighteenth century, and concerned evictions

(Boland, 1973: 114). The play that emerged was quite different, and may have been a reaction, not just to Bloody Sunday itself, but to the Widgery Tribunal, which many claim was merely an institutional cover-up on the part of the British Establishment. One incidental feature of the play that links it clearly with Bloody Sunday is the image in the opening scene. Skinner, Lily, and Michael are lying across the front of the stage: "*a priest enters right, crouching like the photographer and holding a white handkerchief above his head*" (*Plays I*: 107). To anyone who has seen film footage of the events, the crouching priest with the handkerchief is iconic; Fr Eamonn Daly led a small group through the shooting in just such a position, and this is one of the images that received world-wide attention at the time.

One of the most prominent features of *The Freedom of the City* is its use of staging techniques. Lighting changes, sound effects, voiceovers, flexible stage spaces and contrapuntal scenes, and allowing characters to exceed their characterisations have all appeared in Friel's work before and after this play, but never to the same, almost frenzied, extent. The scenes switch quickly between the Guildhall interior and the tribunal high overhead, and are punctuated by the comments of a sociologist, a forensics expert, a pathologist, a television reporter, the press, and the shifting positions of the balladeer and the priest. The perspective that results makes one think that one is a witness to the truth of the situation happening inside the Mayor's parlour, a truth to which the other commentators in the play have no access. This is theatrically flamboyant, but politically dangerous. It places blame for the killings unambiguously with the authorities, in particular with the soldiers.

One of the points made by Friel was that the play was a study of poverty (Boland, 1973: 114). If one can separate the politics from the dialogue, this is largely true. Much of the conversation in the parlour is about the way in which the

characters live. As is usual with Friel's characters, the types
are recognisable. Lily comes from a long line of female survi-
vors, from O'Casey's Juno to Keane's Moll. She is garrulous,
has too many children, and a layabout husband who pretends to be chronically ill. She has the breezy, whimsical attitude to life that many of O'Casey's characters have, even if
their end is to be, in the dramatic sense, tragic. The impression she creates initially is one of comic dimwittedness. Her
life and opinions appear to have been pieced together un-
critically from scraps of half-knowledge and urban folklore.
In one of her first conversations, her train of thought proves
particularly difficult to derail:

Lily	Did you get a thump of a baton, young fella?
Skinner	Gas.
Lily	Maybe he got a rubber bullet in the stomach.
Skinner	Only gas.
Lily	He might be bleeding internal.
Skinner	Gas! Are you deaf? (*Plays 1*: 113)

She then proceeds to tell a story about a wound on a police
officer's head which bled profusely but apparently caused no
harm. She also subscribes to the beliefs, among others, that
CS gas can cure stuttering, that all orphans are musical, and
that bodies do not age in outer space.

Much is made of her family situation. She has 11 children
and a husband she calls "the Chairman", a forceful piece of
irony, as not only are they diametrically opposed to the lifestyle of the company board, but her husband spends most of
his day in a chair by the fire, a situation that cannot fail to
remind an audience of Juno and Captain Boyle. She has encouraged a culture of dependency around her. She tells of
the day her husband and herself went on a day-trip to Bun-
doran with her Downs-syndrome child. The rest of the fam-

ily sat at the table at teatime and waited for her to return, rather than fend for themselves (139). It appears as if her own activity, her job as a cleaner and her ministrations to her family, have encouraged inactivity in others. She even extends this to Skinner, with an offer to feed him if he turned up on her doorstep.

We have considered the similarity between Lily and Juno. Christopher Murray, in a comparison of the play with the work of O'Casey, does not take these similarities into account; indeed, he is more interested in enumerating the differences between the two playwrights. He states that a comparative approach might "beg the question of Friel's originality as an artist" (1999a: 16). I cannot agree. The fact that Friel takes a situation, or a recognisable character, and uses them in a different way, or for a different end, is the very definition of his originality as an artist. Were he to pro-duce something entirely different and entirely unrelated to anything that had gone before, it would leave the audience without a reference point, and resemble the deliberately disorienting plays of Beckett. Murray does concede, how-ever, that Lily is "a Juno figure" (18). The fact that the play is not set in Lily's tenement is important, but it does not ne-gate the similarities that exist. Skinner has some of the nervous energy and edginess of the Covey in *The Plough and the Stars*, and Michael's aspirations to better himself are analogous to Jack Clitheroe's ambitions in the Citizen Army.

The use of comedy is another important comparison. O'Casey described most of his Dublin plays as tragedies, and *The Silver Tassie* as a tragicomedy. Humour, however, is in-terwoven throughout the plays as an indication of the resil-ience of the spirit of the tenement dwellers despite the world outside. The humour in *The Freedom of the City* is simi-lar to O'Casey, but also similar to that provided by O'Donnell in *Making History*. It is the juxtaposition of the individual with the progress of history. This is the most important similarity, and one not mentioned by Murray. The three characters are caught up in an action which is much bigger than they are, and about which they have only partial or flawed understanding. Each is doing what they must to survive: Lily has developed a bovine forbearance and a cheerful exterior; Skinner lives off the system while railing against it; while Michael longs to be assimilated by the bourgeoisie and studies to be acceptable. Were it not for the fact that the audience is already aware of the end of the play, and that Lily will be killed horribly, she would be simply a buffoon, the stock comic charlady. It is this one poignant fact that alters the perspective, not just on Lily, but on all three.

Skinner represents another type of poverty, quite distinct from Lily's clinging to destitute respectability. He sees himself as outside the system, and this justifies his attempts to take advantage of it whenever possible. He lives, and dies, as he says "in defensive flippancy" (150). He misuses the parlour, deliberately stubbing out a cigar on the leather desk-top, and defaces the portrait of Sir Joshua. Michael thinks that Skinner might be "a revolutionary" (132), a quaintly ironic name from one who, by his own account, was on every civil rights march since 1968. Like Michael, he is unemployed, but unlike Michael, he has no particular desire to work.

Skinner's nickname may shed some light on the status of the play as a study in poverty. I emphasise that what follows is pure conjecture, but, I hope, no less interesting for that. Adrian Casimir Fitzgerald (Skinner) may have acquired his nickname by being thin (skin and bone), or Friel may have had in mind the behavioural experiments of the American psychologist B.F. Skinner. Skinner developed the theory of Operant Behaviour, where an organism, in the process of interacting with its environment, encounters positively or negatively reinforcing stimuli. In other words, the behaviour is followed by a consequence, and the nature of the consequence changes the organism's propensity towards repeating or avoiding the behaviour in the future. As part of his research, Skinner constructed a maze (known as a Skinner-box), into which he placed laboratory rats. He then observed the lengths of time it took for the rats to learn simple tasks, dependent on positive and negative stimuli. Skinner, in *The Freedom of the City*, is a perfect example of one who has been negatively conditioned by his environment, a detail that is commented on in general terms by Dodds. In fact, when one takes into account the number of theories that are applied to the three in the mayoral parlour, the play as a whole begins to take on the shape of a luxurious, imperial rat-maze, studied at second hand from a wide variety of perspectives. Of course, this is only a partial reading of the play, and takes no cognisance of the characters themselves. As a means of exploring the play's commentary on modern Ireland, however, it is a useful exercise. The interior world of the play becomes then a baseline story, onto which the ideologies of the exterior world are superimposed.

The first of these is the voice of the tribunal. A quite different model of reality is constructed by the judge, whose voice resounds throughout the play, having no less than eight scenes, four of which are soliloquies. He speaks first and last, so one is left with an impression of an enveloping authority, one which is interested in maintaining a particular order. His questioning of the policeman in the opening scene illustrates the way in which his mind works. Certain questions are to be asked in order to produce particular answers. Other questions are deemed irrelevant, and are not allowed to be asked. His lack of interest in social motivation is important, if, as Friel claims, the play is about poverty. With this in mind, it is possible to read the opening scene as one in which the judge's antipathy is towards the poor rather than towards the nationalist community. His ignorance of the phrase "[n]o fixed address" (109) is evidence of his detachment from the actuality of life on the streets.

This voice of the judge is unrepentantly imperial, military, and hermetic, beginning with the assumption of its own correctness. In this respect, it parallels the Widgery Tribunal, in which, as McGrath points out, the judge accepted the evidence of the soldiers whenever there was a conflict (1999: 106). The judge in the play states his terms of reference as: "to form an objective view of the events which occurred . . ." (*Plays 1*: 109). Given the status of ambiguity and the impossibility of fathoming human action in Friel's plays, we can safely read these lines ironically. This ironic search for disinterest, in a site where it cannot exist, becomes one of the main themes of the play. The irony is compounded by the reference to "Londonderry", a name used by loyalists and the British establishment. To the nationalists, the city is simply "Derry". The judge unconsciously declares his partiality. The alternatives he considers likely for the actions of the three main characters likewise betray an ideological refraction. The tribunal is to decide whether the three were "callous terrorists", or whether the scheme had only occurred to them on the day. Other alternatives do not present themselves; whichever is chosen, the invaders of the Guildhall are maliciously culpable.

The scene with Brigadier Johnson-Hansbury portrays the judge in no better light. He presents to the Brigadier the contention of the defence lawyers, that the soldiers were operating a *de facto* shoot-to-kill policy, but accepts without equivocation the Brigadier's explanation. Significantly, he uses the phrase "to teach the ghettos a lesson" (134), as distinct from teaching a lesson to the Paddies, or Tagues, or any other of the pejorative terms for Catholic that have developed in the North. On his third appearance, the judge sums up his assessment of civilian versus military evidence. His "On the other hand . . ." (142) before introducing the military evidence is very telling. The evidence produced by Dr Winbourne is sufficiently ambiguous to allow for interpretation. Of course, as Winbourne is attached to the Army Forensic Department, one might look at his interpretation of the evidence with some scepticism.

The first soliloquy in Act 2 presents an interpretation of the evidence, and one which is, at face value, reasonable. The judge is considering the defence's claim that the choice of the Guildhall as a place of refuge was accidental: "And if the choice was fortuitous, why was the building defaced . . . Would they have defaced a private house in the same way?" (149). It is a practical question. The audience has seen precisely how this has come about, but that information is not available to the judge. By interpreting the facts in a narrow manner, and by ignoring the socio-economic factors that contributed to Skinner's minor vandalism, the judge can come to no other conclusion. He is undoubtedly prejudiced and ideologically biased, but it is uncertain whether this bias and prejudice have come about for class reasons, or for reasons of race, religion, and empire.

The judge's penultimate scene is the one in which he interviews Professor Cuppley, who carried out the post-mortem examination on the bodies. The horror of the scene lies in the blunt manner in which the facts are presented. It completes a picture of how the judge has interpreted his brief: "essentially a fact-finding exercise" (109). Nowhere in the recitation of the gruesome wounds inflicted on the victims does either man question the appropriateness of the response. Facts, as interpreted by the tribunal of inquiry, speak for themselves once they are established.

The final speech of the play is taken almost *verbatim* from the report of the Widgery Tribunal into Bloody Sunday. It was this report and its obvious bias which inflamed the feelings of the already furious nationalists of Derry. Both this tribunal and Widgery made the grossly insensitive point that if the ban on the march had been respected, then the shootings would not have taken place. Both took the word of the soldiers over the other witnesses; both failed to find any evidence that the soldiers had opened fire first. True to his implicit bias at the beginning of the play, the judge is not conducting a social survey. That is left to Dodds, the sociologist.

No other character in the play has exercised as much critical space as Dodds. William Jent has produced a useful overview of the range of critical commentary on Dodds (1994: 572–5), but here is a brief summary: Pine emphasises Dodds's role as the universal voice of the particular crisis represented on stage, but, according to Jent, trivialises his (Dodds's) role by referring to him as "the sociologist-ex-machina". Winkler notes the ambiguity of his role, as the intellectual voice of poverty studies, filling out the play's range of appeal, and thinks his analysis is "chillingly accurate"; Deane includes him in his list of the play's "displaced voices". Grene dismisses Dodds, contrasting the academic theory with the reality of the situation; Schneider claims that Dodds "explains everything and understands nothing"; while McGrath sees him as evidence of Friel's entry into postmodern, and, we presume, decentring discourse.

Jent himself proposes that Dodds "enacts . . . the cultural program of which the play is itself an expression" (575). Jent notes his detachment from the play, and the fact that he addresses the audience, the only character in the play to do so, but his claim that Dodds "delivers his lecture on the dynamics of poverty and oppression in the real world outside the theater" cannot be considered. Dodds certainly addresses *an* audience, for which the actual audience in the theatre serves as surrogate, but he is, as much as any other character, a part of the play; he is in the script. He does not participate in the main action, nor is he a part of the frame of officialdom encompassing that action, but he is nonetheless one of the many voices with hypotheses that pertain to the main action.

The opinions expressed by Dodds are taken with few changes from a work by the American anthropologist Oscar

Lewis, *La Vida: a Puerto Rican Family in the Culture of Poverty*. Jent points out, quite correctly, that this gives the social issues in the play an international perspective. The fact that he talks directly to the audience is significant only in the fact that it is one more theatrical technique employed by Friel, that of the public lecture. It seeks to give a theoretical framework and a connection with a world beyond Ulster.

Critical discussion has also taken place on the status of Dodds' information. Since it is taken from a scholarly work on anthropology, one assumes that it meets the criteria for such work; it is certainly intellectually coherent. So is Dodds "serious or satirical" (Jent, 1994: 576)? Does Dodds subvert Lewis, or is he, as Jent maintains, Friel's proxy on the stage? All of these positions assume that there is an authoritative centre to the play, a normative perspective from which all others can be judged. Given that Friel is, in other works, careful to present us with people who deceive themselves and others, this assumption is a precarious one. Friel has a tendency to decentre authority, and to allow a myriad of conflicting opinions to speak for themselves. Granted, the play is too close to its subject, and the anger that produced it is still palpable, but even within that anger, Friel's artistic preoccupations can be discerned.

A case can be made even for the discourse of the tribunal. Deane describes the soldiers' discourse as "bogus" (Deane, 1984: 18), and, indeed, compared with the events inside the Guildhall, their account is in error. The three did not emerge firing, indeed could not have, as they had no weapons. However, at no time are we told that the soldiers are lying, or that the tribunal is corrupt. It is one obvious interpretation, given a knowledge of the Widgery Tribunal, and one which is difficult to dislodge. It is at least possible that the official discourse of the tribunal in the play is one which is believed by the soldiers and by the judge, in the same way in which, for example, Trilbe Costello and Mr In-

gram construct alternative versions of their own past in *Cass
McGuire*. As a play, *Cass McGuire* is concerned with shutting
out reality, or constructing alternative realities. On one
level, everybody is lying to everybody else. Even the title is,
to some extent, a lie, a fact on which Cass herself comments. Tellingly, at one point in the play, Trilbe claims: "We
know what is real, Catherine" (29). In a similar vein, the forensic pathologist, Dr Winbourne, makes the statement: "I
don't know what constitutes conclusive evidence" (*Plays 1*:
142). It is too easy to accuse Friel of partisanship in his
scenes at the tribunal. He may well have felt sympathy with
the nationalist plight, but themes of conflicting evidence
abound in his work. Friel's sympathy may be based on social
rather than political affiliations. Likewise, Dodds is constructing a model of reality, into which aspects of Lily, Michael, and Skinner fit, but which will never be a complete
enough or complex enough model to encompass the whole
reality.

The television reporter, Liam O'Kelly, is another differ-
entiated, commenting voice. His report is demonstrably mistaken. Of course, one might equally claim it to be bogus or
deliberately misrepresented, as the discourse of the soldiers
and the tribunal is claimed to be. The fact is that Friel does
not give his audience or reader any motivation for the
discourse of any of the commenting characters, and such
motivation as is ascribed to them comes from extrinsic
knowledge. O'Kelly's contribution to the discourse is to
produce a fictional set of circumstances, in which the Guildhall has fallen into the hands of terrorists, and to compare it
with the fall of the Bastille during the French Revolution.
Official, imperial voices are silent; his only source of information is "usually reliable spokesmen from the Bogside"
(118) (that is, from the Catholic/nationalist area of the city).
The reporter's discourse represents itself as incomplete and
one-sided, and yet suggests that its information is accurate.

The same kind of information is re-released a number of scenes later by the Army Press Officer, this time without an attribution of source: "At approximately 15.20 hours today a band of terrorists took possession of a portion of the Guildhall. . . . It is estimated that up to forty persons are involved" (126). Journalistic uncertainty is crystallising into official truth.

O'Kelly's second soliloquy is close to the end of the play, placed beside the official report of the tribunal with which the play concludes. His speech is crafted to resemble television reportage, but is sprinkled with ideological markers. The Mass is celebrated by "the four Northern bishops", meaning, of course, the bishops of the four northern *Catholic* dioceses (167), suggesting an event of such moment that it can only be marked by the presence of all the bishops. The omission of the word "Catholic" is itself an ideological bias, suggesting, as it does, that only Catholic bishops would be of significance to, or considered by, a Southern audience. Bach's *Prelude and Fugue* is not only "beautiful", but also "triumphant", and in that way, "appropriate". Friel can get away with some rather obvious use of pathetic fallacy by placing the words in the reporter's mouth: "an icy rain is spilling down on all those thousands of mourners" (167). The mourners who wait patiently and in silence along the "narrow ghetto streets" suggest a long-suffering and noble race enduring yet another atrocity. The city is referred to as: "this ancient, noble, suffering city of St Colmcille". The definition of the city by reference to the saint is historically important. We have already seen the different uses of "Derry" and "Londonderry" as semiotics of religious and political affiliation. The origin of "Derry" is the Irish "Doire", an oak forest. In Irish, the city is often referred to as "Doire Choilm Chille", the oak forest of Colmcille (or Columba), referring to the city's mythical foundation by the saint in the sixth century. In this way, the city is named for its origins, bypassing seven centuries of Norman and British rule and connecting it with its Catholic, monastic foundations. By inference, the suffering came later, after the city's association with the saint had ceased.

The list of dignitaries is almost absurd. The presence of the Cardinal Primate, as archbishop of Armagh, is possible, but the presence of the "spiritual leaders of every order and community in the country" is unlikely. Friel exaggerates the religious presence in order to mark the occasion as a public relations coup for the Catholic/Nationalist side of the divide. The attendance of the entire Dáil and Senate is equally unlikely. The idea of an entire government decamping to another state for a politically motivated funeral is untenable.

Friel's real motivation for the hyperbolic commentary comes late in the speech, as O'Kelly is describing the cortège: "And lastly the remains of Adrian Fitzmaurice — I beg your pardon — Adrian Fitzgerald . . ." (168). Amid the exaggerated splendour of the funeral, and the suggestion of political and religious martyrdom, O'Kelly can still get the name of the putative martyr wrong, the first step into anonymity.

The Balladeer also provides an interesting perspective on the Guildhall. His two ballads are placed strategically in the text. The first occurs after O'Kelly's initial report on the occupation of the Guildhall, and uses similar, if exaggerated, information. The second ballad opens Act 2, and plunges the audience again into the web of misinformation and bias surrounding the central story. The political ballad is the successor of the *aisling*, and the sentimental nationalist ballad is probably more popular now than when it first appeared. Although not all are contemporary with the events they portray, it would be difficult to persuade their audience that they represent anything but the truth of 1798, 1916, or even 1981. Of these, the most famous are "Who Fears to Speak of '98?", "The Boys of Wexford", and the messianic "Wolfe Tone will Come Again". Others such as "Father Murphy", "Henry Joy", and "The Rights of Man" are still accessible.

They connect the rebellion with the myth of the sleeping hero, or of Christ, and remind the listener of Ireland's catalogue of wrongs at the hands of the British. It matters little that few of them are authentic; they are enmeshed with events in the popular mind.

The first ballad used in *The Freedom of the City* is to the tune of "John Brown's Body", a triumphant march rhythm. Friel describes the Balladeer as *"aggressive-drunk"* (148):

> A hundred Irish heroes one February day
> Took over Derry's Guildhall, beside Old Derry's quay.
>   (118)

The ballad displays the usual disdain of the genre for factual accuracy, and embodies the need to rhyme and scan at all costs. Furthermore, it illustrates the next step in the process of mythologisation: "forty" has now become "a hundred". More sinister is the chorus of children:

> Three cheers and then three cheers again for Ireland
>   one and free,
> For civil rights and unity, Tone, Pearse and Connolly. (118)

The children sing of Tone, Pearse, and Connolly as if the three represented the same social and political aims. Tone's aim was a secular, integrated Ireland; Pearse's a Gaelic and Catholic one, Connolly's, a socialist state. The usurpation of all three by sentimental Republicanism is well represented in the chorus, and points to a fundamental division in Irish society.

The second ballad, to the tune of *Kevin Barry*, is slower, more a lament than a triumph. The original ballad is concerned with the torture and execution of an 18-year-old student during the War of Independence, the first IRA man to be executed in that war (Connolly, 1998: 39). One stanza of that ballad is particularly emotive, beginning: "Another

martyr for old Ireland, another murder for the crown . . .".
The discourse of Friel's analogous ballad is, unsurprisingly,
laden with republican propaganda.

The characterisation of the three as "volunteers" re-
quires explanation. The IRA routinely refers to its active
members as "volunteers"; hence the ironic title of Friel's
later play. The term, describing membership of an unofficial
military organisation, originates in the eighteenth century,
when the Volunteer force was exclusively Protestant, and
formed to defend Ireland from invasion during the American
Revolution (Johnston, 1980: 150–1). The United Irishmen,
before the 1798 rebellion, attempted to include Catholics in
the Volunteers, but were largely unsuccessful. These original
Volunteers were subsumed and superseded by more ex-
treme Protestant organisations. The Irish Volunteers were
founded in 1913, with the aim of arming themselves to pro-
tect Home Rule. There was considerable involvement by the
Irish Republican Brotherhood, forerunner of the IRA, in the
founding of the organisation. "Volunteer", then, has a long
and emotive history, and to refer to those killed as "volunteers" is making a specific political and paramilitary point.

As is typical of these ballads, none but the purest motives
are ascribed to those killed by the "Saxon bullet": "They
took a stand against oppression, they wanted Mother Ireland
Free . . ." (148). These sentiments are as patently untrue
from the perspective of the audience as are the claims of the
soldiers. In this respect, the Balladeer is analogous to
Lombard in *Making History*. Truth is not necessarily the only
criterion on which to base what is, essentially, political hagiography. From an intertextual point of view, Friel's opinion of
Mother Ireland is undercut by the subversion of the image in
The Enemy Within. Equally, the statement that the names of
the "bold three" will not be forgotten is subverted by the
fact that their names are not mentioned in the ballad, and the
fact that O'Kelly accidentally misnames Skinner.

The last two lines are of particular interest, as they both connect the ballad to the generic concerns of its analogues, and, I believe, destabilise the genre using irony:

> They join the lines of long-gone heroes, England's
> victims, one and all.
> We have their memory still to guide us; we have
> their courage to recall. (148)

Memory and recollection play an important part in the political, and, indeed, tribal composition of modern Ireland. The Provisional IRA claims its mandate from the rebels in 1916, who in turn claimed to be the successors of Wolfe Tone. It was Pearse himself who commented in one of his most famous speeches at the graveside of Jeremiah O'Donovan Rossa, who died in 1915: "the fools! the fools! the fools! they have left us our Fenian dead; and while Ireland holds these graves Ireland unfree shall never be at peace."

The first line of the ballad couplet undercuts the notion of memory and tradition by positing a long line of dead heroes, all of whom died at the hands of the British, like some kind of supernatural republican queue. This is typical of the emotional ballad genre, whose words are, on the surface, enticements to commit to a cause, but which will not stand critical scrutiny because of their careless structure, and the relentlessness of their scansion and rhymes.

The tradition is additionally undermined by the fact that both appearances of the Balladeer are characterised by drunkenness. At first he is "*[u]nsteady on his feet but his aggressive jubilance makes him articulate*" (118). For his second ballad: "*As before, he has a glass in his hand . . . this time he is maudlin-drunk*" (148). The juxtaposition of republican, anti-British, sentiment and alcohol is not uncommon in modern Ireland. In the second ballad vignette, the Balladeer is dressed as for a funeral, giving credence to the inference that the ballad is being sung at the post-funeral gathering.

The priest is another significant voice to weave itself into the complex web of ideologically motivated comment surrounding the events in the Guildhall. Friel treats him with the most open contempt of any of the voices. His two sermons, given the non-linear structure of the play, could be alternative versions of the same sermon, rather than two sermons representing a *volte-face* on the part of the church. They both begin in the same words: the priest announces the solemn requiem mass which is to be held in the church the following day. He notes his own action in administering last rites to the victims, and comes to the question: "Why did they die?" It is at this point that the two sermons diverge. In the first, the fusion of religion and nationalism is apparent. The priest's message is openly political:

> They died for their beliefs. . . . They sacrificed their lives so that you and I and thousands like us might be rid of that iniquitous yoke and might inherit a decent way of life. And if that is not heroic virtue, then the word sanctity has no meaning. (125)

Obsolete phrases such as "that iniquitous yoke" characterise a clumsy rhetoric that is ironically crowned by the *non sequitur* of the last sentence. The peroration continues with a litany of imaginations to be fired, sinews to be stiffened, and dreams to be dreamed in an accumulation of banal clichés. The exhortation at the end of the sermon is that the congregation might have the courage to continue the struggle that the victims represented.

In the second version, the "iniquitous yoke" has been transmuted into "certain imperfections in our society" (156). The implication is that the peaceful protest organised by decent citizens had been subverted by "evil elements". These the priest identifies with Communism. Instead of noble visionaries, the three are now victims of a communist conspiracy. The sermon ends, not with an exhortation to arise and follow, but with a quotation from the Sermon on the Mount: "Blessed are the meek for they shall possess the land" (156).

Friel has made it impossible to decide whether there are two sermons or one. It is unclear whether the priest has changed his mind, or been told to change his mind, whether the sermons exist as examples of clerical thinking at the beginning of the Northern Ireland troubles, or whether the speeches are an example of the ability of the Irish to hold two contradictory beliefs and believe both. Traditionally, the hierarchy in Ireland was on the side of the *status quo*. Individual priests or prelates may have spoken with a reforming voice, but, for the main part, the clergy, since the foundation of the state, have been conservative. Certainly, the sermons represent a vested interest in the Guildhall intruders, whether as exemplars to be followed or as warnings to be avoided.

One group of voices remains to be examined: the victims themselves. In a very theatrical manoeuvre at the beginning of Act 2, Friel allows each of the characters to transcend their role, and to speak about the moment of their deaths. Michael, who speaks first, is consistent in death as he was in life. He is sure that the soldiers will not shoot, he is sure that it is a mistake, as he appears to believe that the discrimination against Catholics is a mistake, one that could be rectified by persuasion or by example. His words: "I became very agitated, not because I was dying, but that this terrible mistake be recognized and acknowledged" (149).

Lily is the one who moves furthest outside the character that Friel has constructed for her. She speaks articulately and persuasively, using a vocabulary that was not hers in life: "The moment we stepped outside the front door I knew I was going to die, instinctively, the way an animal knows" (150). She is also the voice whose expression of regret is least authentic. Her regret is that never once in her life: "had an experience, an event, even a small unimportant happening been isolated, and assessed, and articulated" (150). This is consistent with the view advanced by Dodds that the poor live in a kind of existential present, but the suddenly articulated regret for her lack of exploration of her life is distinctly middle-class. The inference is that the middle-class approach to life is the normative one, and that Lily, having been given a glimpse of this paradigm, dies of grief. Given that Friel had been engaged in decentring the voices of authority throughout the play, this speech strikes a dissonant note. Murray's assertion that this is a "language of liberation . . . through which Lily . . . could somehow answer the glib sociological commentary of Professor Dodds" does not quite fit, given the characterisation of the non-existential life as middle-class (Murray, 1999: xviii). It may be that Friel was attempting to evoke a class-free Socratic ideal of the explored life, but the *glissement* between the language and his possible intention does not allow this to happen.

On the other hand, Skinner's analysis of his death is consistent with the opinions he expressed in life. He has known all along that a price would be exacted for their trespass upon the holy of holies, and they pay that price "because the poor are always overcharged" (150). He specifies that it is the poor who suffer, not the Catholics or the Nationalists. The fact that these were much the same group is not an issue for Skinner. His death-speech crystallises a great deal of his "revolutionary" discourse in the Mayor's parlour. For Skinner, the "us-and-them" is a social and economic struggle, not a religious and political one. His comment that the authorities were serious about them, while they were "unpardonably casual" about the authorities is notable because of the year in which the play is set, 1970.

Although it is two years before Bloody Sunday, on a day on which nothing momentous happened in the Northern

Troubles, 1970 saw the coming into existence of a number
of organisations which have helped shape the North. The
Ulster Defence Regiment (UDR) was created as a locally
recruited regiment of the British Army to replace the Protestant B-Specials. Ian Paisley was elected to Stormont and
Westminster for the first time, beginning a long career in
sectarian-fundamentalist obstructionist politics. The British
Army introduced the use of rubber bullets. On the Nationalist side, the Social Democratic and Labour Party (SDLP) was
established. Its then deputy leader, John Hume, was to have
a deep and lasting effect on Northern politics, not least because of his belief in the non-violent democratic process. It
was also the year of the Arms Trial in the South, where two
cabinet ministers, Charles Haughey and Neil Blaney, were
dismissed by the Taoiseach, on suspicion of having attempted to import arms into the North for the use of Re-
publicans. They were acquitted at trial. In other words, 1970
was the year in which the British and Irish establishment became very serious indeed about the agenda of the minority
in the North, and Westminster made a number of changes
to the way in which the province was governed. Their assumption that the violence would cease once justice could
be seen to apply even-handedly was mistaken.

Friel has, to an extent, written a play about poverty, and
the way in which poverty is treated by officialdom. The elements he has assembled to write that play are perhaps still
too close, and the anger engendered by the events of 30
January 1972 still burns. In some respects, the reception accorded to the play resembles the objections to *The Plough
and the Stars* in 1926. It was considered that carrying the
tricolour into a public house, particularly when one of the
onlookers was a prostitute, was an insult to the sacrifice of
1916. These events have passed into history and allowed a
more detached view of the play. The same will undoubtedly
happen to *The Freedom of the City*.

In contrast to the self-consciously theatrical construction
of *Freedom*, Friel's next play on nationalist themes, *Volunteers*, first produced in 1975, is presented as a realistic piece.
It juxtaposes two significant events in 1970s' Ireland: the
debate over the political status of IRA prisoners and the
Wood Quay controversy.

In Dublin in the 1970s, while excavating for the foundations of a site for the proposed headquarters of Dublin Cor-
poration, the remains of a Viking settlement were discovered. The developers, anxious to proceed with their project,
were less than sympathetic to the suggestion that their office
block should now be located elsewhere, in order to allow
access to a significant archaeological find. Archaeologists, historians, and a sizeable section of Dublin opinion opposed the
building. Protests, site invasions, and sit-ins were staged, in-
junctions sought and a loud public debate took place. The
episode, in the words of George O'Brien, "raised questions
about the relationship of heritage to property, of representatives to their electorate, and of present to past. . . . the
Wood Quay affair also contributed to the anxious investigation of Irish cultural identity which has been the main feature
of intellectual life in Ireland" (O'Brien, 1997: 177). An archaeological survey took place, and the offices were subsequently built on the site, although on a smaller scale. The
project was not completed until the late 1980s.

Volunteers opened in 1975 at the Abbey Theatre. Again,
reviews were unfavourable. Fachtna O'Kelly described the
reaction of the critics as "universal put-downs" (O'Kelly,
1975: 118). Although it did not attract the opprobrium that
attached to *The Freedom of the City*, the adverse publicity en-
sured that it was, for many years, one of the least produced
of Friel's plays, one that did not appear on the London stage
until the late 1980s.

The plot of *Volunteers* is typical of much of Friel's work,
in that the story is of less importance than the interaction

between the characters, and the wider symbolism of the situation in which they find themselves. Briefly, the play is set in an archaeological dig, on a site that is shortly to become a hotel. In order to finish within the time they have been given, the archaeological team have enlisted the help of five IRA prisoners, who are brought to the site by a warder, Wilson. Because the IRA men have volunteered for the dig, they are ostracised by their fellow-prisoners. The three main incidents in the plot are: the premature ending of the dig; the disappearance of Smiler, one of the volunteers, who is brain-damaged from a police beating; and the announcement by Keeney that their fellow prisoners have sentenced them to death for assisting the authorities, a crime the kangaroo court that condemned them sees as treason.

The set is one of the most heavily symbolic that Friel has created, confronting both the characters onstage and the audience with the uncertainties of Ireland's past, and the ambiguity of its present. The opening lines of the stage direc-tions make the multiple functions of the set clear: "*The action takes place in a huge crater or, as Keeney describes it, 'a huge womb' or a 'prison yard'*" (*Volunteers*: 9). In this womb, or prison, are the remains of a Viking wattle-and-daub house, and the skeleton of a Viking, whom they have named Leif. Offstage left is a cesspit, and above the whole set "*we can see rooftops, TV aerials, etc*" (9). They have also discovered the pieces of an early thirteenth-century jug, of French ori-gin, which George has painstakingly reassembled. The set is then a cross-section of Irish history from the Viking inva-sions of the ninth century to the TV aerials of the twentieth. It includes the continental influence represented by both the Viking remains and the French jug; it is both nurturing womb and restraining prison. Within this visible metaphor, one of the main themes of the play is the question of Irishness, and of its constituent parts.

None of the characters is what he appears to be at first glance. Each of them is suspended between their tribal origins and their aspirations. George, the technician, is neither digger nor academic, but "*prefers to be associated with the academics*" (11). Wilson, the warder, is attempting to climb socially through his daughter, and is affronted by the casually patronising attitude of the English music examiner. Des, the archaeology student, has, by definition, aspirations towards the status of the non-appearing but often invoked Dr King, but espouses socialism. His convictions and dedication to the workers is easily swayed by King's explanations.

The IRA volunteers are equally deceptive. It is likely that one of the issues troubling Friel at the time of the play was the personality of someone who would become an illegal paramilitary, and the motivation behind their enlistment in "The Cause". In *The Freedom of the City*, the judge had no difficulty in believing that a mother of 11 who worked as a cleaner could also be a violent subversive. Friel clearly has, and has worked to humanise the faces behind the balaclavas. This is not to suggest that he approves of their actions, or has written an *apologia* for the IRA. There is a reference by Wilson to them at the beginning of the play as "[b]loody trash" and "bloody criminals" (14), but beyond that they are allowed to speak for themselves. Smiler has had subversion thrust upon him, rather than achieving it. His story, told by Keeney, is one of loyalty to the wrong idea. Working as a stonemason in a quarry in Donegal, Smiler began a protest march to Dublin because one of his fellow-workers was interned. He was easily arrested and taken to Dublin, where beatings at the hands of the Gardaí resulted in brain damage.

Knox appears to have a Big House background; he speaks of servants and private lessons. After the collapse of this way of life, Knox discovers companionship in a life as a messenger for the IRA. Pyne was a sailor. Of his recruitment and operational profile, we are told nothing. Both Butt and

Keeney appear to be intelligent men. Butt is interested in
the project, and manages, using the information he has
gleaned on the dig, to conclude that the chart of Viking ship-
ping used by the dig team is incorrect, a conclusion Des has
to admit may be right. Keeney himself worked in a bank,
quotes Keats and *Hamlet*, and has a clear if cynical grasp of
the socio-political situation through which he moves.

All this said, the play remains enigmatic and elusive. Dantanus describes it as "an extremely difficult play to extract
meanings from" (1985: 190). Given the hostile reception
accorded to its predecessor, and the accusations levelled
against it of being a pro-IRA play, it may be that Friel is being
more cautious in *Volunteers*. From start to finish, the play
probes ideas, tests them, subjects them to ridicule, subverts
them, but never yields answers in the same way that *The
Freedom of the City* appears to. The question of Irishness is
posed by association, by the non-verbal symbolism of the
set, by the selection of characters, by the juxtaposition of
incidents. The difficulty in uncovering meaning may be part
of the meaning. Towards the end of the play, Keeney makes
a deliberately rambling speech which is emblematic of the
manner in which meaning may be extracted from the play:

> There was a definite something about him that day
> — it was a Tuesday, I remember, a warm, breathless
> day — an unrest, a disquiet — it's difficult to define.
> And perhaps I'm investing that last meeting with a
> significance it didn't in fact have. (83)

Much of the play is an invitation to invest actions or
speeches with significance, or to disregard the significance of
others. Friel provides no markers as to his intentions, nor is
any point made conclusively. Keeney's speech continues with
a detailed description of Leif propping himself on one elbow,
and eagerly looking for the answer to the question that was

troubling him: "was Hamlet really mad?" The bathetic ending to the story is cautionary. Friel probes an issue, then drops it without warning.

The main force behind this probing is Keeney's anarchic behaviour. He announces himself on his first entry as a political animal, by reciting a limerick about Parnell's adulterous relationship with Katherine O'Shea, which led to his ruin. Although it is delivered in a light-hearted manner, and never referred to again, the "Parnell split" divided Ireland into pro- and anti-Parnell factions. Keeney thus begins with an invocation of that most typical of Irish political events: the split. Not to be outdone, Pyne, described by Friel as Keeney's apprentice (17), adds a limerick of his own on the possibility that Leif died in a conflict between Christianity and paganism. Religion is introduced into the political arena.

Keeney and Pyne "improvise" a comic double act, as the work begins on the site. Keeney begins an ironic and caustic meditation on the fate of Leif, one which has parallels with his own situation. Leif has been found with a leather noose around his neck, and a hole in his skull:

> D'you think now could he have done it to himself? . . . Or was the poor eejit just grabbed out of a crowd one spring morning and a noose tightened round his neck so that obeisance would be made to some silly god. Or . . . maybe the poor hoor considered it an honour to die — maybe he volunteered: Take this neck, this life, for the god or the cause or whatever. Of course acceptance of either hypothesis would indicate that he was — to coin a phrase — a victim of his society. (28)

In this speech, Friel sets up a hypothesis of his own. Are the volunteers really volunteers in any accepted sense of the word, or has their absorption into the violence of subversion been brought about by the conditions in which they existed? This is part of the thesis of *The Freedom of the City*. Keeney's proposition that Leif could have been plucked from the crowd and sacrificed introduces an interesting and disturbing modern parallel: the suggestion that perpetrators of Irish urban terrorism may not always be willing participants, but become involved either through coercion, or through the imperatives of their upbringing. At the same time, the cliché "to coin a phrase" devalues the status of the remark. As a result, there is no way of assessing the authority of Keeney's hypothesis.

The republican paramilitary agenda is often referred to as "The Cause", and Keeney's dismissal of it with a "whatever", in addition to his status as dig volunteer, suggests a weariness with the ideology. The juxtaposition of "the cause" with a "silly god" equally suggests a feeling that the ideology may be obsolete. In an essay called "Digging Deeper", Seamus Heaney, to whom the play is dedicated, expands on this idea:

> The play is not a quarrel with others but a vehicle for Friel's quarrel with himself, between his heart and his head. . . . It is more about values and attitudes within the Irish psyche than it is about the rights and wrongs of the political situation, and represents a further digging of the site cleared in his *Freedom of the City*. (Heaney, 1980: 216)

Heaney's assessment is acute, not just in terms of Friel's play, but of his own output also. Digging as a metaphor allows Heaney access to the past, and connects spatial and temporal measurements (O'Brien, 2001: 10-13). The dedication to Heaney is at once an act of *homage* and a siting of the play in the same metaphorical landscape. The archaeological dig allows access to a past of fact and symbol in the same way that the figure of Heaney's father does in *Digging* (Heaney, 1966: 13-14).

The quarrel between the heart and the head is an apt characterisation of the play, and helps to explain the lack of a readily identifiable centre. One critic of the original production asked irritably: "Your point, Mr Friel — your point?" (O'Kelly, 1975: 118). I have argued in relation to *Freedom of the City* that, despite the obvious outrage in the play, Friel is continuing with his attempt to decentre authority. In *Volunteers*, we see this decentring taken to extremes, where the authority of the play is dissipated to such a degree as to be unidentifiable. This hypothesis both confirms my position on *Freedom of the City*, and explains some of the difficulties inherent in *Volunteers*. The archaeological dig is a metaphor for the meditation of the play, and also the method by which one can reassemble its fragmented meanings.

One of the explorations of Irishness which can be pieced together from the play is the disputed notion of Irish history. The dig, as we have noted, is a metaphor within which the exploration happens. Keeney launches into an impression of Dr King speaking to a group of imaginary schoolchildren. He quickly and accurately explains the nature of the business of archaeology, while Pyne, playing the part of the teacher, parrots the ends of his sentences for the "children". Physically, this is an image of the degeneration of cultural ideas, from the researcher, through to the teacher who repeats scraps of it. There may be an element of criticism of the process of cultural transmission. Friel, after all, worked as a teacher in Derry, in a system segregated by religion and cultural tradition. The versions of history taught in Protestant and Catholic schools were likely to have been very different, even if the textbooks were similar. There is certainly a deep irony at work.

Keeney describes the strata of the dig: "from early Viking right down to late Georgian . . . a tangible précis of the story of Irish man" (36). Pyne then instructs his invisible children to repeat "Irish man, Irish man". The fact is that

Keeney, and we can presume, Dr King, defines Irish man in foreign terms. The initial age is Viking, named after Scandinavians who probably came from York, where a large outpost had been established, and the final era is Georgian, named after British kings, who were themselves of German extraction. It is difficult to see exactly who an Irish man is, when he came to be so, and how he is involved in Keeney's summary. The point being made is fragmentary, incomplete, in itself archaeological. The notion of Irishness is problematised. When did the invaders become Irish?

The eleventh century *Book of Invasions* describes Ireland's mythical settlements by "Cesair, granddaughter of Noah, Partholón, Nemed, the Fir Bolg . . . the Tuatha Dé Danann . . . and the Gaels or Milesians" (Connolly, 1998: 310). Archaeology states that the earliest settlements were about 7000 BC, and successive waves of prehistoric incursion and later colonisation by Normans, English, and Scots shaped the features of the Irish, and contributed to the national gene pool. In no sense is anyone a pure Celt, or a *fíor-Ghael*. Of course, this is a reconstructive interpretation; Keeney moves his playlet along quickly, returning to his theme, and to the main theme of the play in the lines: "what we are all engaged in here is really a thrilling voyage in *self*-discovery" (37). He then wonders how many want to take that journey. We might infer that of the two models of Irishness, scientific and mythic, the mythic is to be preferred as one that confirms our prejudice and comforts our intolerance. Friel repeatedly returns to this theme, notably in *The Home Place*, where "science" on one hand and the sentimental songs of Tom Moore on the other contend for possession of the Irish psyche.

Early in Act 2, Keeney returns to the theme, but by a different route. Echoing Donovan in *The Communication Cord*, he says "God's in his heavens and the eternal verities are still thumping along" (54). He then destabilises the thought by recounting the story of Vera McLaughlin, a Derry prostitute

who was known as "Eternal Verity". The central meditation
on Irishness instigated by Keeney is, of course, the speculations on the life and death of the skeleton, Leif.

He encourages Pyne to begin, and as he does so, with
the conventional opening "once upon a time", Keeney inter-
jects: "ah sure thanks be to God, lads, it's only an aul' yarn"
(61), again placing the speculations in the realm of fiction.
But Keeney's entire *persona* is structured around the telling
of "aul' yarns", and the assumption of personalities, the
spontaneous mimicry and mockery of those about him. In
the middle of Pyne's story he returns spontaneously to it:
"'Once upon a time' — keep up the protection of the myth"
(62). The injunction tells rather more about Keeney's character than it does about Pyne's story. For Keeney, it appears, the protection of the Irish national myth has broken
down. His defence is to adopt, subvert, and discard new stories, myths, and personalities, as fast as he can.

Pyne's version of Leif's story concerns exogamy, marrying outside the tribe. In his story, Leif marries a Native
American, and brings her back to the city. The tribe think
she is evil; they burn her, and execute Leif. This is a version
of Irishness concerned with the purity of the tribe. Pyne is
further confused by Keeney's question, why did he come
back? For Pyne, the sailor, coming back is so fundamental an
action that he cannot answer it.

Keeney tells a version of the story that is obviously the
story of Knox's involvement with the IRA. In this version,
Knox, or Leif, is merely lonely and destitute, not ideologically motivated. Knox's reaction to this accurate but coruscating summary of his failure is emotional and dissonant. He
bursts into tears. The hiatus is filled by Keeney, who hints at
the commitment of Butt and himself. Butt, he says, is consistent, whereas his "paltry flirtations are just . . . fireworks
that are sparked occasionally by an antic imagination" (71).
He returns to the subject of Leif, proposing quickly a num-

ber of possible situations. He was a slave who could no longer row; he was a blacksmith who wanted a horse of his own; a carpenter who asked to keep one of the houses he had built; an evicted crofter or, as Butt adds pointedly, "he was a bank-clerk who had courage and who had brains and who was one of the best men in the movement" (72). Each set of circumstances imposed on Leif has significance for Keeney, or for Friel. Each has resonances within Irish social and political history. Each is, ultimately, inconclusive.

The symbolism of the reconstructed jug can be seen as emblematic of the difficulty of dissecting the question of Irishness. Keeney's interpretation of it as "Smiler restored, Smiler full, free and integrated" (55) is only one possibility. From the outset, when the jug is introduced and the reconstruction time mentioned, it is earmarked for destruction. The only uncertainty is which of the volunteers will destroy it. Ironically, Butt, who deliberately drops the jug, is the most committed to the dig. His motive appears to be a kind of solidarity with Keeney. George has pompously announced that his report on Keeney to the prison governor will not be favourable; an ironic announcement, as Keeney is to be killed by his fellow-prisoners. Friel is careful to withhold the significance, by indicating that Butt looks at George "*with flat eyes*" (79). As the pieces can be assembled again, albeit with some trouble, the breaking of the jug is more of a gesture than a conclusively destructive action.

If the jug itself is a symbol, it may be, taking a lead from Keeney's comments about Smiler, a symbol of a reconstructed Ireland, or of an authentic vision of the country's past. These are mere speculations, which are themselves undercut by the jug's French provenance. The physical elements of the play that might be taken as symbolic, or even suggestive, are underplayed deliberately. Even the site itself as a womb, or prison, or bomb-crater, has its interpretation delivered in a spirit of burlesque.

The jug is linked with Smiler from the beginning, as it was he who discovered the pieces. Keeney makes the link, but the status of Keeney's pronouncements is highly ambiguous. One symbolic link which may be made is the way in which Smiler's own life is similarly fragmented. He rarely speaks, other than to mouth: "that's right — that's right", as if in perpetual agreement with everyone. At one point in the play he speaks, without warning, a few lines of official-sounding conversation, about delegates and propositions (23), reminiscent of Father in *Aristocrats*. This certainly fits with Smiler's union background, although it is unclear whether these are his own words, or words that he picked up somewhere else. His longest dialogue is with Butt after his reappearance. He tries to explain his absence, but is unable to do so coherently. The stage directions state that he looks "*as if he were trying to capture some elusive intelligence*" (76), an attempt which, given the play's shifting meanings, is unsuccessful. Smiler, damaged by his adherence to his ideology, unable to escape it, compelled to return, may represent all of the other characters in his inability to move on.

It is Smiler's disappearance which is the catalyst for Keeney's revelation about the kangaroo court. He wishes to prevent George reporting Smiler's absence, in order to give him some chance of escaping the summary execution awaiting the rest of them in prison. At one level, it can be seen as an act of humanity on Keeney's part, but, as Smiler returns of his own accord, the gesture is futile. The revelation that they are to die in turn sets in motion the many interpretations of Leif's death, all of which are connected with the lives of the prisoners. The final story finishes just as Pyne leads Smiler back in.

There are a number of points at which *Volunteers* bears comparison with *Freedom of the City*. Its concern with militant republicanism is one, but, whereas in the earlier play the characters were mistaken for subversives, these, for a

variety of reasons, really are. Another point of contact is the
set. The mayor's parlour, embattled and surrounded by
ideologically discontinuous voices, compares to the under-
ground set of *Volunteers*. There is a similar sense of entrapment, and the scientific scrutiny of the dig compares to the
inquiries and reflections on the actions in the Guildhall.
George, Wilson, and Des provide the outside comment.
Between them they represent all shades of opinion. Wilson
opens the play with a racist consideration of genetics:
"speaking from a lifetime of practical experience, you're either born right or you're not" (15). George has an animosity
towards Keeney, and a mild condescension towards the
others. Des, the socialist of the group, considers them fellow-workers, until their spoof letter would threaten his position. He then surrenders to self-interest.

The imminent deaths of the central characters is another
similarity, and one which might form the basis for a final
word on both plays. In *Freedom of the City*, the deaths of Lily,
Michael, and Skinner at the hands of the security forces
were taken by some reviewers and critics as an indictment
of British rule and army indiscipline in Northern Ireland. In
Volunteers, because the deaths will be at the hands of other
republican prisoners, no such criticism can be levelled. Despite any subversive actions that may have been carried out
by any of the five — and we are given no hint as to their
functioning prominence within the IRA — death for taking
part in an archaeological dig is undeserved. It is possible that,
taking the plays in tandem, a comment is being made about
extremist ideologies, and the inherent dangers, not merely
physical, but psychological, in embracing them.

Chapter Six

From Moscow to Ballybeg

> . . . Irish actors have to assume English accents so you end up with being an Irishman pretending you're an Englishman, pretending you're a Russian! (Brian Friel, in interview with Donal O'Donnell, 1981)

Translation is an impossible act. Linguistically, the semantic resonances of any one word cannot be replicated in another language. Even simple structural elements such as the French 'le chat' cannot be entirely translated into English, because there is no masculine definite article in modern English. From a postcolonial point of view, all translation is a political act. W. B. Worthen points to the assertion that translation: "draws our attention not only to the social and political interfaces between literatures and languages, but also to how those borders are configured, and to the cultural work that translating between or across them claims to accomplish" (Worthen, 1995: 22). It is, according to Paulo Eduardo Carvalho: "first an act of hermeneutics and secondly an act of re-writing" (Carvalho, 2006: 263). Translation, then, can never be merely an accurate rendering from one language to another, but is a recognition of alterity of the other language and also a searching for a recognition of the Self in the

Other. It is also, given the necessities of linguistic structures, a re-interpretation of the Other, and, by association, of the Self. Seen in these terms, translation is a natural progression for a postcolonial nation reaching out to the world. Michael Cronin advances the argument even further, in terms that have a resonance for Friel: "the forging of a new national identity implies the forgery of translation, the reading of the translation as if it were the original" (Cronin, 2006: 103).

Irish writers have long been drawn to translation as an act of cultural and political exploration. Frank O'Connor's banned translation of *The Midnight Court* in the 1940s deliberately re-sexualised Gaelic poetry and attempted to bring some earthy maturity to the Celtic Twilight. Tom Paulin's versions of Sophocles and Aeschylus are political statements from any point of view. Seamus Heaney's use of ancient texts to explore contemporary social and political problems is well documented. His aim, according to Eugene O'Brien is: "a reconstruction of language so that the tribe can talk to the other through an acknowledgement of the essential hybridity of language itself" (O'Brien, 2002: 116). There is also, however, a sense in which the tribe talks to itself, using the other as a mirror.

Friel's first play for Field Day was *Translations*, a play about the re-interpretation of topography and the displacement effect it had on the population. The second was his translation into Hiberno-English of Chekhov's *Three Sisters*. The third was *The Communication Cord*, which concerns, among other things, false interpretation of language, and the dangers of attaching sentimental political pieties to linguistic structures. There is undoubtedly a synergy between these plays, a concern for language that goes beyond the knee-jerk reactions of the Gaelic language movements or the political uses of language to define the Self and exclude the Other. All the plays touch on the Saussurean notion of language as a defining force rather than a descriptive one.

Knowing no Russian, Friel eschews the "faithful repro-
duction" (Worthen, 1995: 26) in favour of the "version". As
the epigraph to this chapter suggests, Friel was unhappy with
the existing translations of Chekhov. It is not that he quib-
bled with the accuracy of the translation, but that they had
been translated into a particularly British English idiom. In an
interview with Donal O'Donnell in the *Sunday Press* in 1981,
he made the point that:

> the translations that have been available have been
> British, which results in Chekhov being placed at a
> remove from us. In a way, I think one of the func-
> tions of Field Day enterprises is in some way to 'de-
> colonise' the imagination. (O'Donnell, 1981: 150)

This is, in the broadest sense, a political statement. It is also
a fact of language. Friel had spoken elsewhere of the translations: "redolent of Edwardian England or the Bloomsbury
set . . . . Even the most recent English translation again carries, of necessity, very strong English cadences and rhythms
(Agnew, 1980: 145). The phrase "of necessity" is an important one, as Friel is not criticising previous translations. They
served their constituency, as his does. Theatrical conventions are very strongly conservative, and a practice becomes
the norm. Shakespeare always sounds more 'authentic' in
English Received Pronunciation, despite the fact that the
speech of Elizabethan London was nothing like it. The colonisation of "legitimate" theatre by English accents is under-
standable, but it is still a colonisation, and one that Friel
works, not to reverse, but to circumvent.

One might say that there is a double translation at work
here. Ultimately, Friel is working from Russian literature, but
he is, in the same plays, translating from English. After all, in
Translations itself, the literal process of the play is the translation from English into other English, from the English of

mainland Britain to the English of Ireland, from the English of
the Other to the English of the Self. Friel shows an awareness of the cultural baggage in *Translations*. Captain Lancey,
the English officer, is translated by Owen with cynical shorthand. Lancey details the triangulations, the technical information to be included on the new map, and the scale of "six
inches to the English mile. . ." (*Translations*, 33). Owen renders it as: "A new map is being made of the whole country".
While bathetic comedy and character are being constructed
in the short passage, it is also evident that Friel is aware of
the biggest stumbling block to any translator, that translation, as Cronin notes is always interpretation, and that interpretation is, in many cases, a distortion.

There are three strands to Friel's Russian work. First,
there are the English versions of Russian plays. These are:
Three Sisters, A Month in the Country, Uncle Vanya, and *The
Bear*. Secondly, there are the dramatic adaptations of Russian
novels or stories: *Fathers and Sons, The Yalta Game*, and *The
Bear*. Finally, and most curiously, there is *Afterplay*, a whimsy
in which two characters from *Uncle Vanya* and *Three Sisters*
meet twenty years after the action of those plays has ended.
The Yalta Game, The Bear and *Afterplay* were collected as
Three Plays After, and played together in 2001.

Chekhov, with his careful orchestration of mood and
nuance is very much a playwright's playwright. Turgenev,
Friel states in his introduction to *A Month in the Country*, an-
ticipated Chekhov. He "moved haltingly across unmapped
territory [and] established the necessary environments in
which Chekhov could blossom" (10). This blossoming produced a handful of plays which changed the face of Western
theatre, but which still challenge critics to explain why. They
have little in the way of action, and most of that happens
offstage. The characters are neither comic, nor tragic, neither particularly elevated nor peculiarly base. They exhibit
neither moral strength nor moral turpitude. The settings are

realistic to the point of mundanity. The *dénouements* are un-satisfactory. The plays evade characterization in the same way as Shakespeare's problem plays do.

The image of humanity in Chekhov (and in Turgenev) was shockingly true for its first audiences. Life does not tie up all the loose ends in two and a half hours. Although there are many tragedies, most of humanity will never experience the emotional catharsis of a Lear. The little frustrations of ordinary lives reflected on stage, transformed by art, made somehow worthy of contemplation created an entirely new theatre, as innovative in its own terms as Warhol's baked bean tin as an art-object. When these appear in translation, the limpidity of the realism is clouded. When, as Friel would suggest, the translation is also at one remove, then the plays lose their immediacy and ability to move.

The social background to Chekhov's plays is more than a little similar to Friel's "big house" plays. The big houses were dependent on country estates, worked largely by peasants, who had, a few generations earlier, been serfs. The estates in the Chekhov plays are either poorly managed, or barely give a return. Estate management is a background trope in *Uncle Vanya*. In *Three Sisters*, the Prozorovs are forced to work for a living as their father was in the military, and not landed gentry. Tusenbach, who espouses populist ideas of work, has never actually done any.

The countryside that surrounds the houses is over-whelmingly described in negative terms. Only outsiders like Vershinin in *Three Sisters* can describe the surroundings of the house as "a real Russian climate" (Hingley: 179), al-though Olga complains of the cold and the mosquitoes. While Friel's own attitude to the Irish countryside is am-biguous, Chekhov has constructed an urban-rural divide which appears to favour city life over the country. The te-dium of the provinces is a recurrent theme in Chekhov. As-trov in *Uncle Vanya* remarks: "life here is so dreary and

stupid and sordid" (Hingley, 1998: 119). Serabryakov describes his estate as: "this dead and alive hole" (131). The
Russian countryside continually appears as bleak, wild, un-
productive and unhealthy.

Another factor which may have attracted Friel to the
Russians, in particular to Chekhov, is what he has called in
Give Me Your Answer, Do!: "the Necessary Uncertainty". The
characters and situations in the plays he translates are ambiguous. Their motivations are unclear, their reactions to
situations sometimes opaque. Astrov, in *Uncle Vanya*, is a
complex character to read, and has always attracted attention from theatre critics in productions. Even Vanya himself
is an intricate construction, woven together from tiny incon-
sistencies and suggestions.

Three Sisters appeared in 1981, following the stunning
success of *Translations*. Friel's work on the two texts over-
lapped, and he has stated in interview that the attempt to
encompass Chekhov's play, for someone who spoke no Russian, led him to *After Babel*, which in turn influenced the text
of *Translations* (Agnew, 1980: 145). His approach was to
compare existing translations, and then to recast each line in
a linguistic mould that was closer to the modulations of Hiberno-English. In a way, Friel had already written a version
of *Three Sisters* in *Aristocrats*. There are three O'Donnell sisters (excluding Anna, who never appears); they have an odd
brother and a father whose presence broods over the
house. All have lives which are vestiges of what they might
have been. The same pattern appears in *Living Quarters* and
Dancing at Lughnasa. The theme of stunted lives appears repeatedly in Friel's work, in *Lovers*, *The Gentle Island*, *The Loves
of Cass McGuire* and others.

Friel makes no changes to the broad structure of the
play, and keeps the four acts intact. The play is a long one, a
quarter as long again as anything from Chekhov's mature
period and runs over three hours in the theatre. It covers, in

Friel's version a period of approximately five years in the lives of the Prozorov sisters, Olga, Masha, and Irina, who are originally from Moscow. Chekhov's time-scheme is a little more vague, but internal evidence suggests the play spans a minimum of two-and-a-half to three years. The daughters of an army general, the Prozorovs were based in a provincial garrison town when he died, a year before the opening of Act One. For eleven years they have been dreaming of leaving the provinces and returning to Moscow. Masha is married to Kulygin, a teacher and small-time pedant. Olga teaches in the local secondary (High) school. Irina, by Act Two, is working in the post office. Their brother, Andrey, has ambitions to become a university professor, but is an idler by nature, and becomes tied to the provinces by marrying a local girl, Natasha.

As with Friel's original work, the plot is of considerably less importance than the interaction of the characters and the orchestration of mood and nuance. Although there appears to be a deal of action in the play, most of it takes place elsewhere. The fire in the town, which is the centrepiece of Act Three, happens at a distance, and never threatens the Prozorov household. The duel between Tusenbach and Solony happens offstage, and is reported in an offhand way by Chebutykin. The affairs are reduced to a few kisses and some reportage. Friel's interest in the colonising of language by the translators of Chekhov is mirrored in one of the themes of the play, as Natasha gradually assumes control of the household, ousting the sisters from authority. The theme had appeared earlier in his work in *Aristocrats*, where Eamon, besotted by the traditions and grandeur of Ballybeg Hall, marries into the family. In the same way Willie Driver, tempted reluctantly to take part in the O'Donnells' imaginary game of croquet, declares himself the winner (*Aristocrats*: 59).

Apart from specifically Irish elements in the version, the stolid prose into which Chekhov was traditionally translated had to be addressed. This is Olga's opening speech, translated by Ronald Hingley:

> It's exactly a year ago today since Father died — on the fifth of May, your name-day, Irina. It was very cold then, and snowing. I thought I'd never get over it and you actually passed out, fainted right away. But now . . . . You're wearing white again and you look radiant. [*The clock strikes twelve.*] The clock struck twelve then too. [*Pause*] I remember the band playing when they took Father to the cemetery, and they fired a salute. He was a general, commanded a brigade. All the same, not many people came — it was a wet day of course, with heavy rain and sleet. (Hingley, 1998: 171)

The speech is unashamedly choric and a great deal of back-story is being conveyed. The information she is delivering must be known to the other characters, and lines like: "[h]e was a general" become awkward, and difficult for an actor to deliver naturally. Terms such as "name-day" are heavy and foreign to the ear. The style of acting required, according to Friel was to "stare into the middle-distance and talk desultorily about philosophical questions" (Gillespie, 1981: 156).

Friel takes rather longer over the opening, allowing the cadences of natural speech to intrude: "It's hard to believe it's only a year since Father's death, isn't it? Twelve months to the day. The fifth of May. Your birthday, Irina" (*Three Sisters*, 1992: 11). The "isn't it" turns an indicative statement into an interrogative. By framing the first sentence as a question, he has included the other characters. While not an exclusively Hiberno-English construction, it does correspond to the "*nach ea?*" construction in Gaelic. "Name-day" has become "birthday". He uses interrogatives to tie the speech together: "Do you remember how cold it was? And there was snow falling. I thought then I'd never get over it. And you collapsed — d'you remember? — passed out cold" (11). The choice of "collapsed" and "passed out cold" gives the lines a physicality that the more elegant "fainted right away" lacks. Constance Garnett's "you lay fainting as though you were dead" is faintly romantic (www.eldritchpress.org), whereas "collapsed . . . passed out cold" could equally be applied to a drunk. There is an earthy reality in the lines. The emphasis on "has" in the line following connects it to Olga's assertion that she would never get over her father's death: "But a year *has* gone by and we can talk about it calmly now, can't we? Of course we can. And you're wearing white again and you look . . . radiant!" (11–12). The question turns the speech into an unanswered dialogue rather than choric monologue. Hingley and Garnett also use the word "radiant" to describe Irina. Friel chooses "radiant", but by placing a strategic pause before the word, draws attention to it and makes it a deliberate choice, as if Olga were searching for the right term.

The narration of the ceremony changes from chorus to memory by adding "remember" at the beginning: "Remember the band playing when they were carrying the coffin out of the room here? And firing the salute in the cemetery? General Prozorov, Brigade Commander!" (12). Friel adroitly renders the lines about the general's status by making it explicitly declarative, allowing remembrance to disguise the choric function, while still performing it efficiently.

Introducing the theme of their longed-for return to Moscow, Friel splits the original dialogue between Olga and Irina, resulting in both an increase in emphasis and in the natural rhythms of speech:

Irina To go back to Moscow.

Olga Yes!

Irina	To sell this house, to pack up here and to go home to Moscow.
Olga	Yes! Yes! Home to Moscow! But it must be soon, Irina! It has got to be soon! (13)

By giving Irina two speeches, there is an effective crescendo, which increases the sense of Moscow as the symbolic centre of their lives by adding "home" twice. Moscow functions as the mythical "home place". Exile from the mythical centre has been a recurring theme in Friel's work. In *The Home Place* it figures prominently, but it appears in earlier work also. In *The Enemy Within*, Columba is torn between two centres, one geographical, one religious. In *Crystal and Fox*, Fox longs for a golden time, when everything was as it should be. Cass McGuire returns to her centre after years in exile, only to find it unsatisfactory and unfulfilling. Oileán Draíochta in *Wonderful Tennessee* performs the same function, although Friel deliberately destroys it as a symbol. In *The Gentle Island*, Peter and Shane are convinced that they have found the centre, only to bring ruin with them. Themes of the mystic centre, the *omphalos*, have a destructive currency in Friel.

The Irish cadences that Friel intended to bring to his versions of Chekhov are most apparent in the provincial characters. Perhaps he allows the Prozorovs and their friends to speak a more neutral English in order to make the point that they follow the fashions of another world. In Ireland, the socially aspirational can, on occasion, develop an accent which is called, unkindly, "West-Brit".

Friel's interest in the colonising of language is mirrored in one of the themes, as Natasha gradually assumes control of the household. Natasha is looked down on for her provincial *gaucherie* and garish dress-sense. Friel plays liberally with the lines. In Garnett's version she is described by Masha: "It's not that her clothes are merely ugly or out of fashion, they're simply pitiful. A weird gaudy yellowish skirt with some sort of vulgar fringe and a red blouse. And her cheeks scrubbed till they shine!" (www.eldritchpress.org). Friel shares the unpleasant superiority among the sisters. She and Olga describe Natasha's "poor-but-honest provincial face" (26), the dazzling yellow and greens and purples in her "peccable" dress sense. Finally, Masha explodes: "Vulgar, for God's sake. Plain downright vulgar" (27).

Natasha is the main vehicle for Friel's use of Irish, specifically Northern Irish, rhythms and expressions, although he has written the same kind of dialect for the servant Anfisa, and the Council messenger, Ferapont. Natasha changes accents for social reasons. Her entrance is frantic: "Sweet mother of God, I'm late . . ." (36). Her accent then becomes "*slightly posh*". She replaces her natural phatic phrase with "Goodness gracious", an over-compensation, and when Olga asks after her, she swings wildly into her vernacular again: "As my mother used to say, 'Never felt better and had less'. . . . God but that's a wild big crowd . . ." (37). This has the effect of making Natasha a comic character, eliciting a sympathy which makes her transformation into a domineering harridan more emphatic. The sisters' objections to her also become more pronounced. Masha's interruption of the thought that Natasha is going to marry Andrey is rendered by Hingley: "I'm going to have a little glass of something. Eat, drink and be merry – after all, we only live once" (187). Friel points up the scene more forcibly:

> *Masha deliberately drops her plate on the table.*
>
> **Masha**   I want some wine! Why are you keeping the bloody wine hidden up there?

The stage direction and Masha's line are more explicitly hateful and border, given the sisters' sense of their own social and moral superiority, on vulgarity.

By Act Two, Natasha is already behaving like the mistress of the house. She complains about the quality and conduct of the maids, and begins to bury Andrey under an avalanche of talk. Her new certainty is contrasted with Andrey's indecisiveness, and her garrulous dialect with his "neutral" English. Her speeches are peppered with dialect expressions: "Sweet Mother of God", "the creatures", "the likes of me", "sweating like a pig", "the wee darling" (42–3). When Solony suggests that he would like to fillet her baby and eat him, she retorts: "God but it's easy seen you've never had no manners nor breeding, you pup you!" (59). Friel exaggerates her response for comic effect.

It is in Act Two also that Natasha begins to use clumsy French, long considered the language of civilisation and refinement in Russia, in an attempt to appear more refined than she is. She corrects Masha's manners in a way that would have been unthinkable in Act One. When Masha is berating Chebutykin she says: "Look at him . . . still blathering like a bloody child!" (61). In a swift reversal, Friel puts dialect words into Masha's mouth, suggesting that she too is part-colonised by Natasha's influence in the house. Later in the act, in a vignette created by Friel, Masha becomes deliberately coarse, switching from singing "the baron is drunk" to "the baron is pissed" as Natasha passes through the room (65). The act ends with victory for Natasha. The mummers from the carnival are not granted entrance, Irina is moved from her bedroom, and Natasha leaves for a troika-ride with Protopopov, who will become her lover.

Natasha's use of dialect words and expressions increases in Act Three as her colonising proceeds. Friel also gives her character extremes that do not exist in Chekhov. Seeing Anfisa sitting in the bedroom, she reacts coldly: "How dare you be seated in my presence? Stand up! Be off with you!" (Hingley: 209). Friel replaces the cold delivery: "*Now for the first time she sees Anfisa. Her fury is instant and excessive, al-*

most hysterical" (76). Likewise, when she makes clear to Olga that she, Natasha, is in charge of the house, Friel pushes the reaction into hysteria: "(*Suddenly almost hysterical again*) And don't you ever cross me again! D'you hear me? . . . (*As suddenly in control again*) God bless us and save us, if you don't leave we'll end up having a wee tiff . . ." (78). This is not Chekhov, but it is effective theatre. Natasha becomes a more predatory character, giving Olga cause to fear her.

By Act Four she has become the centre of the household and can ensconce her lover in the drawing-room. There is a sense of the play and the lives of the characters winding down to an unremarkable end. There is more introspection, characters make position statements. One senses that the grip the Prozorovs have on their lives has been loosened even more, and that they have become flotsam, tossed about by any circumstance and unable to take action.

When Andrey describes his wife to Chebutykin, Hingley's: "blind, groping, scruffy little animal" (288) has become: "a mean, myopic, gross, grubbing animal" (*Three Sisters:* 106). He adds "mean", leaving no doubt as to her character. "Gross" is an obvious reference to her manners and breeding, while "grubbing" indicates a frantic scrabbling after something. Friel's choice of adjectives makes her unappealing, but the inference is that her actions are deliberate.

There is a curious alteration in the imagery as Tusenbach is about to leave for his duel with Solony, in which he will be killed. Hingley translates Irina's words to him as: "my heart is like a wonderful grand piano that can't be used because it's locked up and the key's lost" (230). Friel has discarded the musical image in favour of: "all that's needed is the magic key, the code, the password . . ." (109). Codes and passwords are suggestive of secrecy, and are redolent of Yolland's comment in *Translations* that the centre can never be known. The principal characters in *Three Sisters* are never allowed to know themselves completely, and so their introspection becomes, at best, trivial. Their lives are encompassed by forces that move on despite them. They hide behind their eroded gentility and dreams of returning to Moscow while their world gently crumbles about them.

Tusenbach reinforces the sense of triviality, summing up the action of the play: "in the end it's never the great passions, the great ambitions that determine the course our lives take, but some trivial, piddling little thing that we dismiss and refuse to take seriously . . ." (109). The speech as written by Friel is far more resonant than other translations. In Friel's rendering, the speech deliberately encompasses the play. It summarises Chekhov's dramaturgy. Inclusion of words like "manipulated" is an almost direct reference to Natasha, as well as ostensibly speaking about Tusenbach's quarrel with Solony which has led to the duel.

At the end of the play the dreams of the sisters are destroyed, but the calamity of their lives is a small one. They are materially no worse off, their lives will continue. They have been touched by Tusenbach's death, but they are not directly involved. Their tragedy is a small one. Their brave speeches of working and going on are undercut in all versions by Chebutykin. While Irina wishes for knowledge of the reason for their sufferings, he mutters, in Friel's version: "Matters sweet damn all . . . sweet damn all it matters . . ." (123).

By the time Friel came to write *Uncle Vanya*, in 1998, he was working from a literal translation by Úna Ní Dhubhghaill. He had also, by this time, produced his version of Turgenev's *Fathers and Sons* (1987), also from a literal translation, and had refined the technique. The spine of the Gallery Press edition of *Uncle Vanya* proclaims that it is "*after Chekhov*", while the title page states that the play is "*a version of the play by Anton Chekhov*" (*Uncle Vanya*: 5), suggesting that there is some distance between the original and the English rendering. Friel appears to have transcended the wider political issues of translation which were apparent in *Three Sisters*. Irish rhythms and phrases are still in evidence, but they are more organic and less strident. The play has an atmosphere of suffocation and stultification, giving the characters a sense of torpor and *ennui* from which they cannot extricate themselves. The action is precipitated by the return of Serabryakov and his wife to their country estate. It is apparent from Vanya's first entrance that they are a disruptive influence on the long-established rhythms of the household, and this new leisure gives Vanya the opportunity to reflect on his life and to find it empty.

Friel's treatment of Telegin is typical of his handling of the play. Telegin, the ruined landowner who lives on the estate, and on Vanya's charity, is called "Waffles" because of his pock-marked face. Michael Frayn points out that the Russian *Vaflya* is a waffle, but dislikes the name: "To modern English ears it might suggest a taste for meaningless verbiage" (1987: xxv). Friel retains it, but adds precisely those characteristics that Frayn thought might be suggested by the nickname: he makes Telegin waffle:

> my pock-marked face . . . . Lost me my wife as a matter of fact; that [*face*] and a little weakness all the Telegins suffer: victims to perspiration. Lost her to a German. Hans. Marvellous race, your German. Turn their hands to anything. . . . (*Uncle Vanya*: 18)

Telegin's irritation in the original has been diluted. He is nervous and babbles. In almost every speech he has, he says too much, or the wrong thing. The perspiration and the German are new. The perspiration appeared in his first line (14), and re-appears in the inappropriate question: "Do you sweat much yourself?" to Elena (20) and then to Maria as the closing line of the Act (27). There is a significant dra-

matic shift here. Telegin becomes less pathetic, less an index
of Vanya's benevolence, and more a comic character.

Friel adds a curious line late in Act One. As Vanya,
Sonya, and others sit outside drinking tea, the servant, Ma-
rina, comes looking for a speckled hen, which has wandered
off with her chicks, and she is worried that the crows, or
magpies, will get them. She wanders on, and off again. Vanya
says: "The old speckled hen — is she somehow — symbolic?" "Behave yourself", Sonya replies (20–1). Friel is creating a piece of deliberately misleading meta-theatre. The
hen could be symbolic if a commentator chooses to wring
an interpretation from it, or it could merely be, as the subti-
tle of the play indicates, part of a scene from country life. By
drawing attention to it, and by having Sonya issue a rebuke,
Friel is laying a trap for critics.

Act Two is largely composed of three dislocated love-
scenes, emblematic of the fractured relationships in the
household. Serebryakov accuses Elena of loathing him; Vanya
declares his love for Elena, only to suffer a bored rebuff; and
Sonya broaches the subject of love with Astrov, who tells
her he has no emotions left and is too taken up with his
work to love anyone. None of the three reaches a conclusion or contains any kind of closure. In the opening scene,
Serebryakov wakes in the middle of the night, confused and
in pain. Friel accentuates his confusion and ill-temper. In the
original, he wakes in pain but lucid and looks for a copy of a
poetry book. He calls for Sonya, mistaking Elena for her as
he wakes. In Friel's version he is soothed by Elena, with no
mention of Sonya. In the Russian, the sound outside the
window is the watchman tapping. In the Friel version, the
watchman is called Yefim, and he is singing (28). Serabryakov's irritated reaction is very Irish: "Drunken bloody louts
going home from the pub" (28). It is an incongruous line, as
the play is set in a country estate. It is unlikely that anyone
would be passing at night.

The discussion of their fractured relationship that follows has been comprehensively reworked. The spirit is the same: that Elena is married to a deteriorating old man whom she does not love. He resents the situation, but resents his own failing body more. Friel imbues him with more rage, directed uselessly against Yefim's singing, and with more existential *angst* than Chekhov does. Possibly he is attempting to make Serabryakov a more sympathetic character, so that he, even with his privilege, is made to share the fears of the central characters.

The scene between Vanya and Elena has been altered in ways which could well run against the spirit of the original, were Friel attempting a translation. When Elena summarises the problems in the house, she characterises Serabryakov by his roles: professor, father and husband. In Friel, Vanya interrupts her near the beginning of her speech: "What's this — 'the Professor'? You mean 'my husband', don't you?" (33). For the rest of the speech she refers to Serabryakov as "him", and the lines "You loathe my husband and openly sneer at your mother" (Hingley, 1998: 134) are omitted. Friel takes the suggestion that Elena is compartmentalising her husband's roles and deliberately exploits it. The interpolated line makes Elena appear colder, and offers some inducement to Vanya to express his feelings for her. Friel is deliberately making Vanya a more ironic character, pushing him closer in outlook to Astrov, and removing the ambiguity in Elena's speech.

In the Russian original, Vanya objects to Elena's summary. In Friel, he compliments it: "summarised perceptively and succinctly" (33). It may be intended as ironic, it may be sincere, but no privileged reading is available. His declaration of love is, in all the versions, gauche and ineffectual. It is histrionic and silly, and is greeted with languid boredom. Friel pushes the speech into bathos, and gives Vanya the awareness that his grand speech of love is having no effect whatever. It is a much more bitter and sarcastic speech, quite a way from Chekhov. Vanya concludes in exasperation: "Have you any idea at all of what I'm saying to you?" (34). Friel has shifted the bathetic focus from Elena's response to Vanya's frustrated last line.

As the speech ends, Astrov and Telegin enter. Friel inserts a page of dialogue between Astrov and Vanya that could not have been written for Chekhov's theatre. Astrov becomes quite crude on the subject of Elena and Serabryakov, and suggests that he might be persuaded to join her in bed. Telegin is reduced to the role of court jester to Astrov. Instead of just playing guitar, as he does in the other versions, he proposes a German folk song, carrying on the running joke about his obsession with Germans.

The scene between Astrov and Sonya begins differently. In all other translations, Sonya knocks on the bedroom door and calls Astrov back into the room to remonstrate with him on the subject of Vanya's drinking. Sonya thinks that Astrov encourages him. In Friel, he merely returns, having straightened his rumpled clothes. As they speak, Astrov, who also loves Elena, is the one who characterises her as beautiful but useless: "She has no responsibilities, and other people work for her" (Hingley, 1998: 138). From a man crushed with overwork and a sense of responsibility for the future, this is damning.

The opening of Act Three illustrates the difference in outlook between Elena and Sonya. Elena has never been a sympathetic character, and Astrov's characterisation of her in Act Two makes her less so. The comparison Chekhov makes between them at this point distinctly favours the plain and hard-working Sonya over the beautiful and languid Elena. It is also evident that men will choose Elena because of her beauty, whatever Sonya's virtues or Elena's lack of them. Friel plays with the characterisation. When Sonya goes to find Astrov, Elena reflects on the difficulty of holding someone else's secrets. Hingley and Frayn translate the line similarly, that there is nothing worse than knowing another's secret and being unable to help. Friel's line — "People shouldn't burden you with their secrets when there's nothing you can do about them" (52) — makes Elena altogether more petulant. He then goes some way to redeem her in the map-reading scene. As Chekhov structures it, Astrov has one very long speech, expounding on his love of forests and his passionate concern for the decline of the district. Astrov's long speech is structurally important, as its passion makes Elena's lack of interest more offensive.

Friel includes four interjections by Elena, all in the first half of the speech. It may have to do with theatrical style, with the fact that long speeches are out of fashion in contemporary naturalistic theatre. He has left the second half of the speech whole, as if trying to maintain as much of the original structure as possible, but the speech does lose some of its momentum. Robert Tracy regrets the interjections, and sees then as a missed opportunity to "examine solipsism in aborted dialogue" (Tracy, 1999: 70). Friel also softens the ending by having Astrov realise that he is boring Elena. Their short exchange at the end softens the impact of the change of subject. Elena's line: "there's something else I'm anxious about" (56) is less abrupt than: "To be perfectly honest, I was thinking about something else" (Hingley: 149).

The heart of Act Three is the meeting at which Serabryakov proposes selling the estate. In Friel's version, the professor is more assertive. There is ambiguity in other translations as to how much he understands of the impact of his proposal. In Frayn's translation he claims to be "a stranger to the practical life" (1987: 39). Friel alters and expands it: "the world of commerce — as some would have it, the 'real world' — I'm afraid I'm foreign to it and it to me" (*Uncle Vanya*: 61). The word "commerce" has resonances from *Translations*, where Hugh uses it as a pejorative. The inverted commas around "real world" suggest not only a lack of acquaintance, but disdain. When Vanya tries to leave, Serabryakov points out that he is being "unfriendly" (Frayn, 1987: 39) or "annoyed" (Hingley: 152). In each case he apologises for causing offence. Friel makes Serabryakov accuse Vanya of belligerence, and follow it up with: "In character of course but out of place today" (*Uncle Vanya*: 61). Friel also expands Serabryakov's mild antipathy towards the countryside to a more pointed phrase: "Country life is inimical to the life of the intellect" (61) — thereby insulting almost everyone else in the room. In other translations, Serabryakov digresses a good deal in his preamble. Friel omits most of this, making Serabryakov much more brisk, and giving the impression less of a nervous man making a difficult decision, than of a man determined to get his own way. Vanya's initial incredulity is brushed aside with the modern: "Let's keep focused on the first stage" (63).

Friel interpolates a few lines of comic relief from Telegin, before driving to the heart of the matter. He sharpens Serabryakov's reactions to Vanya's summary of the history of the estate: how in law it belongs to Sonya, how his father bought it as a dowry for Vera, and was able to afford it only because Vanya resigned his share of any inheritance, how the balance of the loan was paid by Vanya, who managed the estate for twenty-five years. Serabryakov's protestations of impracticality, in Friel's version, sound more like a conveniently adopted negotiating position.

Vanya becomes steadily more agitated, Serabryakov more obdurate, Telegin becomes so distressed he has to leave. As with a great deal of Chekhov, the emotions are unnecessary and self-generated. Serabryakov has pointed out that he will not sell the estate unless he has agreement. It is the *idea* of selling the estate which outrages Vanya, the idea that the professor's impracticality would extend to indifferent ingratitude and a complete disregard for his work on the estate. The proposal to sell the estate has brought Vanya face-to-face with the reality of his life, and he perceives it as an emptiness, devoid of meaning.

Frayn points out, in relation to the attempted shooting, that "missed again", the traditional translation, does not convey the semantic range of the Russian *promakh*: "A *promakh* is not just a miss; it is any kind of mistake or false move" (Frayn, 1987: xxiv). Vanya refers to his life as a *promakh*, in which the attempted murder is just another failure. Friel's "Oh, for God's sake, how could I miss again" (68) refers to the second shot, but conveys something of the larger idea of a confrontation with a life filled with small disappointments.

The consequences of Act Three are worked out in Act Four, which is largely a series of leave-takings. Friel adds something of his own to each of these. Telegin has more German references, but the joke is wearing thin at this point. When Vanya tells Astrov that he saw him kissing Elena, Friel adds the line: "And that nudged you over the top, didn't it?" (72), giving Vanya an explicit motivation for his attempt to shoot Serabryakov, and his theft of morphia from Astrov. In the original, Astrov is required to thumb his nose at Vanya. Friel's change avoids the awkwardness of the original for a modern audience, but is also less ambivalent.

Elena is altered also. When speaking to Vanya, she virtually orders him to speak to Serabryakov: "Go and see Alexander, he wants a word with you" (Hingley: 162), or: "Go and see my husband – he's got something to say to you" (Frayn, 1987: 52). Friel alters the line to: "Alexander wants to say something to you, Vanya. Speak to him before we go, will you?" (74). In these lines, Elena is softened, while Vanya's interjection makes him harder, reminding her of her distant reference to her husband earlier in the play.

Similarly, in her leave-taking from Astrov, Elena's character is altered. They kiss and embrace "*passionately*" (77). Astrov, instead of enjoining Elena to go after they embrace, asks her to stay. He attempts to hold her as she leaves, shifting the dramatic balance. In the original version the embrace is an expression of mutual attraction, and they decide to part. In Friel's version, Astrov is the active participant, and Elena reacts to him. The vignette of two mature people deciding not to pursue a liaison is replaced with a less subtle reading of the passionate man and the reluctant woman.

Elena's farewell to Vanya is also softened. Hingley translates the stage direction as: "*Kisses him on the head and goes out*" (Hingley: 164). Friel's direction states: "*Elena takes his face in both her hands and kisses the top of his head*" (80). She also refers to him as "Lovely man". The picture of a woman "so drugged with idleness that she can't walk straight" (Frayn, 1987: xvi) is ameliorated by these small changes. In some ways, Elena is moved closer to her virtuous prototype in *The Wood Demon*.

Friel expands the return to work by Vanya and Sonya at the end of the act, filling in little details of the accounts on which they are working. He uses the detail to replace Astrov's commentary from the original. A typically Friel touch is the use of Sonia as chorus, but disguising it by interruption:

Sonya	The name on the left-hand column — goods next — cost on the right.
Vanya	I know.
Sonya	As we've always done it.
Vanya	I know Sonya, I know. (81)

He gives the impression of two people settling into old roles which, although familiar, bring no comfort. Sonya's final speech is more hope than expectation: work as hard as you must in this life, and find peace in the next. Vanya, like Sonya, is condemned to work and to find no rest before death. One of Chekhov's preoccupations in the play is the contrast between work and idleness. The idleness which accompanies Serabryakov and his party is poisonous for the estate, but a return to the old patterns of ceaseless drudgery brings no happiness either. They hope, as in *Three Sisters*, that happiness will be given to a future generation, based, in some unspecified way, on their unhappiness.

There is a brilliant absurdity to *A Month in the Country*, as the characters dance around each other in various *pas de deux*, coming, going, falling in and out of love with one another in a manner that could be characterised as a curious mixture of *A Midsummer Night's Dream* and *The Importance of Being Earnest*. The play includes a number of fine comic set-pieces, the humour of which has stood the test of time admirably. Chief among these are the scene between Doctor Shpigelsky and Bolshintsov, where the latter is instructed in the art of wooing a young woman, and a similar scene where the doctor proposes to Lizaveta, the companion of Anna. Friel has taken the nascent humour of these scenes and broadened it considerably, while maintaining contact with the original.

Friel is equivocal about his play's status as a comedy, claiming that it might "impose a reading on the text and [suggest] a response to it that could be inhibiting to actors and audience" (7). Friel's original plays contain many genuinely funny lines and situations, but their vision is a dark one. Where *A Month in the Country* darkens, and Friel's adaptation emphasises this, is in its negative vision of love. Love brings only misery and uncertainty, while marriage is an arrangement for convenience or escape. "All love is a catastrophe", Michel tells Aleksey in Act Two, Scene Three, and certainly love brings no happiness to the participants. The consequences of their love are not, however, tragic. Michel must leave, but there is a suggestion that he will come back after a time. Aleksey must leave, but his sudden ardent love for Natalya is only an infatuation. Vera is the only one whose situation is bleak. She, at seventeen, will marry Bolshintsov, who is in his fifties, in order to escape from Natalya.

At the heart of the play is the mercurial Natalya, at once fearsome and vulnerable, selfish and sweet, whose shifting moods and opinions are a syntagm of contradictions. She attempts to manipulate Vera, she successfully manipulates the hapless Arkady, she fascinates Michel, and captivates, and is in turn captivated by, Aleksey. By turn she rages, swoons, is coquettish or rudely bored, matriarchal or sisterly. She is the driving force of the drama. She is Elena without the moral sense, Natasha with style, a woman playing with her own and with others' emotions in order to feel something. Near the end of Act Two, Scene Two, when Vera assures her that everything will return to normal, Friel gives her the telling line: "can't you see it's the normal that's deranging me, child?" (103).

Although his two acts with their five scenes incorporate the same action as Turgenev's five acts, Friel has changed the order of vignettes within the scenes, and inserted some others. Some of the detail he includes to give it specifically Irish resonances. In the opening of the play, Vera is playing piano offstage. Friel specifies that the music is that of Dublin-born composer John Field, who spent a great deal of his life in Russia, chiefly in St Petersburg and Moscow. Friel uses Field as a means of closing the distance between the Ireland and Russia. In Turgenev's version, there is no music and Vera is in the garden playing with Aleksey and Kolya. In the same way, Michel is reading from *The Count of Monte Cristo* in French in Turgenev's version, but in Friel's version he reads from Sterne's *Tristram Shandy*, itself a novel of gargantuan improbability.

Irish phrases and rhythms are seamlessly incorporated into the conversations, without the deliberately jarring effects obvious in *Three Sisters*. When Anna is finished telling Herr Schaaf about her meeting with Field, she returns to her cards with a typically Hiberno-English cadence: "And that's my trick, thank you very much" (19). The colloquial use of "and" to return to a subject, and the use of "thank you very much" to express mild indignation are quite familiar. Some lines later, Natalya, sarcastically referring to her husband, asks: "[a]mn't I blessed?", using a very Irish version of "am I not" (19). Arkady, in Act Two, Scene Two, asks Michel: "Have you any idea how destroyed I am?" (91).

Much of the revision is concerned with the expectations of modern audiences, and the fact that, according to Friel, Turgenev was never sure that he wanted his plays to be acted, as opposed to read. This opinion is borne out by some extraordinary, not to say impossible, stage directions. Natalya blushes, Vera flushes crimson on several occasions, while Bolshintsov turns red. On at least one other occasion Natalya turns pale. While these subtleties are possible in the theatre of the mind, there is no actor so accomplished as to reproduce them on stage.

One of the changes Friel has made is to omit the character of Kolya, Natalya's son. He has few lines of any narrative importance, and is more talked about in his absence than appearing on stage. Some of his Act One lines are given to Vera. It is a strategy which causes some slight awkwardness in the kite-flying scene in Act One, scene two. Kolya, who in the original has some interest in the kite, is said to be waiting for the others to arrive at the granary. It is a small point, but not adequately resolved.

In Turgenev's play, it is evident that Michel and Natalya are, in terms of the play's own mores, inappropriately close. They are huddled intimately in Act One, as he reads to her. They flirt, they skirt around the subject of love, and the discussion of Aleksey is designed to make Michel jealous. Later in the act, when they are alone, it becomes apparent that they are in love. Friel's adaptation of the scene gains with the addition of fast-paced witty dialogue, but loses some of the subtlety with which Turgenev constructed the scene. In the original version, Natalya, once they are alone, holds her hand out to Michel, who takes it and presses it. In Friel's version, the stage directions state: "*Michel takes Natalya in his arms from behind*" (28), implying a greater degree of intimacy. Michel, in the original, says to Natalya: "I'm looking at you . . . I am happy" (http://gutenberg.net.au). In Friel's line he makes an explicit causal relationship between the halves of the sentence: "to look at you is a great . . . happiness" (28). In Turgenev, it is apparent that the same sentiment is being conveyed, but the lack of physical contact gives the line an emotional charge and the *frisson* of a forbidden liaison. The *caesura* in Friel's line suggests that Michel is searching for a synonym for happiness, or perhaps "happiness" is a safer way of expressing the emotion he is feeling. Turgenev gives Natalya a line that makes it clear, although they profess love for each other, that they are not engaged in a love affair: "You and I have the right to look everybody in the face" (http://gutenberg.net.au).

Friel also deals broadly with the minor characters. Schaaf becomes another in his canon of stage Germans, each abusing the English language for comic effect. Doctor Shpigelsky's role is also expanded. In Turgenev's version, the doctor has been promised three horses by Bolshintov if he broaches the subject of marriage to Vera with Natalya. Friel hints at the horse theme early in his play. When Natalya asks him to stay to dinner, he replies: "Love to. My horse is as wheezy as myself" (34). The doctor's affection for Lizaveta is also established at a much earlier point in Friel's play than it is in Turgenev's. At his first entrance in the original play, Shpigelsky kisses Anna's hand and sits next to Natalya. In Friel's play, he turns attention almost immediately to Lizaveta (24). In Turgenev, there is no connection between the characters until the opening of Act Four.

Matvey and Katya are also extensively re-written. Katya, in Turgenev's hands, is a chronic eavesdropper, a lurker in bushes and behind pillars. She becomes an audience surrogate, included to mine the feeling of impropriety. Friel largely abandons this use of the character. The first scene between her and Matvey, in Act One, Scene Two, has been lengthened substantially. Turgenev is going over traditional ground. Matvey is much older than Katya, but wants to marry her. He sketches his good points. She thanks him for his solicitations and they are interrupted by Schaaf. The scene has a mildly comic feel which is continued into Katya's scene with Schaaf, who also considers himself a suitor. Turgenev never returns to this theme, so it is never resolved. The pace of Friel's version is faster, the lines are shorter, more urgent, and their dialogue takes the form of patter:

Katya	We have discussed you at length on several occasions.
Matvey	Who has?
Katya	Mother and I.
Matvey	What does that mean?
Katya	She says that the gap between our ages — actually the word she used was "chasm" — is so large —
Matvey	I'm only forty-three!
Katya	And so disquieting —
Matvey	I'm full of vigour!
Katya	Indeed so unbridgeable that the possibility of a permanent and a mutually fulfilling relationship between us is — again to use her own word — "pale". (37)

The invention of the mother and the comically elevated dialogue make the scene sparkle. Friel also resolves their rela-

tionship. In Act Two, Scene One, overheard, in an inversion
of Turgenev's scene, by the doctor and Lizaveta, Matvey recounts his encounter with Katya's mother. The directions
state: "*She* [Katya] *is very angry — or pretends to be*" (74).
According to Matvey, Katya's mother is under the impression that they are to marry. The scene concludes with Katya
storming off: "Get out of my road, you sneaky old . . . pig!"
(75). Friel resolves the theme at the very end of the play,
where they both enter "*beaming and move almost in tandem*"
(108).

Friel has omitted the raspberry scene between Katya
and Aleksey from Turgenev's Act Two (his Act One, Scene
Two). When Aleksey and Vera enter, Katya is singing a love
song as she picks. There is a *frisson* as Aleksey joins in the
song, and, while he and Vera assemble a tail on the kite, Katya's singing forms a background to their dialogue. Her attempt to offer more raspberries to Aleksey is refused, and
she, according to the directions, "*goes off without speaking*".
It is a subtly constructed scene, which makes plain to an audience that Katya has feelings for Aleksey, but that he is unaware of her as anything but a servant. It adds a layer of
complexity to the web of relationships that Turgenev has
created.

There is a corresponding scene in Act Four, when Katya
brings Aleksey a message to meet Vera in the outer room.
He offers her a peach, which she accepts with some confusion. The gift then allows Katya to ask if he is really leaving,
which he denies. The scene is a very brief one, whose main
purpose is to bring Aleksey and Vera together, but it manages, with fine economy, to remind the audience of the Ka-
tya/Aleksey theme and to add further confusion to the
question of whether Aleksey will stay or go. Friel circum-
vents the necessity for the scene as a narrative link by giving
Vera the line: "I was afraid Katya mightn't have got the message to you" (78). Omitting the two brief scenes also gives

the play more pace and drives it towards a conclusion. However, the slow pace of Turgenev's play is part of its charm. One feels the unhurried lives of the leisured class. In Turgenev's hands, the complications in the play have almost the status of a game played on the field of their own lives. In Friel's hands, although the dialogue is sparkling and the writing is tighter, it becomes a series of comic events, and loses something in the transformation.

When Aleksey and Vera do meet in Act Two, Scene One, Friel has wrought several fundamental changes to the encounter. Their meeting follows an encounter between Aleksey and Natalya, in which she told him that Vera loved him. In Turgenev's original, she denies it. Although it quickly becomes apparent that it is true, her denial is another part of the complication of their lives. The response Friel invents has its own complexity: "She's [Natalya] so treacherous. She trapped me into saying things I shouldn't have said. And now I've said it again, haven't I?" (78). The line is an opinion on the character of Natalya rather than an exegesis of the confusion in Vera's mindset, as in Turgenev's version.

A little later in the scene, as the two women become more heated, Vera, in Turgenev, declares: "To you I'm not the ward you are watching over [*Ironically*] like an elder sister . . . . I'm your rival" (http://gutenberg.net.au). Friel's version is more muted, with Vera declaring: ". . . you thought I was a rival. But I'm not a rival, Natalya —— I wish to God I were — but I'm not — I'm not . . ." (81). She asserts her womanhood in both versions, but Friel stops short of Turgenev by not having Vera declare her rivalry. In some ways it is an intelligent change, because Vera's rivalry is imaginary, and never developed in the play. It is also a sympathetic simplification of Vera's character by not allowing her to appear pathetic. Friel has taken a narrative loose end and excised it. The breakdown at the end of the speech allows Vera to exit under the cover of embarrassment. A similar exit exists in the original, but some lines later, after Vera has pressed Natalya to declare her love for Aleksey, Friel's version presents a picture of an altogether weaker Vera.

Throughout Turgenev's play, characters are allowed to comment on the action, whether in a few snatched lines, or in a full-blown soliloquy. Friel has dispensed with the minor ones, and even Michel's first short musing has been cut. The main soliloquies belong to Natalya and Michel. In Act One, as their first scene together is coming to an end, the moment of introspection that Michel is given while alone is not mirrored in Friel: "What does it mean? The beginning of the end, or the end? (*brief pause*) Or the beginning?" (http://gutenberg.net.au).

Michel's soliloquy in Act One, Scene Two is just over a third the length of the corresponding speech in Garnett's translation. It omits the references to Natalya's moods and caprices. One gets the impression in Turgenev's version that the household holds its breath each day to see the kind of humour Natalya will present to them. Friel keeps the core of the speech, Michel's fear of losing Natalya. We are told in the stage directions that he "conducts the . . . conversation with himself at a frantic speed" (46). The speech swings between first and second person, as two sides of a personality argue. The complication that Friel gives it is that the swing is uneven, as if both sides were involved, and it becomes unclear by the end which side is which. It is a much more self-consciously literary speech than in Turgenev.

Friel creates a symmetry between this speech and Natalya's soliloquy in Act One, Scene Three by giving both the form of an internal dialogue. At less than half the length of the original, Friel has cut this to the core also. He excises her remorse at the proposed match between Vera and Bolshintsov, Michel and Arkady have been removed from the speech, so all that remains is the core argument. Natalya persuades herself to ask Aleksey if he really loves Vera.

In Turgenev's version, Natalya is given another, short soliloquy before the end of the act. It is principally a vehicle through which Natalya's internal struggle is made evident. Friel cuts this whole section dramatically short. Aleksey enters with Anna and Arkady, cutting out the need for a whole scene. Arkady, not Natalya, is the one who becomes distressed, at seeing his wife and his best friend in an embrace. He is led away by Anna, and Michel follows. There is a theatrical economy in the cut, but it does lead to some awkwardness, as it seems unlikely that Michel would simply follow them out of the room.

The final soliloquy in Turgenev's Act Three belongs to Natalya. Friel has cut it down to the vacillation on whether Aleksey should stay or go. He ignores the other content, where Natalya considers whether she had the right to speak of Vera's infatuation, and the possibility that Aleksey is deceiving her because he is a man. It is, like the others, a dialogue with the self. This speech loses more than the others, because he omits Natalya's almost paranoid deliberation on the possibility of Aleksey's duplicity. It elides a further contradiction in an already complex and contradictory creation.

As Friel has increased the intensity of the humorous lines, so he has intensified the suffering of the characters. In Turgenev's version, it is difficult to empathise with the various possible pairings, as love happens suddenly and without warning, and the changes are, for the most part, unmotivated and bathetic. Friel's altered characterisations increase the reality quotient of the play, and provoke sympathy. A sense of lives unfinished and unfulfilled pervades the ending of the play. One change exemplifies the increased sympathy the audience is made to feel. In Act Five of Turgenev's version, Vera asks Doctor Shpigelsky about Bolshintsov's character. On being assured that she could mould him to her will, she agrees to marry him. In Friel's version, Vera asks: "I've really only one question . . . is he the kind of man who

would strike me?" (98–9). Violence has not appeared anywhere in the play up to this point. Its intrusion now illustrates Vera's vulnerability and uncertainty. It is a bold stroke,
not because of its suddenness, but due to the fact that the
doctor "*takes her in his arms as if she were a child and rocks
her*" (99) emphasising the poignancy of the situation.

Anna, who in Turgenev's version of the play is a majestic
foil to the action, is given a summary speech by Friel as the
play draws to a close. She and Michel, amid the departures
and revelations, have found themselves together:

> She has the unqualified love of a very good man. But
> for some women . . . that doesn't seem to be
> enough. And instead of that love satisfying, enriching,
> it becomes another form of . . . suffocation. So that
> all their life is dissatisfying, even turbulent. And the
> people who offer their love without reservation . . .
> they are the fortunate ones . . . even though they
> don't believe they are . . . (106–7)

She has, earlier in Friel's scene, revealed to Arkady that his
father had had a mistress in Moscow. She did nothing about
it for the sake of peace. Friel creates a symmetry between
generations. Arkady endures a volatile wife, as Anna had endured an unfaithful husband, while they both love without
reservation. It is a curious kind of good fortune.

In working on Turgenev's *Fathers and Sons*, Friel faced
the challenge of both language and form. Adapting a novel
for the stage necessitates the omission of a great deal of material, and conversion of essential narrative into dialogue. As
a result, even though the novel and the play share a title and
a storyline, they are distinct works.

The necessary changes mean that some streamlining and
simplification take place. In place of the scene at the post-
station, Friel opens the play with Fenichka, Dunyasha and the
baby. With great economy, but with a measured pace, he

introduces Fenichka's origins as a servant, her new but uncertain status as mistress of the house, her strained relationship with Pavel, and Pavel's over-refined, westernised tastes.
All these become matters of importance later in the play.
Dunyasha's dialect is, from the start, very Donegal. Friel settles Irish dialect words, as he did in his other translations,
mostly on the servants, with occasional incursions by the
members of the landed gentry.

The play, like the novel, is about the similarities and contrasts between the older and younger generations. The tensions and correspondences are raised with the same
sureness they were in *Philadelphia, Here I Come!*, but using
very different materials. Arkady is destined to become his
father, a well-meaning estate manager, under the benevolent
thumb of his wife. Turgenev, who was a member of the
older generation when he wrote the novel, appears to be
suggesting that happiness consists in following convention,
and that reform, if it happens, must happen organically. It
ironically falls to Bazarov to have the potential to repeat
Pavel's history, of which he is openly contemptuous, and be
devastated by a colossal passion. Only his early death interrupts that possibility. Richard Freeborn summed up Turgenev's new kind of hero: "his commitment to science and
materialism, his negative cast of mind, his self-assurance,
cynicism, energy, repudiation of aesthetic feeling and everything romantic" (Freeborn, 1991: xii). In other words, Bazarov is a nineteenth-century teenage rebel, albeit that he is
in his early twenties.

The most forceful example of the confrontation between
the generations, in both the play and the novel, is the duel
between Bazarov and Pavel. Bazarov has kissed Fenichka,
and Pavel's sense of decorum is outraged. His challenge is
formal, polite and circumspect, but nonetheless firm. In the
novel, Bazarov reacts with cynical irony, but also with more
than a little pride. Their discussion of the preparations is, in

Freeborn's word, farcical. Friel allows Bazarov a moment of
panic when he realises that Pavel is serious. In the novel,
Bazarov suggests the servant Piotr as second, to Pavel's dis-
approval. In the play, Pavel proposes all the arrangements,
while Bazarov stammers and splutters. It is the only time in
the play when Bazarov's nihilist façade cracks. In fact, in the
novel, Turgenev points out that his nihilism is not a pose,
nor even a conviction, but a fundamental part of Bazarov's
personality. In recreating Bazarov as a hero whose humanity
can be reached, albeit by fear, Friel produces a more modern, more recognisable type. After the duel, the stage directions describe Bazarov as: "*now a fully mature young man —
neither in his clothes nor in his demeanour is there any trace of
the student. His manner is brisk, efficient, almost icy*" (202). The
duel has been a rite of passage for him. It is less so in the
novel, just a means by which he can detach himself further
from those around him. For Turgenev, changes in Bazarov
are made by his passion for Anna, and the inability of either
science or nihilism to account for the way he feels.

Turgenev supplies Bazarov with a set of doting, if somewhat down-at-heel, parents, and Friel captures their essence
to perfection. He compresses the action and conversation of
several days into a single scene. Their religiosity, supersti-
tion, and adherence to the slightest convention provides an
interesting psychological matrix for the emergence of Bazarov's nihilism, and his desire to sweep away all that his
parents represent, or, from his point of view, all that holds
them prisoner. Friel does allow Bazarov to be more at ease
with his parents than Turgenev does. Friel's Bazarov teases
his mother and kisses her hand over lunch, but reverts to
the novel's spleen once his parents have withdrawn.

Fenichka is another part of the generational tension; the
novel's title, *Ottsy i Deti*, literally translates as *Fathers and Children*. Fenichka's social evolution is largely ignored by Turgenev, but Friel turns it into a minor theme. In the novel she

addresses the members of the Kirsanov family formally, but Friel allows this to gradually change in the course of the play. At the opening she is uncertain with Pavel, and intimate with Dunyasha. By Act Two, Scene Three, she is able to sever her allegiance to the household servants, as illustrated by the admonition of Dunyasha in defence of Pavel (224–5).

The novel itself has a well-defined class-consciousness. Bazarov is sensitive about his humble origins and scorns "aristos", even while falling in love with a woman he accuses of being one. Piotr is lampooned for aping the latest fashions, even though he is a servant. Friel's play, however, allows for the possibility of social mobility in the person of Fenichka. Pavel's fussing over the propriety of the relationship between her and Nicolai is quietly dropped, and all that remains is their initially "uneasy" relationship. Richard York has pointed out that Friel's portrayal of the relationship between Russian masters and servants was inaccurate, that the: "sense of hierarchy was . . . much more strongly maintained" (York, 1993: 171). This is something of a red herring, but it serves to highlight the changes Friel has made in the fabric of the work. In many ways, the relationship between Nicolai and Fenichka is the model for that between Christopher Gore and Margaret O'Donnell in *The Home Place*.

Anna Sergeyevna Odintsov is a very complex creation in the novel, introduced over quite a long narrative space. She makes a grand entrance at the governor's ball, and stuns both Arkady and Bazarov with her manner and intelligence. She is much more like the sphinx of Pavel's story. Turgenev describes her as "a fairly strange creature. Having no prejudices, not even having any strong beliefs, she was not on her way to discovering anything" (Freeborn, 1991: 88). Friel describes her as elegant, carefully groomed and circumspect (*Plays 2*: 144), Pavel describes her as "emotionally dehydrated" (134), but the self-containment and grandeur of the novel's character are lost. So too is Arkady's passion for her.

Friel briefly allows him to compete with Bazarov, before surrendering him to Katya. Friel softens her character. In the novel we are told that "She had hardly been able to stand the late lamented Odintsov . . ." (Freeborn, 1991: 88). In the play, she makes it clear that, whatever the drawbacks in their marriage, she misses him (153). At the point in the play at which the statement is made, Bazarov is attempting to impress her with his cold, intelligent wit. It may be that Friel is attempting to warm Anna's character by way of contrast.

Some of Bazarov's complexity is sacrificed to narrative also. In the novel, his declaration of love for Anna, and the incident where he kisses Fenichka, occur more than forty pages apart. Friel telescopes the time scheme, so that both incidents occur in Act Two, Scene One in quick succession, making Bazarov appear more of a serial seducer than a young man caught between his head and his hormones. In Chapter Seventeen, Bazarov's feelings for Anna are dissected forensically, something which the play cannot do. The details of his nihilism can only be touched on in the play, although Friel captures the contradictory essence of a crude philosophy based on rejection of traditional authority-structures — church, state, and family — which Pavel finds so infuriating. Arkady's nihilism is never more than admiration of Bazarov, and a wish to be his acolyte.

Friel does use the discussion of nihilism to emphasise a fascination of his own. Bazarov is berating Pavel for his old-fashioned liberal attitudes. In the novel he says: "Aristocratism, liberalism, progress, principles . . . just think what a lot of foreign . . . and useless words!" (Freeborn, 1991: 49). Friel alters this to: "liberalism, progress, principles, civilisation — they have no meaning in Russia. They are imported words. Russia doesn't need them." He omits the idea of aristocracy as a beneficial influence, and substitutes "civilisation". He intensifies Turgenev's "foreign" by using "imported". The idea of colonisation is close to the surface in this passage.

Russia, Bazarov maintains, is being forced to deviate from her natural course by linguistic and cultural colonisation. Friel would probably have a certain sympathy with this view. Bazarov's solution, however, is change by force, which even in Ireland led to a long and unnecessarily bloody "armed struggle".

Turgenev's novel contains other expertly drawn characters, which Friel omits. Sitkinov, the slavophile, is the means by which Turgenev introduces Anna. As a character he reminds one forcibly of a rat, and is used to poke fun at student pretension and to advance the narrative. It must have been a difficult decision to omit a character who was already innately theatrical. Likewise, he omits Eudoxie Kukshina, the louche, grubby pseudo-intellectual that Turgenev uses as a foil for Anna. The chapter that Arkady, Bazarov and Sitkinov spend in her company mocks the intellectual pretensions of the Russian middle classes, but the requirements of theatrical discourse, and the practical inclusion of an extra set, made her inclusion impossible.

Other details show Friel's practical theatrical sense. In the novel, Bazarov shoots Pavel in the leg. In the play, in order to keep him mobile, the wound is moved to his arm. In the novel, Nicolai has some letters written by Anna's mother to his late wife, and Arkady takes them to her in Chapter Twenty-two. In the play, Nicolai announces in Act One, Scene One that he has been contacted by Anna, who has letters from his wife to her mother. This is the plot device used to bring Anna to the Kirsanov estate. In the novel, Nicolai is in his forties. Friel does not specify an age, but his actions are those of an older man. His benign bumbling is very similar to Christopher Gore. The awful black sherry produced by Bazarov's father becomes the sherry produced by Nicolai to welcome Arkady and Bazarov. Friel uses it as Turgenev does, as an index of the separation of the generations (126).

Act Two, Scene Three is largely an invention of Friel's own. Arkady's visit to Bazarov's parents after his death never happens in the novel, but it provides an opportune vehicle for the remaining narrative. The death, like the duel, happens offstage, as if Friel were basing his dramaturgy on Chekhov, which may well be the case. Bazarov's death is more heroic in the play. Vassily and he were engaged in fighting a typhus epidemic. "Some nights he didn't get home at all", Vassily tells Arkady (215). He becomes infected and dies. In the novel, he asks the local doctor if he can assist the autopsy of a typhus victim, and infects himself accidentally through a cut. Turgenev's version of Bazarov's death emphasises the futility that Bazarov himself was feeling; it is a nihilistic death because it was for nothing. Friel's Bazarov dies for the peasants, in the same way that in the novel he claimed he was attacking the old order for the peasants, whom he despised.

The final scene is less successful. It attempts to tie up the loose ends in the same way as the novel does in the final chapter, but lacks the scope of the third person narrative. Turgenev is able to tell us that Nicolai and Arkady had a double wedding six months later, that Pavel moved to Dresden, that Anna married our of conviction rather than love, that Bazarov's parents visited his grave frequently. Friel contents himself with a soirée to mark Pavel's departure, at which the future is mapped out. It ends with Katya and Nicolai singing: "Drink to me only with thine eyes", an unsatisfactorily sentimental conclusion to the play.

In *The Yalta Game*, Friel attacks Chekhov's story, "The Lady with the Lapdog", with *brio*. Almost all of the principal features of the play are his own, and he has borrowed only the bones of the plot. He falls back on the theatrical device he used so effectively in *Faith Healer* and *Molly Sweeney*, the long monologue, but breaks it with dialogue between the play's two characters. They narrate events in turn, while slipping in and out of the drama themselves. In this way, the play becomes something of a game, self-consciously theatrical like *Dancing at Lughnasa*. In the story the narration, although third person, was from Gurov's perspective, and followed him through the plot. The shared narration provides a balance between the two perspectives, but in doing so sacrifices some of the impenetrability of Anna's character.

The game of the title may be read in several ways. Gurov states that the "great unacknowledged Yalta game" (14) is watching the other tourists, and that it is a game played by everyone out of boredom. The game can be the supposedly casual morals of the transient inhabitants of Yalta, although Gurov in the story dismisses this. It can be, and this is Friel's addition to the story, Gurov's habit of creating imaginary lives for the other inhabitants of Yalta. Initially, this is a device to attract Anna, and works well in doing so. Innocent coffee drinkers metamorphose into crazed heroin addicts for Anna's amusement. This game has the effect of making Gurov a more attractive character than he is in the story. We are told in the opening paragraphs of the original story that he "had been unfaithful to her [his wife] often, and, probably on that account, almost always spoke ill of women, and when they were talked about in his presence, used to call them 'the lower race'" (www.gutenberg.org/files). Despite the fact that he prefers the company of "the lower race", Gurov in the short story is a cynical misogynist for whom the experience of love is an uncomfortable one.

The game is, in essence, as much playing with lives as it is playing with words. Gurov says his degree was in philology, while in the story it is an unspecified Arts degree. Friel has focused attention once again on the status of words in creating reality. It is the creation of fictional alternative realities that attracts Anna to him. The dog of the story's title is petted and fussed over in the play, but is invisible, a creation of words and the theatre. In the story the dog remains unnamed. In the play it is named Yalta by Gurov, so that, when Anna goes home, she brings Yalta with her, a constant reminder of her infidelity and her love for Gurov.

In many of Friel's plays, characters invent their own reality; in *The Yalta Game*, they begin by inventing realities for other people, but the game reaches such an intensity that Gurov half-persuades himself that Anna was his own invention. On his own after Anna has left Yalta, he warms to the idea that the affair never happened: "Maybe it was no more actual than the fictional lives I invested the people in the square with" (27). Gurov argues with himself, much as Natalya and Michel did in *A Month in the Country*. Although he berates himself for callousness in attempting to consign Anna to the realm of the fictive, the speech concludes curiously: "there was one element I was happy to consign to the imagined. That damned dog was definitely make-believe. Definitely never any Yalta" (28). Friel is playing with theatrical conventions. He has used invisible characters before, most famously Gar Private in *Philadelphia, Here I Come!* In *Dancing at Lughnasa*, the seven-year-old Michael never appears, and the other characters address empty space. His lines are spoken by the adult Michael, who, although visible to the audience, is invisible to the other characters. Gurov has petted the dog, and attempted to feed her a biscuit. Obviously, from the point of view of the audience, there is no dog, but the conventions of the stage demand that they accept its existence. To then deny the existence of the dog in such a vehement manner casts doubt over the authority of any of the narration. From that point on the dog is never mentioned again. It ceases to exist on the word of Gurov.

Back in Moscow, the game "inverted itself" (29). His former reality now becomes imagined, and what he can imagine, his memories, become real. Anna, on the other hand, imagines Gurov arriving at her door, or meeting her in the street. By means of this inversion of actuality, their affair becomes not only inevitable, but the only reality they have.

Finally, the game is the affair begun by Gurov and Anna, which segues into a situation from which they cannot escape. Gurov in the story sets out to seduce Anna as a relief from boredom. He is embarrassed by her shame after their first sexual encounter; his eroded moral sense sees it as "strange and inappropriate". The same elements are present in the play, but the balance suggests that Friel's Gurov, although outwardly cynical, is more easily moved: "Gurov felt bored already, listening to her. He was irritated by the naive tone, by this remorse, so unexpected and inopportune; but for the tears in her eyes, he might have thought she was jesting . . ." (www.gutenberg.org/files). Friel's Gurov is surprised rather than irritated: "the emotion was genuine. Completely" (22). The following day, Anna joins in the Yalta game, inventing suggestive actions for a couple across the street.

In Chekhov's story, the end is uncertain. They hope for a time in which they will not have to meet in secret:

> in a little while the solution would be found, and then a new and splendid life would begin; and it was clear to both of them that they had still a long, long road before them, and that the most complicated and difficult part of it was only just beginning. (www.gutenberg.org/files/13415/13415.txt)

It ends on a note of self-deception, with a slightly moral tone. They are, after all, no happier than they were before they met, and their lives are considerably more complicated. In the play, it is Anna who voices this self-deception. Gurov, aware that it will end, does not tell her so (35). She is aware that "we would have to stumble on together for a very long time; because the end was coming even though it was still a long way off" (35). For her, the end is the end of their need for secrecy, for Gurov, the end is the end of the affair.

The Bear is probably Chekhov's best known short work, often anthologised and beloved of amateur theatre. It is, by any standards, a slight piece. Chekhov himself referred to it as "a piffling little Frenchified vaudeville" (Frayn, 1988: xxxi). By and large, Friel is faithful to the original, but he increases the intensity of the play. Every detail is magnified, every passion exaggerated. In the original play, Smirnov, when describing his love life, declares that he has refused twelve women, and nine have refused him. In Friel's version this becomes: "Married three times. Lived with ten others at different times; jilted four and was jilted by six. Fought duels over five" (*Three Plays After*: 52).

He coarsens the language, presumably because *damn* or its equivalent will not resonate with a modern audience as foul. He moves Elena's calling Smirnov a bear to an earlier point, so that she can also call him a bastard. He turns Elena's exaggerated grief for her husband into vengeance, a guilt-trip aimed beyond the grave. Looking at a photograph of her dead husband, she tells Luka: "But *I* shall be faithful unto the grave — I shall prove to him that *I* am capable of love. And he'll see at last from beyond the tomb exactly what sort of woman I was" (Frayn, 1988: 22). Friel's version pushes the emotion a little further: "I shut myself off . . . totally faithful to you, and there you are, still looking beyond me with your slithery eyes and your weak smile . . ." (46). The change from third person narration to direct address makes her dislike of the husband she loved, her determination to make him feel guilty even after he is dead, more intense. It paves the way for her temper and her passion moments later.

The scene in which they prepare for their duel is still a fine set-piece of comic invention, with much opportunity for both actors to provoke laughter. The dialogue is sharp, witty, and rapid. Friel has echoes of it in his version of the duel between Pavel and Bazarov in *Fathers and Sons*, but here it is unambiguously comic. Friel adapts the scene so that Smirnov's admiration for the pistols gradually transfers to Elena. It is a well-worn comic device, but highly effective. The end of the play, in which Elena and Smirnov fall for each other is highly improbable, but, according to the play's peculiar internal logic, it is also inevitable.

The most curious piece in *Three Plays After* must be *Afterplay*, in which Sonya from *Uncle Vanya* and Andrey from *Three Sisters* meet in a café in Moscow in the 1920s. There is always a curiosity about the lives of characters in drama beyond the final curtain, but modern criticism frowns on such speculation, considering it an impertinence. Art is untrammelled by such self-imposed limitations. *Afterplay* is a sequel in that it happens long after the original plays, but it looks backwards rather than forwards, and its poignancy lies in the way things have happened, rather than in any new action.

The play received mixed reviews. *Sunday Times* critic John Peter claimed it added "nothing to the original". Alan Bird called it "bland and prosaic". *The Washington Post*'s Peter Marks called the play "an indulgence" and made the point that if one were not familiar with the original plays, then much of the allusion of the text is lost. Philip Fisher reported that the play was "beautifully and tenderly written, and significantly adds to the Chekhov canon". The reviews exhibit a mystification with Friel's work that is not unusual.

It is true that *Afterplay* is opaque without knowledge of the originals. There is much allusion to the past lives of the characters, and a corresponding loss to an audience. Friel attempts to compensate by making both fill in enough of the back-story to make it comprehensible. One loses the sense of a Chekhovian presence without this information. What is left, however, is pure Friel.

Two people meet in a run-down café in Moscow. Andrey says he is a violinist, rehearsing *La Bohème*, his wife is dead and he has "a very gifted daughter and an absolutely brilliant son" (*Three Plays After*: 73). He is, in fact, a street musician, whose wife has left him, whose daughter has all but lost contact with him and whose son is in a Moscow jail. Sonya, who claims that the bank and the Ministry of Agriculture were backing forestry on her estate, is in financial difficulties and may lose it all. She drinks, is terrified of the future, and may be fabricating the extent of her relationship with Astrov.

Andrey and Sonya lie about themselves. Both are obsessed by and trapped in the past. Buried in the smalltalk and the revisions of their pasts and presents lies an irremediable unhappiness. They take comfort in each others' company, in their mutual misery, for a short time, and then move on. The play is another facet of Friel's work on communication. In earlier plays, lies acquired the status of reality, and truth became a mobile, indefinable entity. Here, infused with Chekhovian realism, the characters cannot quite bring themselves to believe their own lies, or even to hold on to them for very long. Their notions of themselves are stripped away, not by the harshness of life or the cruelty of circumstance, but by the innate goodness of the characters themselves. Andrey remains the ineffectual, bumbling, but ultimately benign character he was in *Three Sisters*. Sonya, although ground down by hardship, has the same fortitude she showed at the end of *Uncle Vanya*. She will go on.

The play is also about the stranglehold the past has on the present, another theme Friel has visited before. In *Aristocrats*, the O'Donnells are forever recalling their glorious past, in *Living Quarters*, the Butlers are condemned to reliving it. "And a complete break with the past — that would be such a release, wouldn't it? (*Three Plays After*: 78), Sonya says, speaking of her plan to plant trees on her estate. She does not appear to realise that planting trees feeds directly into her obsession with Astrov.

To contemplate the futures of Chekhov's characters, Friel has created a 1920s Russia in which, as Bird has pointed out, the Bolshevik Revolution appears not to have happened. Sonya can still go to the bank, her estate is still in private ownership. One presumes that a busker in a bourgeois dress-suit would be unwelcome on the streets of Moscow. Bird uses it as a criticism of the play, but it is a necessary condition if the play is to exist at all. The estate would have been taken after the revolution and turned into a collective. Natasha would be unlikely to live in a mansion on the bank of a river (85). Bobik would be in a labour camp, or executed. By removing political interference from their lives, Friel has allowed the characters to play out their own personal tragedies rather than be carried along by historical ones. The play allows for a combination of the strengths of both playwrights: Friel's gift for characterisation, and for allowing his characters to express themselves through falsehood; and Chekhov's unwavering humanity and attention to the small details of commonplace lives.

Friel's Russian translations begin with an expressed desire to incorporate Irish voices, expressions, and rhythms into a domain that had been dominated by received standard English. From the initial line-by-line translation, one can see an increase in confidence, where the playwright's instincts begin to take over from the cautious "translator". *Uncle Vanya* contains far more of Friel than does *Three Sisters*, and he allows himself additional latitude in the translations and adaptations of Turgenev. The result is a number of plays which are made accessible to an Irish audience, and which have been liberated from starched Edwardian prose. More importantly, it is, as Friel might put it, keeping a kind of piety with the past.

Afterword

The Friel canon, while embracing many different theatrical forms, has at its centre a recognisable constellation of obsessions to which Friel returns from different perspectives, as if to examine them from every available theatrical angle. Plays about memory gradually metamorphose into plays about the nature, construction, and deconstruction of external reality, or about the ways in which even false memories of the past construct the Self of the present. Plays about communication grow into plays about the slippage of language and the difficulty of capturing meaning. In his later work, both the words he uses and their possible meanings become unstable, melting away into music, or exploding into atavistic dance. Plays about the nature of Irishness become plays about the near-impossibility of defining what Irishness was, is, or might become. Translations from Russian become, in effect, translations from English. From the outset, loyalty was a contested ideal in Friel's plays, and the later plays deepen and complicate the argument. Belief system are interrogated in many ways. Political beliefs, religious sentiment, personal loyalties all become unpicked. In all the plays, the themes overlap and interweave, turn back on and interrogate each other, becoming a dialogue that progresses throughout Friel's lifetime in the theatre.

A statement of themes makes the plays sound austere and cerebral, yet part of the stagecraft of Friel is that he is able to present a range of recognisable characters and plausible plots, clothing his intellectual probing in everyday conversation and, for the most part, realistic settings, whose symbolism is all the more resonant for being based on commonplaces. When he does stray into the impossible, when dead characters speak or when settings are at once real and imaginary, they are still recognisable and provide touchstones for an audience. Humanity is still the centre of his concern.

It is possible, across the range and years of Friel's work, to observe, not without some faltering, the growth of a master dramatist. His handful of masterpieces compare with the best of late twentieth/early twenty-first century world drama, while his lesser plays are of interest for the light they shed on the evolution of one of Ireland's finest modern playwrights.

Bibliography

The Plays of Brian Friel

[Note: The dates listed here refer to years of publication, not of first production. For production dates, see the Chronology.]

Aristocrats (1980; reprinted 1999), Loughcrew, Oldcastle, County Meath, Ireland: Gallery Press.

Communication Cord, The (1989; reprinted 1999), Loughcrew: Gallery Press.

Crystal and Fox (1984), Dublin: Gallery Press.

Dancing at Lughnasa (1990), London: Faber and Faber.

Enemy Within, The (1979; 2nd edition 1992), Loughcrew: Gallery Press.

Faith Healer (1991), Loughcrew: Gallery Press.

Fathers and Sons (1987), London: Faber and Faber.

Freedom of the City, The (1992), Loughcrew: Gallery Press.

Gentle Island, The (1973; reprinted 1993), Loughcrew: Gallery Press.

Give Me Your Answer, Do! (1997), Loughcrew: Gallery Press.

Home Place, The (2005), Loughcrew: Gallery Press.

Living Quarters (1992), Loughcrew: Gallery Press.

London Vertigo, The (1990), Loughcrew: Gallery Press.

Lovers: Winners, Losers (1984; reprinted 1999), Loughcrew: Gallery Press.

Loves of Cass McGuire, The (1984; reprinted 1992), Loughcrew: Gallery Press.

Making History (1989), London: Faber and Faber.

Molly Sweeney (1994), Loughcrew: Gallery Press.

Month in the Country, A (1992), Loughcrew: Gallery Press.

Mundy Scheme, The, in *Two Plays* (1970), New York: Farrar Strauss and Giroux.

Performances (2003), Loughcrew: Gallery Press.

Philadelphia, Here I Come! (1965), London: Faber and Faber.

Plays 1 (1996), *Philadelphia, Here I Come!, The Freedom of the City, Living Quarters, Aristocrats, Faith Healer* and *Translations*, edited and introduced by Seamus Deane, London: Faber and Faber.

Plays 2 (1999), *Dancing at Lughnasa, Fathers and Sons, Making History, Wonderful Tennessee* and *Molly Sweeney*, edited and introduced by Christopher Murray, London: Faber and Faber.

Three Plays After (2002), Loughcrew: Gallery Press.

Three Sisters (1981; 2nd edition 1992), Loughcrew: Gallery Press.

Translations (1981; reprinted 2000), London: Faber and Faber.

Uncle Vanya (1998), Loughcrew: Gallery Press.

Volunteers (1989), Loughcrew: Gallery Press.

Wonderful Tennessee (1993, repr. 1996), Loughcrew: Gallery Press.

Yalta Game, The (2001), Loughcrew: Gallery Press.

Other Primary Works

Chekhov, Anton (1916), *Plays by Anton Tchekov*, translated by Constance Garnett, New York: Macmillan.

Chekhov, Anton (1987), *Uncle Vanya*, translated and introduced by Michael Frayn.

Chekhov, Anton (1988), *Chekhov: Plays*, translated by Michael Frayn, London: Methuen.

Chekhov, Anton (1998), *Uncle Vanya*, translated by Marian Fell, edited by Kathy Casey, Ontario: Dover.

Chekhov, Anton (1998), *Five Plays*, translated by Ronald Hingley, Oxford: OUP.

Chekhov, Anton (1998), *Three Sisters,* translated by Constance Garnett, www.eldritchpress.org/ac/sisters.htm.

Chekhov, Anton (1999), *Uncle Vanya*, translated by Marian Fell (unacknowledged), www.gutenberg.org/dirs/etext99/vanya 10h. htm

Chekhov, Anton (2003), *Plays by Anton Chekhov,* second series, translated, with an introduction, by Julius West www.gutenberg.org/dirs/etext05/8pla210.txt

Chekhov, Anton (2004), *The Lady with the Dog and Other Stories,* translated by Constance Garnett, www.gutenberg.org/files/13415/13415.txt

Heaney, Seamus (1966), *Death of a Naturalist,* London: Faber and Faber.

Turgenev, Ivan (1991), *Fathers and Sons*, translated and introduced by Richard Freeborn, Oxford: Oxford UP.

Turgenev, Ivan (2003), *A Month in the Country*, translated by Constance Garnett, http://gutenberg.net.au/ebooks03/03008 31h.html

Turgenev, Ivan (1998), *Fathers and Children*, translated by Richard Hare, www.eldritchpress.org/ist/fas.htm

Secondary Works

Agnew, Paddy (1980), "Talking to Ourselves" in Delaney (2000), pp. 144–8.

Andrews, Elmer (1995), *The Art of Brian Friel: Neither Dream Nor Reality*, London: Macmillan.

Andrews, J. H. (1992–3), "Notes for a Future Edition of Brian Friel's *Translations*", *Irish Review*, Vol. 13, pp. 93–106.

Barker, Francis, Peter Hulme, Margaret Iverson and Diana Loxley, eds. (1986), *Literature, Politics, and Theory: Papers from the Essex Conference 1976–84*, London: Methuen.

Bertha, Csilla (1999), "Six Characters in Search of a Faith: The Mythic and the Mundane in *Wonderful Tennessee*", *Irish University Review*, Vol. 29, No. 1, pp. 119–135.

Bhaba, Homi K. (1986), "The Discourse of Colonialism", in Barker et al. (1986), pp. 148–172.

Boland, Eavan (1973), "Brian Friel: Derry's Playwright", in Delaney (2000), pp. 112-16.

Burke, Patrick (1999), "'Them Class of People's a Very Poor Judge of Character': Friel and the South", *Irish University Review*, Vol. 29, No. 1, pp. 42–7.

Carvalho, Paulo Eduardo (2006), "About Some Healthy Intersections: Brian Friel and Field Day" in Morse *et al*, pp. 251-269.

Comiskey, Ray (1982), "Rehearsing Friel's New Farce" in Delaney (2000), pp. 163–7.

Copleston, Frederick, S.J. (1962), *A History of Philosophy*, Vol. 2:i, New York: Doubleday.

Coult, Tony (2006), *About Friel: the Playwright and the Work*, London: Faber and Faber.

Cronin, Michael (2006), *Translation and Identity*, London and New York: Routledge.

Dantanus, Ulf (1985), *Brian Friel: The Growth of an Irish Dramatist*, Gothenburg: Acta Universitatis Gothoborgensis.

Deane, Seamus (1984), "Introduction" in *Selected Plays of Brian Friel*, London: Faber and Faber, pp. 11–22. Reprinted as *Plays 1* (1996), London: Faber and Faber.

Delaney, Paul, ed. (2000), *Brian Friel in Conversation*, Ann Arbor: University of Michigan Press.

Dineen, Patrick S. (1927), *Fóclóir Gaedhilge agus Béarla: An Irish-English Dictionary*, Dublin: Irish Texts Society.

Friel, Brian (1971), "Self-Portrait: Brian Friel talks about his Life and Work, in Delaney (2000), pp. 98–108.

Friel, Brian (1972), "Plays Peasant and Unpeasant", in Murray (1999), pp. 51–6.

Gillespie, Elgy (1981) "The Saturday Interview: Brian Friel" in Delaney (2000), pp. 153–7.

Gussow, Mel (1991), "From Ballybeg to Broadway", in Delaney (2000), pp. 202–12.

Harris, Claudia W. (1997), "The Engendered Space: Performing Friel's Women from Cass McGuire to Molly Sweeney", in Kerwin (1997), pp. 43–76.

Heaney, Seamus (1980), "Digging Deeper: Brian Friel's *Volunteers*" in *Preoccupations*, London: Faber and Faber.

Heaney, Seamus (1999), *Beowulf*, London: Faber and Faber.

Jent, William (1994), "Supranational Civics: Poverty and the Politics of Representation in Brian Friel's *The Freedom of the City*", *Modern Drama*, Vol. 37, pp. 568–87.

Joyce, James (1917; reprinted 1992), *A Portrait of the Artist as a Young Man*, Ware, Hertfordshire: Wordsworth Classics.

Joyce, James (1977) *Ulysses*, Harmondsworth: Penguin.

Kavanagh, Patrick (1964; reprinted 1972), *Collected Poems*, London: Martin Brian & O'Keeffe.

Kearney, Richard (1997), "Language Play: Brian Friel and Ireland's Verbal Theatre" in Kerwin (1997), pp. 77–116.

Kerwin, William, ed. (1997), *Brian Friel: a Casebook*, New York and London: Garland.

Kilroy, Thomas (1999), "Friendship", *Irish University Review*, Vol. 29, No. 1, pp. 83–9.

Krause, David (1997), "The Failed Words of Brian Friel", *Modern Drama*, Vol. 40, pp. 359–73.

Maxwell, D.E.S. (1973), *Brian Friel*, Lewisburg: Bucknell UP.

McGrath, F.C. (1999), *Brian Friel's (Post)Colonial Drama: Language, Illusion and Politics*, New York: Syracuse UP.

Morse, Donald E., Csilla Bertha and Mária Kurdi (2006), *Brian Friel's Dramatic Artistry*, Dublin: Carysfort Press.

Murray, Christopher (1999), *Brian Friel: Essays, Diaries, Interviews: 1964–1999*, London: Faber and Faber.

Murray, Christopher (1999a), "Friel and O'Casey Juxtaposed", *Irish University Review*, Vol. 29, No. 1, pp. 16–29.

Ó hAodha, Micheál (1974), *Theatre in Ireland*, Oxford: Blackwell.

O'Brien, Eugene (2001), *Seamus Heaney: Creating Irelands of the Mind*, Dublin: The Liffey Press.

O'Brien, Eugene (2002) *Seamus Heaney and the Place of Writing*, Gainesville: University Press of Florida.

O'Brien, Flann (1939; reprinted 1980), *At Swim-Two-Birds*, Harmondsworth: Penguin.

O'Brien, Flann/Myles na gCopaleen (1975), *An Béal Bocht*, 4th edition, Dublin: Dolmen Press.

O'Brien, George (1997), "*Volunteers*: Codes of Power, Modes of Resistance", in Kerwin (1997).

O'Casey, Seán (1966; reprinted 1980), *Three Plays*, London: Pan.

O'Connor, Ulick (1981), "Friel Takes Derry by Storm", in Delaney (2000), pp. 158–60.

O'Donnell, Donal (1981) "Friel and a Tale of Three Sisters", in Delaney (2000), pp. 149–52.

O'Kelly, Fachtna (1975), "Can the Critics Kill a Play" in Delaney (2000), pp. 117–19.

O'Toole, Fintan (1982), "The Man from God Knows Where" in Delaney (2000), pp. 168–177.

O'Toole, Fintan (1993), "Marking Time: From *Making History* to *Dancing at Lughnasa*", in Peacock (1993), pp. 202–14.

Peacock, Alan (1993), *The Achievement of Brian Friel*, Gerrards Cross: Colin Smythe.

Pine, Richard (1990), *Brian Friel and Ireland's Drama*, London: Routledge.

Pine, Richard (1999), *The Diviner: The Art of Brian Friel*, Dublin: UCD Press.

Roche, Anthony, ed. (2006), *The Cambridge Companion to Brian Friel*, Cambridge, CUP.

Rushe, Desmond (1970), "Kathleen Mavourneen, Here Comes Brian Friel", in Delaney (2000), pp. 79–88.

Saussure, Ferdinand de (1981), *Course in General Linguistics*, ed. Charles Bally and Albert Sechehaye, trans. Wade Baskin, New York: Fontana.

Smith, William and John Lockwood, eds. (1987), *Chambers Murray Latin–English Dictionary*, London and Edinburgh: Chambers/John Murray.

Stoppard, Tom (1980), *Dogg's Hamlet, Cahoot's Macbeth*, London: Faber and Faber.

Synge, John Millington (1968; reprinted 1982), *Collected Works*, vol. 4, edited by Anne Saddlemyer, Washington: Catholic University of America Press.

Tracy, Robert (1999), "The Russian Connection: Friel and Chekhov", *Irish University Review*, Vol. 29, No. 1, pp. 64–77.

White, Harry (1999), "Brian Friel and the Condition of Music", *Irish University Review*, Vol. 29, No. 1, pp. 6–15.

Worthen, W. B. (1995), "Homeless Words: Field Day and the Politics of Translation", *Modern Drama* 38, pp. 22-41.

York, Richard (1993), "Friel's Russia" in Peacock (1993), pp. 164–77.

Irish History and Culture

CAIN: Conflict Archive on the Internet (Chronology of the conflict), http://cain.ulst.ac.uk/othelem/chron.htm

CAIN: Conflict Archive on the Internet (Widgery Tribunal) http://cain.ulst.ac.uk/events/bsunday/irgovt2e.htm

Connolly, S. J. (1998), *The Oxford Companion to Irish History*, Oxford: Oxford UP.

Dowling, Michele (1997), "'The Ireland that I would have': De Valera and the Creation of an Irish National Image", *History Ireland*, Vol. 5, No. 2, pp. 37–41.

Dréacht-Bunreacht / Draft Constitution (1937), Dublin: Stationery Office.

Dudley Edwards, Ruth (1979), *Patrick Pearse: The Triumph of Failure*, London: Faber.

Guy, John (1990), *Tudor England*, Oxford: Oxford UP.

Herity, Michael, ed. (2000), *Ordnance Survey Letters: Donegal*, Dublin: Four Masters Press.

Johnston, Edith Mary (1980), *Ireland in the Eighteenth Century, Gill History of Ireland, Vol. 8*, Dublin: Gill and Macmillan.

Kee, Robert (1976), *The Most Distressful Country, Vol. 1 of The Green Flag*, London: Quartet.

Kee, Robert (1976a), *The Bold Fenian Men, Vol. 2 of The Green Flag*, London: Quartet.

Kee, Robert (1976b) *Ourselves Alone, Vol. 3 of The Green Flag*, London: Quartet.

Keogh, Dermot (1994), *Twentieth-Century Ireland: Nation and State, New Gill History of Ireland, Vol. 6*, Dublin: Gill and Macmillan.

Kiely, Benedict (1982), "A Sense of Place" in Mac Réamoinn, pp. 93–110.

Lee, J.J. (1989; reprinted 1992), *Ireland 1912–1985, Politics and Society*, Cambridge: Cambridge UP.

Mac Réamoinn, Séan, ed. (1982), *The Pleasures of Gaelic Poetry*, London: Allen Lane.

Morgan, Hiram (1990), "Making History: A Criticism and a Manifesto", *Text and Context*, Vol. 4, pp. 61–5.

Morgan, Hiram (1993), *Tyrone's Rebellion*, Woodbridge, Suffolk: Boydell Press for The Royal Historical Society.

O'Brien, Eugene (2000), "Northern Ireland: The Omagh Bomb, Nationalism and Religion", *History Behind the Headlines*, Vol. 2, pp. 221–35.

O'Brien, Eugene (2001), *Examining Irish Nationalism in the Context of Literature, Culture and Religion: A Study of the Epistemological Structure of Nationalism*, Lewisburg, New York: Edwin Mellen Press.

O'Faoláin, Seán (1942), *The Great O'Neill*, London: Longmans, Green & Co.

Ó Tuama, Seán and Thomas Kinsella, eds. (1981), *An Duanaire 1690–1900, Poems of the Dispossessed*, Portlaoise: Dolmen Press.

Wichert, Sabine (1999), *Northern Ireland Since 1945*, 2nd edition, Harlow: Longman.

Reviews

Bird, Alan (2002), *The London Theatre Guide*, London, 24 September.

Fisher, Philip (2002), *The British Theatre Guide*, London.

Marks, Peter (2005), *The Washington Post*, Washington DC, 15 March.

Peter, John (2002), *The Sunday Times*, London, 22 September.

Peter, John (2002), *The Sunday Times*, London, 29 September.

Index